Popular Dictatorships

Electoral autocracies – regimes that adopt democratic institutions but subvert them to rule as dictatorships – have become the most widespread, resilient and malignant non-democracies today. They have consistently ruled over a third of the countries in the world, including geopolitically significant states like Russia, Turkey, Venezuela, Egypt, Indonesia, Nigeria and Pakistan. Challenging conventional wisdom, *Popular Dictators* shows that the success of electoral authoritarianism is not due to these regimes' superior capacity to repress, bribe, brainwash and manipulate their societies into submission, but is actually a product of their genuine popular appeal in countries experiencing deep political, economic and security crises. Promising efficient, strong-armed rule tempered by popular accountability, elected strongmen attract mass support in societies traumatized by turmoil, dysfunction and injustice, allowing them to rule through the ballot box. *Popular Dictators* argues that this crisis legitimation strategy makes electoral authoritarianism the most significant threat to global peace and democracy.

ALEKSANDAR MATOVSKI an Assistant Professor in the Department of National Security Affairs at the Naval Postgraduate School and an Associate at the Davis Center for Russian and Eurasian Studies at Harvard University. He was previously National Security Advisor in the Government of North Macedonia.

3/3/22

Popular Dictatorships

Crises, Mass Opinion, and the Rise
of Electoral Authoritarianism

ALEKSANDAR MATOVSKI
Naval Postgraduate School, Monterey, California

CAMBRIDGE
UNIVERSITY PRESS

CAMBRIDGE
UNIVERSITY PRESS

University Printing House, Cambridge CB2 8BS, United Kingdom

One Liberty Plaza, 20th Floor, New York, NY 10006, USA

477 Williamstown Road, Port Melbourne, VIC 3207, Australia

314–321, 3rd Floor, Plot 3, Splendor Forum, Jasola District Centre,
New Delhi – 110025, India

103 Penang Road, #05–06/07, Visioncrest Commercial, Singapore 238467

Cambridge University Press is part of the University of Cambridge.

It furthers the University's mission by disseminating knowledge in the pursuit of
education, learning, and research at the highest international levels of excellence.

www.cambridge.org
Information on this title: www.cambridge.org/9781316517802
DOI: 10.1017/9781009047500

© Aleksandar Matovski 2021

First published 2021

Printed in the United Kingdom by TJ Books Limited, Padstow Cornwall

A catalogue record for this publication is available from the British Library.

ISBN 978-1-316-51780-2 Hardback

To my mother and father
To Eli
And to Mila

Contents

Figures

Tables

Acknowledgments

This book is the product of a long gestation. Although it began to take shape as a dissertation in the Department of Government at Cornell University, its roots lie in my "extended exposure" to electoral authoritarianism throughout my upbringing and professional life as a think-tank researcher, government official, and scholar. Living through the breakdown of the former Yugoslavia and its aftermath made me confront a very different reality from that which the post–Cold War era of unprecedented democratization had seemed to promise, and also very different from the standard understandings of authoritarianism. The new dictatorships that spawned after the Yugoslav collapse attracted the support of popular majorities and regularly trounced their political alternatives at the polls. What stuck with me throughout the years was that ordinary people, including many that I knew, voted for these "strongmen" not because they had been indoctrinated, forced, or bribed. They did so because they sincerely believed these leaders were the only ones that could be relied upon to guide their countries through the new era of extraordinary turmoil.

Some years later, I found that these sentiments were not a fluke of Yugoslavia's peculiar background and fiery disintegration. As a government official and researcher, I had a unique opportunity to closely witness the rise of another wave of electoral autocrats not only in the Balkans, but also throughout Eastern Europe, the former Soviet Union, the Middle East, and beyond. The forces that propelled them to power appeared eerily familiar: deep crises and conflicts that delegitimized other political alternatives and produced anguished electorates, yearning for strong-armed, but popularly accountable leaders, who would restore order, resolve their problems, and supply the emotional gratification of vanquishing corrupt politicians, traitorous elites, or disliked minorities, thought to be responsible for the country's woes. This distinctive mass appeal of elected autocrats has been the motivating puzzle that guided my research. Was the attractiveness of elected strongmen in dysfunctional societies responsible for the unprecedented spread of these regimes and the democratic recession they have spearheaded since the mid-2000s? Could it account for why these regimes have outlasted the traditional, unelected dictatorships despite allowing more freedoms, legalizing oppositions, and holding elections?

I could not have hoped to transform these intuitions and observations into a coherent study without the generous support of my mentors, colleagues, friends, and family members, who propelled me through the years of painstaking research. I am particularly indebted to Valerie Bunce, who has provided indispensable advice and support at every stage of this project and was a constant source of encouragement as I navigated around numerous hurdles. This book began as a very broad-ranging and ambitious endeavor to investigate a largely unexplored area of authoritarian politics, and Val's remarkably patient, generous, and astute mentorship was crucial in steering it toward a coherent, well-rounded final product. Sidney Tarrow has left an indelible mark on this study by providing a unique mix of incisive critiques, precious advice, and unrelenting support. I owe him my gratitude for being my harshest critic and my kindest advocate. Peter Enns has been invaluable in helping me develop a theoretical framework and a research design that bridge the gap between the study of popular opinion and of authoritarianism. His selfless advice, support, and friendship helped me overcome many obstacles and bring this project to a conclusion. Christopher Anderson provided key guidance in framing the project in its critical early stages and pushed me to better articulate the mechanisms of authoritarian legitimation, and to avoid the pitfalls of opinion research in autocracies. I am extremely grateful to Andrew Little, who offered very perceptive critiques and suggestions on my research design and key propositions, helping me transform my dissertation into a book manuscript.

This project benefited tremendously from the year I spent at the Hoover Institution at Stanford University, where I had the opportunity to interact with brilliant scholars who provided precious insights, inspiration, and advice. I am particularly indebted to Michael McFaul, Kathryn Stoner, John Dunlop, Norman Naimark, and Stephen Kotkin for reading portions of my research and for their excellent feedback. I am also grateful to Secretary George Shultz for taking the time to talk about my research and to share some of his timeless wisdom about understanding and dealing with autocracies. The experience at Hoover and its reflections on this project would not have been the same without the stimulating conversations I had there with Niall Ferguson, Larry Diamond, Stephen Haber, Richard Allen, Michael Bernham, Alvin Rabushka, Kenneth Judd, Annelise Anderson, Thomas Hendriksen, and Erik Wakin. I owe special thanks to Paul Gregory, who was a constant source of encouragement and support, and to Gustavo Del Angel, Michael Albertus, Carlo Prato, Aila Matanock, and Brett Carter for being such great companions during our year together at Hoover.

At the Davis Center for Russian and Eurasian Studies at Harvard University, I had the good fortune of interacting with a remarkably talented and generous group of scholars, who helped me refine my study theoretically and empirically and were a wellspring of encouragement and support. Tim Colton has been a vital resource, both directly, by sharing data and providing incisive comments and advice on my research, and indirectly, by being an inspiration with his trailblazing work on Russian politics and mass opinion. I learned a great deal from Mark Kramer, and Rawi Abdelal and Alexandra Vacroux have been immensely supportive both during my fellowship and throughout my continued association with the Davis Center. I thank Nadia Boyadjieva, Tornike Metrevelli, Maria Sidorkina, Inna Melnykovska, Yuval Weber, Olena Nikolayenko, Daria Boltokova, Anna Graber, and Elina Kallas for their valuable feedback, as well as for their sincere camaraderie, which has made the research and writing process much less solitary.

I completed the concluding stages of my research during my immensely rewarding time at Williams College, and I am particularly grateful to James McAllister for his steadfast support and encouragement throughout this entire period, and to Mark Reinhardt for helping me tackle important hoops and obstacles in my final year. Jim Mahon and Sam Crane are fantastic colleagues and friends, who have shared quite a bit of their time discussing authoritarian politics with me and commenting on my research. Michael MacDonald, Chad Levinson, Darel Paul, Justin Crowe, Galen Jackson, Mason Williams, Nicole Mellow, and Nimu Njoya read and listened to portions of my work and provided insightful comments, advice, and encouragement, which helped shape my study. Olga Shevchenko, Lisa Koryushkina, Steve Nafziger, Julie Cassiday, Yana Skorobogatov, Bill Wagner, and Vladimir Ivantsov provided a superb interdisciplinary perspective – both individually and within our *kruzhok* on Russian politics, history, and literature – helping me broaden and contextualize my research.

This book has been also enhanced through countless additional exchanges with many more scholars throughout the years. In my study of authoritarianism in Russia and beyond, I have benefited tremendously from the insights, feedback, and support I received from Henry Hale, Mark Beissinger, Joshua Tucker, Thomas Remington, Brian Taylor, Steven Fish, Grigore Pop-Eleches, Samuel Greene, Graeme Robertson, Scott Gehlbach, Karrie Koesel, Jessica Pisano, Tomila Lankina, Maria Repnikova, Bryn Rosenfeld, Kiril Kalinin, Natalia Forrat, Regina Smyth, John Reuter, Maria Lipman, Sergei Guriev, and Andrei Kozyrev. My warmest gratitude also goes to Elizabeth Plantan and Manfred Elfstrom for being a keen critical audience and a sounding board for my ideas over the years. When refining the broad theoretical framework and empirical scope of this book, I also greatly benefited from conversations with Milan Svolik, Tom Pepinsky, Ken Roberts, Nic van de Walle, Steven Levitsky, Kenneth Greene, Andreas Schedler, Barbara Geddes, Beatriz Magaloni, and Lucan Way. One of the core pillars of this book – the analysis of popular opinion trends in electoral autocracies – would be poorer in nuance without the shrewd critiques and advice of William Mishler, Jon Krosnick, and Adam Levine.

I had the privilege of presenting portions of this research and receiving extremely valuable audience feedback at about two dozen conferences, professional talks, and workshops, including the annual meetings of the American Political Science Association, the Midwest Political Science Association, the International Studies Association, the Association for Slavic, East European, and Eurasian Studies, and the International Conference of Europeanists, as well as at the political science departments and research institutes of Cornell University, the New Economic School in Moscow, Stanford University, Harvard University, the University of Notre Dame, Indiana University Bloomington, Colgate University, and Williams College. The insightful comments and helpful suggestions that I received at these venues helped me develop and refine my project through its various stages.

Popular Dictatorships draws on the analysis of a large amount of empirical data, and from fieldwork conducted in Russia, which I was only able to complete thanks to the generous grants and fellowships from several institutions. For the financial support that enabled most of the data collection and fieldwork for this book, I would like to thank the Einaudi Foundation and the Cornell University Institute for European Studies, as well as the American Council of Learned Societies and the Andrew W. Mellon Foundation. They provided the bulk of the funding for my empirical investigations through the Mario Einaudi Graduate Fellowship and the Mellon/ACLS Dissertation Completion Fellowship. I have also received additional financial support from the Council of European Studies Pre-Dissertation Research Fellowship and the Cornell Graduate School Research Travel Grant. My immense data trove would not have been transformed into the analyses I present in this book without the generous support of the National Fellows Program at the Hoover Institution at Stanford University, the Davis Center Postdoctoral Fellowship at Harvard University, and the Mellon Postdoctoral Fellowship at Williams College.

The volume that you are holding in your hands took its final shape at the Naval Postgraduate School, and it would have been impossible to complete on schedule in the *annus horribilis* of 2020 without the amazing support of my colleagues at the Department of National Security Affairs. I am particularly grateful to Clay Moltz, Maria Rasmussen, and Naaz Barma, who spared no effort to help me integrate at NPS, and to ensure that I had the necessary opportunities and support in the last steps toward completing my book. I am also highly fortunate to have had the extremely kind and energetic support of Rachel Sigman, Chris Twomey, Covell Meyskens, Misha Tsypkin, Erik Dahl, Chris Darnton, Emily Meierding, Mariana Giusti Rodríguez, Afshon Ostovar, and Anne Clunan, who helped me make a very smooth transition to NPS and complete a myriad of tasks to finalize my manuscript.

Last, but certainly not least, I owe a special debt of gratitude to anonymous reviewers at Cambridge University Press and Oxford University Press, who gave my manuscript a meticulous read and provided immensely valuable comments and observations. Their thoughtful critiques and suggestions pushed me to refine the theory and analyses, and to fully develop my discussion of the book's implications. I would also like to thank David McBride and John Haslam for soliciting such high-quality reviews. John Haslam in particular has my profound gratitude for shepherding me through the publication process and for being an amazingly efficient and responsive editor throughout what must have been the most challenging period for the industry in living memory.

At the very end, I reserve my deepest gratitude for the members of my family who literally made all of this possible. I owe everything to my mother and father, who invested their all and spared no sacrifice to make my every success possible. My mother, Ljupka Matovska, has been the inspiration behind all my achievements and a central pillar of support that has helped me weather all the storms in my life. My father, Nikola Matovski, instilled in me an attitude of dogged perseverance and a lifelong interest in politics that has set me on this path to exploring its thorniest mysteries. I am eternally grateful to my wife, Eli Matovska, for sharing this adventure with me, with all its burdens, and for being by my side through the finest and bleakest moments. And Mila has my infinite love for being the best motivation any parent can ever hope for.

1 | A "Perfect Dictatorship?" The Puzzle of Electoral Authoritarianism

One of the most ridiculous aspects of democracy will always remain . . . the fact that it has offered to its mortal enemies the means by which to destroy it.

> - Josef Goebbels, Nazi propaganda minister, 1933–1945

"The perfect dictatorship," the Nobel-Prize-winning novelist Mario Vargas Llosa quipped in 1990, "is not the Soviet Union, but Mexico." Ruled by the Institutional Revolutionary Party (PRI) since 1929, Mexico had a regime that was not an overbearing totalitarian dictatorship, but an electoral autocracy: a hybrid system that embraced all the institutional trappings of democracy, including democratic constitutions, parliaments, and regular multiparty elections, but subverted them informally. The secret of electoral authoritarianism's success, according to Vargas Llosa, was that it could impose itself without the people even noticing – under the cloak of a popular mandate, won at the ballot box. Its core appeal was that it could avoid the excesses of both liberal democracy and unchecked dictatorship. In Mexico, PRI's electoral authoritarianism ushered in an era of unprecedented stability as it simultaneously curbed the country's factionalism and maintained a system of elections and term limits, which ingeniously avoided personal dictatorship by retiring its dictators at the end of their six-year presidential terms (Castañeda 2000).

Vargas Llosa's warnings about the malicious tenacity of electoral authoritarianism became prophetic soon after his famous remark. The Soviet Union collapsed in 1991 and Mexico's far less imposing dictatorship outlived it by another nine years, ruling continuously for seventy-one years until its demise in 2000. But more importantly, the electoral authoritarian model perfected in Mexico proliferated beyond anyone's wildest expectations. As I show in Figure 1.1 below, electoral autocracies were the only type of undemocratic regime that paralleled the unprecedented

1

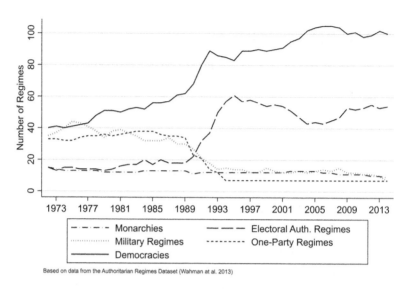

Figure 1.1 Regime types by year, 1973–2014

spread of democracies after the Cold War.[1] As traditional, unelected dictatorships have crumbled with breakneck speed across the world, the overwhelming majority of regimes that have remained authoritarian, and virtually all new autocracies that have emerged since 1989, have been electoral autocracies. Electoral authoritarianism has been stunningly successful where the seemingly far more robust and menacing totalitarian single-party regimes and military dictatorships have faltered. It spread not when democracy was in retreat, but during its greatest expansion.

The optimism spurred by the largest wave of democratization initially led scholars and commentators to discount the threat posed by these regimes. Electoral autocracies were dismissed as "democracies with adjectives"[2] – inherently unsustainable, transitional regimes, set to eventually become full democracies (Carothers 2002). By the

[1] This data is drawn from the updated Authoritarian Regimes Dataset (ver. 6.0, downloaded from https://sites.google.com/site/authoritarianregimedataset (accessed 05/25/2021); see Wahman, Teorell, and Hadenius (2013)).

[2] The most common referents for these regimes included "delegative democracies" (O'Donnell 1994), "illiberal democracies" (Zakaria 1997, 2007), "ambiguous" or "hybrid regimes" (Diamond 2002). Other less frequently used terms to describe these regimes have included "weak," "partial," "façade," "virtual," "pseudo," and "semi" democracy (Carothers 2002; Collier and Levitsky 1997).

mid-2000s, however, it was clear that electoral authoritarianism was both far more durable and far more assertive than previously thought. As the number of electoral autocracies increased, the global rate of democratic transitions almost halved and dictatorships more than doubled their rates of survival (Kendall-Taylor and Frantz 2014).

Then, in the aftermath of the 2009 global financial crisis and the mounting backlash against liberalism and globalization, electoral authoritarianism emerged as a full-fledged alternative to democracy and a mechanism for an authoritarian resurgence on a much greater scale than had previously been thought possible. In 2020, Freedom House (2020) registered fourteen straight years of consecutive decline of civil rights and political freedoms across the globe. The driving force of this democratic erosion was made up of popularly elected authoritarian incumbents who finagled democratic institutions and procedures to gradually dismantle checks and balances, curtail the freedom of the press, and extinguish the independence of the judiciary and the state administration. Some of the sharpest, and most sustained and malignant reversals toward electoral authoritarianism occurred in countries like Hungary and Poland – members of the European Union (EU) and North Atlantic Treaty Organization (NATO) and seemingly permanent converts to democracy. Even the core Western democracies appeared to be vulnerable to the threat of backsliding into electoral authoritarianism, as populist authoritarian parties and leaders surged at the polls (Norris and Inglehart 2019), and incumbents willfully undermined long-standing democratic norms and institutions (Levitsky and Ziblatt 2018).

How is this possible? How can autocracies that provide so many opportunities for their defeat by legalizing oppositions, allowing criticism, and holding elections, become so durable and menacing? This book argues that to address this puzzle, we must consider a paradoxical and disturbing possibility, largely unaccounted for in the current literature: that electoral autocracies may have a broad and *genuine popular appeal* in certain contexts. This appeal allows them to hijack the democratic process – to win favor among majorities or substantial pluralities and maintain power through the ballot box, and with minimal coercion. This is the same appeal, I argue, which made Mexico's electoral autocracy appear "perfect" to many of its citizens: the widespread perception that its alternatives – liberal democracy and closed dictatorship – were worse.

The most distinctive and yet least appreciated aspect of electoral authoritarianism, as this book will show, is that it has appeared in the wake of the deepest crises in the countries that have been ruled by such regimes. Far more often than other regime types, electoral autocracies have emerged after periods of unmanageable conflict, state collapse, socioeconomic decline, and general political dysfunction, when societies are desperate for order and stability to be restored, and when other alternatives have become delegitimized. Rooted in collective traumas from unmanageable turmoil under these alternative systems, support for electoral authoritarianism is not a product of ideological indoctrination or cultural predispositions toward undemocratic rule among certain nations or social classes. Instead, the motives for consenting to electoral authoritarian rule are far more mundane. Ordinary people support these hybrid regimes for what they think are instrumental reasons, and often reluctantly: as the least objectionable governing option when all others have become exhausted.

Posing as tough, efficient, and popularly accountable "strongmen" (so far, in an exclusively masculine sense),[3] electoral authoritarian leaders – the likes of Vladimir Putin in Russia, Recep Tayyip Erdoğan in Turkey, Viktor Orbán in Hungary, Hugo Chávez in Venezuela, Alberto Fujimori in Peru, and many more – rise to power by taking advantage of such contexts and sentiments. These elected dictators attract genuine popular support by claiming they are uniquely capable of imposing order and addressing grievances in troubled societies because they combine the best and avoid the worst of both democracy and authoritarianism. They offer popular accountability without the divisions, conflict, and uncertainty of liberal democracy, and strong, uncompromising, and effective government without the arbitrary behavior and violence of unchecked dictatorship. I claim that this ability to compellingly justify their rule as a pragmatic solution for

---

[3] Throughout the book, I purposefully avoid a more gender-balanced description such as would be implied by the use of the alternative "strongwoman" label. This is because the appeal of electoral authoritarian incumbents that I describe has had a distinctive masculine, "macho," and even a misogynistic and homophobic connotation (O'Donnell 1994; Gudkov 2011; Sperling 2014, 2016; E. A. Wood 2016; Heydarian 2017; Michelutti 2017a). Moreover, leadership in dictatorships, including regimes of the electoral variety, has thus far remained a completely undisputed realm of absolute male dominance. To emphasize this pattern, I refer to these regimes and their leaders by using only the masculine, "strongman" label.

their nations' acute problems is the most fundamental tool of power for elected autocrats. Above all, it allows these regimes to win and maintain power through democratic means and with relatively little coercion, defusing resistance and criticism about their authoritarian nature.

This account sheds a very different light on the nature of electoral authoritarianism from how it is currently understood. These regimes do not subvert democracy by simply *faking democracy*, as is commonly assumed. Instead, the secret of their success lies in the ability to *hijack democracy* in societies beset by turmoil and despair. This is a crucial point. Electoral authoritarianism did not blossom after the Cold War just because the spread of democracy forced dictatorships to hide behind a democratic façade. Instead, as I show in the chapters that follow, these regimes were boosted, more than anything else, by the spread of instability and the proliferation of new, fragile, crisis-prone countries. This backdrop enabled autocrats to turn democracy against itself: to attract real popular support by posing as guarantors of order and justice, and to claim democratic legitimacy won at the polls.

This ability to usurp democracy is a defining feature of electoral authoritarianism, and sets it apart from all other forms of dictatorship. It is also the key reason why these autocracies were the only ones that thrived in the era of unprecedented democratization, when traditional, closed dictatorship crumbled. Their foundation – the appeal of popularly endorsed strongmen in troubled societies – not only allows these regimes to win elections and pose as democracies, but also enables them to behave as autocracies. It empowers authoritarian incumbents to repress their political opponents with impunity, censor the media, bend and break laws, and ride roughshod over legislatures and courts – all in the name of the supreme imperative of restoring order and justice in their troubled societies.

These coercive tactics have a strong tendency to backfire when used by unpopular regimes. However, they can have the opposite effect when deployed by electoral autocrats who have compellingly justified their rule as a response to a national emergency. Majorities that believe that authoritarian rule is necessary to impose order or to address their grievances would not only condone the use of violence and coercion by these regimes; they might also become more supportive of their rulers after such tactics are employed, as their strongman leadership is keeping the promise of tough-mannered, effective rule. Thus, while a dictatorship cannot coerce people into liking it, an elected dictatorship, which the voters genuinely like for its hard-line tactics, can coerce with impunity – and become even more popular for it. A widely supported electoral autocracy can become, in other words, a repressive dictatorship of the most insidious, popularly mandated sort, resembling the tyranny of the majority foreseen by James Madison (1787).

For this reason, I argue that the popular appeal of electoral authoritarian regimes has a massive confounding influence on all other aspects of electoral authoritarian rule. For one, popularity is absolutely essential for these regimes' ability to rise to power, before they have the coercive and other resources to control their populations. And once they assume control of the state, the "strongman" popular appeal of elected autocrats enables them to stay in power by democratic means even as they use coercion against their opponents. Hence, we must, at a minimum, develop a basic understanding of this legitimizing strategy and control for its effect. We must shed light on the origins and inner logic of this appeal, the background circumstances that enable it, and the mechanisms through which it affects popular opinion and the trajectories of electoral authoritarian regimes. This book is an attempt to make a step in this direction.

What Is Electoral Authoritarianism?

[T]he approach of democracy appeared a chaotic storm against which a dam had to be built[.]

Carl Schmitt (1988)

Electoral autocracies have been broadly defined as regimes that adopt democratic institutions, like regular multiparty elections, legislatures, and judiciaries, but sabotage these in practice to rule in an authoritarian fashion (Schedler 2006). The key distinguishing feature of these regimes is that political "[c]ompetition is ... real but unfair" (Levitsky and Way 2010a, 5). They therefore easily stand out from traditional closed dictatorships, like monarchies, single-party regimes, and military juntas, which do not provide institutionalized means for contesting power. The main difficulty in identifying electoral autocracies, as well as in identifying their appeal, is to distinguish them from democracies (Kailitz 2013, 46). This, to a large degree, is because part of the purpose of these regimes is to mislead: to act as "democracy's doubles," claiming genuine popular legitimacy to defuse domestic and international pressures for democratization (Krastev 2006).

The key conceptual challenge here is that the tactics electoral autocracies use to masquerade as democracies – their "menu of manipulation" (Schedler 2002) – vary significantly across regimes and over time. While some regimes use crude and direct methods of electoral falsification, like ballot stuffing or vote buying, others rely on more sophisticated and surreptitious methods to reduce the opposition's competitiveness *long before* the ballots are cast. They use administrative leverage to deny their oppositions funding and media access, they gerrymander electoral districts or otherwise tweak the electoral rules in their favor, and so on. Also, electoral autocracies resort to different manipulative strategies over time. Some might use cruder, more direct tactics at the beginning of their rule and become more sophisticated later. Other regimes may follow the opposite pattern, often because an unexpected oppositional mobilization compelled them to use all available means to cling on to power. Ultimately, all electoral autocracies change their "menu of manipulation" as they learn from each other's experiences, adopting new tactics that have proven effective elsewhere and abandoning those that have failed.

The only constant feature of electoral authoritarianism, in other words, is that it constantly changes the ways in which it pursues a single underlying goal: limiting democracy. A few, or even one of these manipulative tactics, if employed systematically, may be *sufficient* to identify a regime as electoral authoritarian. But none of them is individually *necessary* for a regime to be identified as such. This is why electoral authoritarianism is such an elusive concept: there are great many different ways in which it manifests itself. To paraphrase Tolstoy's oft-cited maxim, while all democracies are democratic in the same way (by meeting the same basic standards of democracy), each electoral autocracy is authoritarian in its own way (in terms of how exactly it subverts democratic institutions).[4] Hence, to be valid and consistent, a measure of electoral authoritarianism must be both

---

[4] Svolik (2012) makes a similar argument about all types of nondemocratic regimes, including closed autocracies, arguing that each is necessarily different because it departs from democratic norms of governing in its own way. However, unlike military dictatorships, single-party regimes, and monarchies, which have relatively fixed repertoires for subverting political competition, electoral autocracies have much broader "menus of manipulation."

comprehensive and *versatile*: it must consider a very broad array of tactics that can be used to substantially curb democracy, and it must recognize that their many different combinations all amount to electoral authoritarianism.

I employ these criteria to select the most appropriate indicator of electoral authoritarianism. I do so by adjudicating between two broad regime classification schemes. The first distinguishes electoral autocracies from democracies, based on the presence or absence of a minimal set of fixed institutional criteria for a country to be considered democratic. In what is perhaps the most commonly used dataset crafted in this "minimalist" tradition, Boix, Miller, and Rosato (2012) employ a dichotomous measure where democracy is distinguished by the presence of free and fair elections, and a minimal level of suffrage (see also Miller (2017)). Another popular measure in the minimalist tradition, developed by Cheibub, Gandhi, and Vreeland (2010), similarly identifies democracies based on the presence of multiparty elections, but instead of attempting to judge their fairness directly, it employs an alteration in power criterion, whereby a regime is classified as democratic (often retroactively) if ruling parties and candidates have lost elections and have been replaced by the opposition.

The downside of both minimalist approaches is that their narrow focus on the bare-bones essentials of democracy and on the integrity of the electoral process misses the more subtle manipulations of broader democratic principles which are increasingly prevalent in electoral autocracies. Due to the learning mechanism I mentioned earlier, most of today's electoral authoritarian regimes do the "heavy lifting" in suppressing democratic competitiveness outside of the electoral process – by abusing the administrative and economic resources of the state, manipulating the judiciary and the legislative process, establishing control of the media, and other nonelectoral machinations that degrade the capacity of autonomous social actors to compete, long before the ballots are cast (Schedler 2002; Levitsky and Way 2010b; Bermeo 2016). As one authoritarian regime connoisseur put it: "[t]oday, only amateurs steal elections on election-day" (cited in Bermeo 2016). Against this backdrop, a minimalist, election-focused indicator of democracy is prone to misclassify many electoral autocracies that have adopted sophisticated ways of masquerading as democracies.

The second major approach to identifying electoral autocracies is to separate them from democracies on the basis of composite democracy indices – such as those provided by Freedom House and the Polity Project – which record adherence to much broader set of democratic norms, ranging from various institutional prerequisites to respect for the rule of law, freedom of the press, and individual liberties. In this scheme, regimes are dichotomously classified as democratic when their score on these composite indices is above some particular predefined cutoff point, usually justified by empirical comparisons with other classifications. The most prominent regime dataset using this approach was developed by Wahman, Teorell, and Hadenius (2013), and it defines electoral autocracies as regimes that hold elections in which oppositions are allowed, but whose average combined Freedom House and Polity IV scores fall below a threshold of 7.0.

The main issue with this classification is that it uses a cutoff point for separating electoral autocracies from other regimes that is somewhat arbitrary, rather than strictly derived from substantive criteria (Bogaards 2010; Cheibub, Gandhi, and Vreeland 2010). Another critique of this approach is that a specific ranking on a multicomponent democracy score cannot be attributed to any consistent set of components of democracy. For instance, two countries may have the same score because they satisfy the same number of disparate democratic norms (K. S. Gleditsch and Ward 1997).

While these criticisms are valid, the flaws they detect are, in fact, advantages when it comes to identifying electoral autocracies. First, the composite index regime classifications are much better able to register the shifting strategies used to subvert democracy, precisely because they are based on a broad range of different democratic standards that are weighed equally. For instance, when an electoral autocracy shifts its tactics from ballot stuffing to more subtle approaches like media control or abuse of the judiciary, the seeming improvement in one area (integrity of the electoral process) will be compensated for by the decline in another (freedom of the press or rule of law), and the composite index measure will still accurately classify this regime. A minimalist, election-centric classification scheme, on the other hand, will be more prone to miscategorizing this regime as a democracy.

Second, even the minimalist measures of democracy, which are presumably based on a consistent standard of election integrity, are, in practice, affected by potentially significant biases, subjectivity, and arbitrariness. This, to a large degree, is because these indices directly or indirectly draw their core conclusions from interpreting election reports, which as a rule lack a common standard of coverage and are often inconclusive, or skewed for political reasons (Hadenius 1992; Kelley 2009). By virtue of its greater breadth, the composite index score classification is, on the other hand, less prone to be swayed by the biases inherent in any of its individual components, or the sources used to construct them (on this, see Bollen and Paxton 2000). From the same vantage point, the seemingly arbitrary numerical threshold for democracy in the composite scale may – again paradoxically – ensure better measurement consistency across cases. Because it is uniformly applied across the board, the numerical-cutoff-point measure of democracy may suffer from fewer subjectivity and interpretation biases than the minimalist alternative, which attempts to size up each regime's adherence to democratic standards individually, on a case-by-case basis.

Based on these considerations, as a key dependent variable for this book's empirical analyses, I use the composite index regime indicator from the Authoritarian Regimes Dataset (ver. 6.0) of Wahman, Teorell, and Hadenius (2013), covering the 1960–2014 period.[5] Despite its potential drawbacks, this measure satisfies both the comprehensiveness and versatility criteria for accurately identifying electoral authoritarian regimes better than the alternative. As such, it provides the best match with the definition of electoral authoritarianism as a political system that rules within a democratic constitutional framework but subverts it informally, using many different combinations of manipulative tactics that can shift over time.

The Strongman Appeal of Electoral Authoritarianism Regimes

In a crisis, you don't need governance by institutions. What is needed is somebody who tells the people that risky decisions must be taken ... and who says to them follow me ... Now strong national leaders are required.

Viktor Orbán, Hungarian Prime Minister
(cited in Lendvai 2017)

Electoral autocracies come from backgrounds that seem so incomparably diverse that searching for a single common factor, explaining their

---

[5] Although the Authoritarian Regimes Dataset documentation states that it covers the 1972–2014 period, it has a starting year of the regime variable that goes back to 1960. I use it to extend the regime measures to the 1960–2014 period, achieving greater coverage in this fashion.

rise and persistence, looks like a fool's errand. These regimes have emerged in countries as dissimilar as Singapore and Nigeria, Venezuela and Hungary, Peru and Turkey, and Russia and Zimbabwe. Their institutional underpinnings have varied between highly personalistic arrangements, like that under Robert Mugabe in Zimbabwe, to anti-personalistic, party-based dictatorships, such as the one in Mexico under the PRI. Their leaders and ideologies have ranged from the flamboyant leftist populism of Hugo Chávez to the steely nationalistic anti-populism of Vladimir Putin; from Recep Tayyip Erdoğan's religious-based appeal in Turkey to the impassionate, technocratic style of Singapore's Lee Kwan Yew. And as I have argued in the previous section, each of these regimes tends to be electorally authoritarian in its own way, relying on its own, custom-made "menu of manipulation" to keep democracy at bay.

Yet despite this bewildering diversity of electoral authoritarian rule, there is something strikingly familiar in the way in which these regimes have conducted themselves. All these regimes, without exception, have projected an image of a strong-armed, but popularly elected party or leader, who can provide the stability and efficient governance their country needs. And they have all framed their tough image as a response to their countries' most severe crises and periods of instability.

The regimes in the electoral authoritarian "Hall of Fame" have all religiously adhered to this legitimation strategy. The basic appeal of the PRI regime in Mexico – the world's longest-lasting electoral autocracy – laid in its ability to restore order after the country's bloody revolution and then maintain an unprecedented degree of political and economic stability for a Latin American country, all while being broadly representative and minimally coercive (Castañeda 2000).[6] Similarly, the world's second-oldest (and still thriving) electoral autocracy in Singapore established and sustained its rule on a promise to end the bitter class and ethnic strife in a divided society. Both before and after it delivered Singapore's "economic miracle," the primary appeal of the People's Action Party (PAP) regime was the extraordinarily stable order it created with minimal coercion (Slater 2010, ch. 8).

---

[6] Showcasing its image as an indispensable guarantor of order, the PRI was referred to in public by regime representatives and supporters as the "party of the state" in Mexico (Dominguez and McCann 1998).

Among the post–Cold War electoral autocracies, the core appeal of the Russian electoral autocracy under Vladimir Putin has been based on his promise to usher in a new era of stability after the disastrous post-Soviet decline in the 1990s – an image reinforced by successes in reining in the restive province of Chechnya and the country's unfettered oligarchs, improving the economy, and restoring Russia's standing on the world stage (Treisman 2011a; Matovski 2020). Putin sustained his impressive popularity using slogans such as "raising Russia from its knees," "a strong leader for a great country," and "strong president – strong Russia." In the wake of the bloody collapse of Yugoslavia, Serbia's strongman Slobodan Milošević justified his electoral authoritarian regime as the only force that could protect his compatriots at home and abroad. The appeal of Milošević's Socialist Party was summarized by its pithy campaign slogan: "With us, there is no uncertainty" (Gagnon 2004). Peru's Alberto Fujimori achieved unprecedented popularity and electoral dominance based on his pledge to dismantle the "false democracy of elites," deemed responsible for his country's deep structural crisis in the 1980s, and on his government's successes in taking on the brutal Shining Path insurgency (Levitsky and Cameron 2003). Venezuela's Hugo Chávez fashioned himself as a popular *caudillo* who would rescue his country from economic decline, rising inequality, and the corruption deemed to be caused by the neoliberal politics of the mainstream parties and "American imperialism" (Hawkins 2010; Corrales and Penfold-Becerra 2015).

Since the 2000s, Recep Tayyip Erdoğan has cast himself in the role of Turkey's strongman "savior" by taking advantage of the country's long stagnation under its previous secular establishment, and by exploiting anxieties about the Kurdish insurgency, the war in neighboring Syria, and the failed military coup against his rule (Cagaptay 2017). In the crucial 2014 presidential election which entrenched Erdoğan's power, his party rallied support with a blunt message: "if you want bread, vote for Erdoğan" (Brookings 2014). In Egypt, the legitimation strategy of the NDP party under Hosni Mubarak – propped up by perpetual emergency rule and justified by foreign and domestic security threats – was best condensed in its austere campaign slogan: "continuity for the sake of stability" (Singerman 2002). Egypt's next strongman, Abdel Fattah al-Sisi, exploited fears of chaos after the Arab Spring to rally popular support for a military coup and to establish another ham-fisted electoral authoritarian regime. "At least we are not Syria!" has been the most salient catchphrase of the Sisi regime – and is the best explanation why Egyptians have put up with it, despite the dire economic situation (*The Economist* 2015a). Even beyond these (in)famous cases, one would be hard pressed to find an exception to this pattern: an electoral autocracy that *does not* primarily justify its rule as a tough, decisive and popularly mandated response to a political, economic, and security crisis, or latent instability. This legitimation strategy makes electoral autocracies appear remarkably similar. Indeed, as I demonstrate in Chapter 4 of this book, it is so ubiquitous that we could reliably identify these regimes based on their rhetoric alone.

Despite the prevalence of this behavior, the possibility that electoral authoritarian parties and leaders sustain their rule by appealing for popular support – much like their democratic counterparts – has been routinely overlooked in political science.[7] There are several reasons for this. The first is practical: popular appeals and mass attitudes are notoriously difficult to study in authoritarian settings, and until fairly recently, there were few resources and opportunities to explore their impact. The second obstacle is normative: there is a strong, instinctive bias against the notion that popular support for authoritarianism can be a product of anything other than intimidation, brainwashing, and bribery. We cringe at the idea that ordinary people may willingly consent to authoritarian rule, because thinking otherwise would give legitimacy to such regimes.

The third key reason why the strongman appeal and other legitimation strategies of electoral autocracies have not been seriously considered is conceptual. Quite simply, the rhetoric of elected strongmen does not resemble any recognizable ideological and programmatic platforms observed in either traditional, closed dictatorships, or democracies. Unlike their democratic counterparts, strongman electoral authoritarian incumbents do not regularly vie for votes based on policy proposals or issue stances. And unlike their totalitarian predecessors, they do not seek to attract popular support with utopian ideologies. Instead, electoral autocracies have primarily relied on what looks like a hodgepodge of relatively shallow nationalist, religious, and populist platforms, designed to take advantage of particular grievances in their

---

[7] On this issue, see Burnell (2006), Gerschewski (2013), Kailitz (2013), Mazepus et al. (2016), Dukalskis and Gerschewski (2017), Kailitz and Stockemer (2017), von Haldenwang (2017), and von Soest and Grauvogel (2017).

countries, and to appeal to the lowest common denominator. Seen from the standpoint of the traditional campaign and legitimation theories, these appeals seem too superficial to attract stable popular support. Discounted as the most "ideologically homeless" regime type (Schedler 2013, 55), electoral autocracies are generally not considered to have a coherent and compelling popular appeal which could sustain their rule.

I argue that this interpretation is wrong for two reasons. First, it overlooks the unique circumstances in which electoral autocracies rise, and how these contexts shape political competition and legitimation. A central empirical finding of this book is that at a far greater rate than any other regime type, electoral autocracies have emerged in the wake of the greatest political, economic, and security crises in their countries' histories. These are periods when societies reject traditional ideological and programmatic appeals, and put a premium on strong-armed, but popularly accountable leadership, which promises to restore national unity and stability by all means necessary. To put it differently, electoral autocracies emerge when the rules of legitimation are inverted: when substantive platforms and ideologies are shunned, and tough, decisive, and pragmatic leadership, unburdened by partisan dogmas or allegiances, is seen as the only reliable source of authority. The standards for evaluating these regimes' legitimation strategies must, therefore, be reversed too.

Such scenarios seem to squarely fit Max Weber's insight that in times of great strife, the charismatic authority of individual leaders and parties becomes a more stable form of legitimacy than that of well-defined policies, ideologies, and laws. According to Weber, when unprecedented disasters strike, doctrines and principles that have guided societies in the past tend to offer neither answers nor solutions. Faced with uncertainty and despair, societies abandon established ideas and follow "ideal" leaders, who appear to have the skill and vision to somehow transcend the current problems (Weber 1946).

The appeals of elected strongmen, from this standpoint, are mistakenly assumed to be "formless" not because they lack a firm set of guiding principles, but because they believe that traditional political ideologies and platforms stand in the way of effective government, which is necessary in their troubled countries. As Shevtsova (2003) shrewdly observed in the Russian case, electoral autocracies are defined by the view that their beleaguered societies do not need fixed ideologies, policies, or even rules of politics; what they do believe is needed are strong, competent, and decisive "fixers."

This is why the strongman appeal of electoral authoritarian regimes cannot be discounted as "cheap talk." Instead, I claim that it is a fully fledged legitimation formula and governing doctrine. And this legitimation script and doctrine is based on much more than Weber's pure, personality-driven charisma. Even in highly personalistic electoral autocracies, the core pillar of legitimacy is not the current leader's personal charm, but the *argument* that dysfunctional societies should be governed by tough, uncompromising leadership, empowered to impose order and justice by any means necessary. Elected strongmen take advantage of the wide appeal of this doctrine to justify their rule as a form of emergency rule: a popularly mandated suspension of democracy to deal with an unmanageable crisis. The state of emergency rationalization,[8] exemplified by Viktor Orbán's statement quoted at the beginning of this section, transforms what might otherwise appear as naked personalized tyranny into a compelling governing philosophy and mandate. From this standpoint, the "charisma" of any particular strongman is not much more than a bit of personal flair attached to this legitimation formula – something that may multiply its appeal but can never replace it.

Electoralism is the other core pillar of this strategy for justifying authoritarian rule. It allows strongmen to credibly commit to staying accountable to the majorities they vie to protect. This distinguishes electoral autocracies from other dictatorships that claim to rule in the name of the people and to defend them from grave danger.[9] For as long

---

[8] This legitimation strategy has also been made explicit in cases when electoral autocracies have resorted to formally declared emergency rule. The most extreme case is that of Egypt, which has been under emergency rule for much of its postcolonial history (Singerman 2002; Brown and El-Sadany 2017), and it has also been deployed to significant effect in Turkey, after the failed coup against Recep Tayyip Erdoğan in 2016 (EU 2018). However, most electoral autocracies have by and large avoided the explicit use of constitutional state of emergency provisions – preferring to use the supreme emergency justification for rule rhetorically, but to exercise unlimited executive power informally.

[9] In particular, the state of emergency justification has been a core legitimation strategy of dictatorships since the Roman republic (Nicolet 2004). Napoleon Bonaparte was the first modern leader who established an autocracy justified as emergency rule through a series of plebiscites, staking a claim that it legitimately represented the will of the people (Woloch 2004, 42). Later, the Nazi and many other dictatorships relied on this legitimation strategy to establish absolute rule of

as they hold regular multiparty elections, autocrats are fundamentally limited in how much they can rely on coercion and manipulation to compensate for the lack of genuine popular support. Above all, allowing people to vote in a regime that is unpopular defeats the purpose of authoritarianism: instead of suppressing discontent and opposition, elections provide focal points for mobilizing it (see e.g. Tucker 2007).

But elections cannot constrain dictatorships that are *popular*. Instead, they enable them. A strongman regime that is genuinely supported by majorities as an indispensable provider of order and justice can break institutional norms, restrict freedoms, and repress its opponents with far greater impunity than an unelected dictatorship. This, I argue, is the key "missing link" in current understandings of electoral authoritarianism. If most people are convinced that the violations of democratic principles in the name of order, stability, and justice are acceptable, and signal their beliefs at regular elections, then the regime overseeing this state of affairs cannot be easily resisted, or even branded as undemocratic. Electoral legitimation transforms popular personalistic or party-based dictatorships into majority tyrannies: a far more sinister and resilient threat to democracy.

Taken together, these observations suggest that the mass appeal of electoral autocracies is a key systematic explanatory factor, and not just an idiosyncratic feature of these regimes. The campaigning strategies of elected strongmen are more than a jumble of populist overtures, rabble-rousing statements, and personal bravado. Instead, they reflect a fully fledged legitimation formula and governing doctrine. They do not simply call for strong, charismatic leadership in times of crisis, but also explain: (1) what charismatic leadership is in such circumstances (tough, effective, and uncompromising party or leader); (2) how it should be selected and replaced (through regular elections); (3) how it should govern (through the forceful use of executive power, unhindered by checks and balances); and (4) why it is the best alternative for nations recovering from deep crises (it is the most benign and pragmatic choice between democracy and complete dictatorship).

a single ruler or party (see Schmitt 2014, Fraenkel 2017, and Ullrich 2017, ch. 14). But unlike today's electoral autocracies, these regimes never adopted *regular multiparty elections* to signal continued popular approval for this form of rule. Electoral autocracies, in other words, are the only kind of authoritarian regime to sustain the (quasi) emergency rule legitimation of dictatorship within a nominally democratic institutional framework.

While pure charisma is a unique and inimitable product of extraordinary personal appeal, this doctrine of strongman authority provides a general legitimation formula, which can be emulated by different leaders and parties in different countries.

To succeed, however, this legitimation strategy also needs favorable conditions and a captive audience. This is the second key insight of this study. A strongman legitimizing doctrine, no matter how compelling, is not enough, because under normal circumstances, societies are too divided by various particularistic interests, outlooks, and allegiances for a majority-backed strongman regime to emerge (see Dahl 1963, 132–133, 146). Only shared collective traumas from unmanageable crises can neutralize this diversity of opinions and interests and make electoral authoritarianism a compelling choice across society.[10] Without these painful experiences of turmoil and existential insecurity under alternative regimes, there is nothing to ensure that the supply of strongman electoral authoritarian leadership is met by broad popular demand for it. Or to put it simply: no crises, no autocracy-sustaining strongman appeal.

Other Analytical Approaches to Electoral Authoritarianism

This book is an attempt to address a fundamental gap in the current understanding of electoral authoritarianism: the failure to appreciate the role of these regimes' distinct popular appeal in their rise and persistence. It is useful, from this perspective, to briefly trace how this omission has shaped the literature on electoral autocracies.

All efforts to understand electoral authoritarianism, as I have argued earlier, must resolve its central puzzle: why are autocracies that legalize oppositions, hold regular multiparty elections and rule in a democratic institutional framework more durable than closed, tightly controlled dictatorships? There have been three major approaches to this issue. The first and most influential one has argued that paradoxically,

---

[10] Slater (2010) makes a similar point that the strongman appeal of autocracies is only convincing when populations have traumatic experiences of turmoil under a democratic order. According to Slater (2010, 14): "[a]ll dictatorships may attempt to construct a shared sense that democracy equals chaos while authoritarianism equals stability, but only some possess the historical raw material [in the form of experiences of unmanageable upheaval under a more democratic order] to succeed at making such claims broadly credible."

adopting nominally democratic institutions can actually stabilize dictatorships. Studies in this tradition have underlined that multipartyism, legislatures, and elections increase incentives for various elite and opposition groups to participate in the authoritarian system and to be co-opted by the regime (Brownlee 2007; Gandhi and Przeworski 2007): they defuse violent and subversive oppositions (Schedler 2013, 35), compel key constituencies to compete for patronage within the institutions of the system (Lust-Okar 2008), and provide mechanisms through which autocrats can credibly commit to deliver it (Boix and Svolik 2013). Through more transparent institutions and controlled pluralism, autocracies can better monitor the elites (Blaydes 2008) and the population (Morgenbesser 2016), as well as the performance of their subordinates (Gehlbach and Simpser 2015). Such institutions therefore allow dictatorships to better pinpoint their opponents and to repress them far more selectively, avoiding the potential backlash from indiscriminate coercion (Frantz and Kendall-Taylor 2014). And by winning elections with big margins, autocracies compellingly demonstrate their unparalleled dominance and firm grip on society, deterring current and future challenges to their rule (Magaloni 2006).

The core idea of this neo-institutionalist approach (Gerschewski 2013), in other words, is that democratic institutions enable authoritarianism to use its coercive tactics better – to better bribe, brainwash, repress, and intimidate their societies into submission. Electoral autocracies, from this point of view, are not resilient because they are more legitimate or genuinely popular, but because adopting nominally democratic institutions allow them to deceive many into believing so, and to more effectively subjugate the rest. For all the emphasis on quasi-democratic institutions, they are little more than a clever façade; the true force that sustains authoritarianism is still coercive power.

At the macro-level, this line of thought implies that electoral autocracies will thrive in environments that give them maximum leverage to control their population through clientelism, propaganda, repression, and similar tactics. In particular, low levels of economic development are assumed to be especially conducive to the rise of electoral authoritarianism, as such contexts make impoverished populations more dependent on patronage (Magaloni 2006; Miller 2017). Similarly, access to substantial resource rents and other non-tax revenue like foreign aid could allow electoral autocracies to survive by maintaining robust patronage networks (see e.g. Ross 2001 and Morrison 2009). And where such clientelistic inducements are insufficient, states with greater repressive capacity can better sustain electoral authoritarianism by deploying overpowering violence and intimidation against their oppositions (Albertus and Menaldo 2012).

The second major approach to electoral authoritarianism argues that electoral autocracies are more likely to thrive where societies and oppositions lack access to external influences and resources that can help them to mobilize and overcome these regimes' manipulative and coercive power. In this regard, Levitsky and Way (2010a) point out that the rise of electoral authoritarianism is best predicted by a country's "linkage" to the West, in the form of political, economic, social, and cultural ties, as well as its exposure to Western "leverage" – pressure aimed to promote democratic behavior.[11] Sensitivity to such external pressures, as other studies have shown, tends to be geographically and temporally clustered (K. S. Gleditsch and Ward 2006), and driven by waves of democratic diffusion and retrenchment (Beissinger 2007; Bunce and Wolchik 2011). The driving force behind the success or failure of electoral autocracies, from this perspective, is the exposure of these regimes to the external influence of other democracies. The domestic determinants of electoral authoritarianism, such as the oppositional structure and mobilization potential, play an important but secondary role, mediating the impact of these external factors (Waldner and Lust 2018, 106).

The third explanation of electoral authoritarianism ties the persistence of these regimes to their strong economic and other performance. This performance legitimacy argument is the only one that explicitly tackles the possibility that electoral authoritarianism can enjoy genuine majority support. This popular consent is rooted in an "authoritarian bargain": societies trade in their political freedoms for strong economic growth delivered by these regimes (Desai, Olofsgård, and Yousef 2009). A notable example of this line of reasoning is provided in Treisman (2011a), who argues that the

---

[11] On this, see also Brinks and Coppedge (2006), Hyde (2007), Djankov, Montalvo, and Reynal-Querol (2008), Wright (2009), and Kelley (2012). Conversely, contexts that create bonds of mutual assistance and cooperation between authoritarian regimes has been used to help "diffusion-proof" electoral authoritarianism against democratization (Koesel and Bunce 2013; von Soest 2015).

impressive popular support of Vladimir Putin's electoral authoritarian rule during his first two terms in office was owed to Russia's sustained economic recovery in this period. The performance legitimacy mechanism has also been applied comparatively, in relation to other regime alternatives and on the international level. Miller (2015b) and Cassani (2017b), for instance, argue that electoral autocracies can claim greater performance legitimacy than closed dictatorships because on average, they have been more successful in delivering various economic and social benefits and services. Miller (2016), in turn, shows that the attractiveness of authoritarianism relative to democracy has grown when such regimes are perceived to have a superior record of economic performance. From this comparative point of view, examples of electoral authoritarian overachievers such as Singapore influence people to support similar regimes in their own countries.

Despite their valuable insights, these paradigms have been unable to account for several key aspects of electoral authoritarianism. First, the arguments that electoral autocracies are sustained by their more nuanced, efficient, and institutionally channeled coercive power or by their superior economic performance cannot explain how many of these regimes rise to power, before they have access to the patronage, propaganda, and repressive resources of the state, and before they have clear records of economic achievement. In particular, the idea that authoritarian regimes secure popular consent with repression, propaganda, and clientelism runs counter to the fact that the vast majority of electoral autocracies today have entirely nonviolent and democratic origins. Unlike military dictatorships and other closed autocracies, contemporary electoral authoritarian regimes have overwhelmingly emerged without any use of coercion whatsoever. They are established *after* elected incumbents – many of whom were outsiders with few allies and resources – have gradually dismembered democracy through the democratic process itself – often with substantial popular support (Svolik 2013; Bermeo 2016; Levitsky and Ziblatt 2018). The external influence paradigm, in turn, has a problem explaining why some of the most striking cases of backsliding toward electoral authoritarianism in recent years have emerged in countries like NATO and EU members Hungary and Poland, where Western influences and democratic pressures are very high.

Second, the neo-institutional, performance legitimacy, and external influence accounts of electoral authoritarianism cannot fully explain the collapse of these regimes. Here too, the issue is simple: if coercion and manipulation, economic performance, and isolation from democratization pressures are central to keeping incumbents in power in electoral autocracies, why are they unable to prevent or crush the popular revolts that unseat them? The standard response in the existing literature is that electoral autocracies collapse when economic crises diminish these regimes' resources and capacity to control their populations with clientelism and repression, or insulate them from foreign influence (see e.g. Diaz-Cayeros, Magaloni, and Weingast 2003, Magaloni 2006, and Greene 2007).

However, this argument cannot account for the opposite paradox: why have many prominent electoral authoritarian regimes stubbornly persisted in the wake of catastrophic economic crises and an increasingly urban, educated, middle-class citizenry? The world's longest-lasting electoral autocracy, that of the PRI regime in Mexico, for instance, retained its popular support for years despite its failing performance and credibility.[12] Serbia's strongman Slobodan Milošević maintained electoral dominance for more than a decade, despite inflicting several disastrous wars and crippling international sanctions on his population (Palairet 2001; Gagnon 2004). The "Bolivarian" electoral autocracy of Hugo Chávez in Venezuela has long outlived its charismatic founder, although it failed on its promise of bringing welfare to the poor, squandered the country's oil wealth, wrecked the economy, and presided over incessant blackouts, shortages of basic goods, and staggering crime rates (Rodriguez 2008; Corrales and Penfold-Becerra 2015; *The Economist* 2017a). Zimbabwe's ailing electoral autocrat Robert Mugabe doggedly clung on to power until he was ninety-two years old, surviving rising opposition and succession struggles, and presiding over record-breaking hyperinflation and the complete devastation of the country's economy, law and order, and public services (Bratton and Masunungure 2008; *The Economist* 2017b). Such

---

[12] As Greene (2007, 19–20) points out, "76% of voters evaluated the PRI's economic performance negatively beginning more than a decade before it lost power; however, during the 1990s, up to 57% of voters who were the most dissatisfied with the PRI's performance still planned to vote for it." Morgenstern and Zechmeister (2001) find similar results as late as in 1997, three years before the PRI's electoral defeat.

stunning cases of regime survival completely defy performance legitimacy explanations. They also cannot be fully attributed to more efficient
clientelism, as these resource-strapped regimes increasingly lacked the
means to reward even their loyal supporters. Similarly, legions of
suffering citizens cannot be reliably kept in line with selective repression alone.

In the ultimate analysis, accounts centered on manipulation and
coercion struggle to explain not just the rise and downfall of electoral
authoritarianism, but also how these regimes reach and stay at the
height of their power. In this sense, the most successful and robust
electoral autocracies, as the literature admits, are the ones that need not
resort to repression, clientelism, propaganda, and vote fraud to win the
ballots. Dubbed *hegemonic* electoral autocracies, these regimes are
genuinely popular, regularly win oversized majorities of 70–75 percent
of the vote, and are long-lasting (Roessler and Howard 2009; Schedler
2013). Hegemonic regimes use coercive tactics as a last resort or to
boost their already high vote margins (Magaloni 2006, 11; Simpser
2013; Gehlbach and Simpser 2015). On the other hand, the electoral
autocracies that collapse do so in spite of, and indeed because of, their
heavy reliance on authoritarian tactics like coercion, patronage, and
vote fraud. These so-called *competitive* electoral authoritarian regimes
do not command strong popular support; they are unstable and more
likely to serve as stepping stones to democracy than as precursors of
robust authoritarianism (Hadenius and Teorell 2007, 150–153). This
contrast between hegemonic and competitive electoral autocracies
indeed demonstrates that coercion and the stability of electoral
authoritarianism generally have a negative, *inverse* relationship. The
more a regime relies on clientelism, propaganda, repression vote fraud,
and so on, the weaker it is.

In a similar vein, relatively high economic performance seems to have
undermined, rather than stabilized electoral autocracies in many cases.
This has been especially true for hegemonic electoral autocracies. The
first major protest wave against Vladimir Putin's reign in Russia, for
instance, was led by the biggest beneficiaries of the economic recovery
under his reign – the educated urban middle class – and took place
during a period of relatively robust growth (Treisman 2014; Dmitriev
2015). Similarly, the ruling PAP party in the world's top-performing
electoral autocracy in Singapore has been experiencing a consistent
decline in its vote share relative to the opposition since the early

2000s. This shift has been occurring despite – or as some would argue, because of – the fact that Singapore's economic performance in this period was so high that the country overtook the United States in terms of GDP per capita (*The Economist* 2015b). These and other examples suggest that the relationship between sustained economic achievement and electoral authoritarian resilience has been more in line with modernization theory – that societies turn against authoritarianism as their income, education, and urbanization levels increase (Inglehart and Welzel 2009) – than the performance legitimacy argument.

To summarize, there are at least three paradoxes of electoral authoritarianism that the existing literature cannot resolve. First, electoral autocracies typically emerge and consolidate their power with little or no coercion and manipulation, without an impressive record of economic and other achievements, and often in places with substantial exposure to external democratization pressures. Second, electoral autocracies that struggle and ultimately collapse often do so in spite of their vast coercive and manipulative capacity, relatively solid economic performance, and isolation from Western influence. Third, relying even on sophisticated forms of coercion and manipulation tends to be an indicator of weakness – not strength – of electoral authoritarianism. The regimes that most heavily use these tactics tend to be the most vulnerable ones. The most robust electoral autocracies, on the other hand, rule with very little resort to coercion and manipulation, and by winning in relatively clean elections.

This obvious mismatch between institutionalized coercion, economic performance, international influences, and authoritarian stability strongly suggests that there is a crucial omitted variable lurking in the background: the popular appeal of electoral authoritarian parties and leaders. When this appeal is high, fledgling authoritarian leaders like Alberto Fujimori in Peru or Hugo Chávez in Venezuela have won elections against long-established competitors and ushered in electoral authoritarianism before they had meaningful coercive power under their control. Other popular autocrats, like Hungary's Victor Orbán, have set up electoral authoritarian regimes at the heart of the EU and NATO, effectively negating their countries' exposure to Western influences and democratization pressures. Once in possession of the considerable coercive and remunerative resources of the state, popular electoral autocracies, like Vladimir Putin's regime in Russia during his first two presidential terms, have had relatively little use for them. As long as their popular appeal has persisted, these regimes have dominate their societies through the polling booth and with minimal use of force and forgery. And once the tide of popular opinion has turned against them, even the most robust and long-lasting electoral autocracies, like the PRI regime in Mexico, have eventually collapsed, despite of – or indeed because of – their heavy reliance on institutional manipulation, and the repressive, clientelistic propaganda and other resources still at their disposal.

The Confounding Influence of the Popular Appeal of Elected Strongmen

The previous discussion is not meant to suggest that institutionalized coercion, economic performance, and foreign influences do not play meaningful roles in these regimes. Quite the contrary, they are both defining features of electoral authoritarianism and crucial "force multipliers" which enable authoritarian forces to achieve a much greater margin of control than they could muster with their popular appeal alone. And in some critical junctures, when opposition threatens to snowball, these mechanisms – the strategic use of coercion in particular – play the role of the proverbial finger in the dike, protecting authoritarianism from being easily swept away.

However, as the current literature admits, no regime can be sustained by coercion and manipulation alone over the long run – or for that matter, its economic performance and relative isolation from foreign influences – unless it retains some degree of sincere popular support by satisfying the broader aspirations of its citizens (Wintrobe 1998, 2018; Geddes 1999; Acemoglu and Robinson 2006). Thus, at any given point in time, the impact of coercion and institutional manipulation – as well as of external influences and economic performance – is shaped by preexisting mass attitudes toward the regime. The main purpose of propaganda, clientelism, repression, vote fraud, and similar tactics from this standpoint is to boost or to fill gaps in the popular appeal of authoritarian incumbents. Their effectiveness, particularly when used systematically over the long term, is limited by what people are predisposed to believe and justify, and by the potential for popular backlash.[13] Because coercive power operates in a social milieu supplied by mass sentiments and the legitimizing appeal of electoral authoritarianism, these attitudinal factors condition its effects on the rise and survival of these regimes.

The same could be said about the effects of adopting nominally democratic institutions in autocracies, which according to neo-institutionalist accounts, allow these regimes to monitor, coerce, and coopt their societies in a more selective, efficient, and targeted fashion. Because multipartyism, parliaments, and elections create opportunities for oppositional mobilization long before they provide such benefits for authoritarian incumbents, the decision to adopt these institutions is bound to be endogenous to the preexisting strength of the regime (see Negretto 2013, Pepinsky 2014, and Knutsen, Nygård, and Wig 2017) – particularly its ability to control their populations without much resort to coercion. Hence, a large portion of

---

[13] The case in point is the use of repression by electoral autocracies. As Wintrobe (2018) observes, electoral authoritarian incumbents resort to systematic violence to strengthen their genuine popularity, not to compensate for the lack of it. They tend to repress certain *disliked minorities* – ethnic, racial, religious, and other ostracized social and opposition groups – as a way to win the support of popular majorities. For this strategy to work without undermining the regime, these minorities must obviously be small enough. The majority, in turn, must either be hostile toward these groups and approving of their treatment, or, at a minimum, it ought to be apathetic about their plight – sentiments that clearly depend on preexisting opinion patterns that strongmen seek to exploit. Similarly, the study of clientelism and patronage strongly suggests that the scope and effectiveness of these tactics depends on the preexisting appeal of their regimes. As vote buying and patronage tend to only sway passivized regime supporters, weak opponents, and undecideds (see e.g. Stokes 2005, Bratton 2008, Nichter 2008, Calvo and Murillo 2013, and Gutiérrez-Romero 2014), a sufficient number of people must remain in these categories for the clientelistic appeal of autocracies to make a meaningful difference. The most common effect of clientelism, for these reasons, is to increase the vote margins of incumbents that would likely prevail without relying on this tactic. In the same vein, the studies of vote fraud show that the electoral autocracies with the greatest capacity for falsification are those that do not need it to win; their overwhelming popularity is the key factor that convinces countless bureaucrats to rig the ballots – signaling that the regime will remain in power after the elections to reward their loyalty and to protect them from punishment (see Simpser 2013, Gehlbach and Simpser 2015, and Rundlett and Svolik 2016). Finally, the effectiveness of propaganda has also been shown to depend on favorable mass dispositions toward the regime. It tends to backfire when it does not play on people's preexisting sentiments, and generally mobilizes entrenched sympathies for the regime or the opposition, instead of changing people's opinions (see e.g. Mickiewicz 1999, 2008, Gehlbach 2010, Knight and Tribin 2018, and Peisakhin and Rozenas 2018).

what appears like an independent effect of institutions may in fact be a product of the original appeal of the regimes that have adopted them (on this, also see Smith 2005). In the extreme, institutions and coercive strategies are only the most easily observable symptoms of the social forces that sustain authoritarianism (see Pepinsky 2014, 650), which have little independent causal effect of their own. At a minimum, background factors are bound to have a strong moderating influence on the influence of authoritarian institutions, as well as on the coercive power channeled through them.[14]

This book's key point of departure is that the existing literature correctly identifies many key drivers of electoral authoritarianism but overlooks the most fundamental background factor that ties them all together: the genuine popular appeal of these regimes in troubled societies. In the analytic framework I propose, coercive power still plays an essential role, and pseudo-democratic institutions also help autocracies apply it with greater efficiency and precision. Electoral authoritarian regimes are still propped up by their economic performance, as well as by their resilience to democratic diffusion and external pressures. However, these factors operate in a broader context, defined by the distinct appeal of elected autocracies as guarantors of order and justice in troubled societies. When this appeal is salient and these

---

[14] In electoral autocracies, there are at least three strong indicators that institutions are shaped by the popular appeal of these regimes at least as much as those regimes are shaped by them. First, when they have sufficient support, electoral authoritarian regimes have proved supremely capable of ignoring institutions that were supposed to constrain their behavior (Pepinsky 2014, 635). Second, when armed with supermajorities, electoral autocracies have routinely manipulated institutions – they have redrafted constitutions, packed the courts, and changed laws on libel, campaigning finances, and so on – to gain tactical advantages over their oppositions (Magaloni 2006). Third, the claim that adopting nominally democratic institutions like elections, multipartyism, and parliaments has a stabilizing role on authoritarianism does not square with the findings of cross-national empirical studies, which have shown that regimes that exhibit high institutional inconsistency – electoral autocracies in particular – tend to be the least stable regimes on average (Gates et al. 2006). In other words, as far as the institutional effects registered at the aggregate level are concerned, adopting democratic institutions should make autocracies *less*, not more stable. But that is clearly not the case in many electoral autocracies (Knutsen, Nygård, and Wig 2017). What drives this discrepancy? Clearly, looking at institutions alone cannot address this question. To determine the independent causal effect of authoritarian institutions, we must control for the confounding influence of social consent, which might have produced the electoral authoritarian regime – as well as its institutions – in the first place.

factors are aligned with it, their effects are greatly amplified. When the strongman appeal is diminished, the use of coercion, high economic performance, and resistance to democratization pressures have weak or negligible impact, at best. At worst, they may be counterproductive and hasten the downfall of electoral authoritarianism.

Not accounting for this contingent relationship creates a significant blind spot, limiting our understanding of these regimes. Even more troublingly, it severely biases the existing accounts of electoral authoritarianism, because the factors that keep elected autocrats in power, according to the current literature, are not independent of these regimes' mass appeal. In particular, popular support confounds the effects of coercive and manipulative tactics in two fundamental ways. I depict these in the directed acyclic graphs[15] in Figure 1.2 below.

Seasoned observers of electoral authoritarian politics will find the pattern in the left panel of this figure very familiar. Deep systemic crises increase the attractiveness of strongman parties and candidates, promising to restore order and address injustices. This genuine popularity among crisis-weary and aggrieved populations, in turn, gives authoritarian political actors a direct route to win elections – without any use of repression, clientelism, propaganda, and vote fraud – a paradox that is largely unaccounted for in the current literature. At the same time,

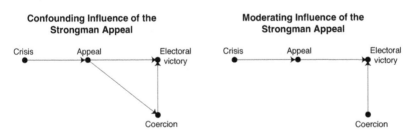

Figure 1.2 The relationship between crises, "strongman" popular appeal, coercion, and electoral victory of authoritarian parties and leaders

---

[15] Directed acyclic graphs (DAG) are a versatile, nonparametric tool for specifying causal relations between variables (see Pearl 2009). Quite simply, the nodes in the DAG graphs represent variables, and the directed vertices among them capture the hypothesized causal relationships. These graphs are "acyclic" in that they do not allow for simultaneous causation and reciprocal relationships (i.e. two variables cannot be connected with arrows going in both directions). For an excellent introduction to the use of DAGs in the social sciences, see Morgan and Winship (2007).

the strongman appeal and mandate to restore order and prosperity justifies and encourages these regimes' use of coercion and manipulation – tactics they can abuse to stymie their opponents further and win with larger electoral margins. Thus, by affecting the outcome both directly as well as indirectly (through the repressive tactics and other machinations it enables), the strongman appeal confounds the relationship between coercion and securing electoral victory. What we typically attribute to the coercive power of electoral autocracies, might, as a result, be an indirect consequence of these regimes' popular mandate to restore order, or address grievances and dysfunction.

Even if the effects of repression, clientelism, propaganda, and other coercive strategies are independent of the strongman appeal of electoral autocracies, they are bound to be moderated (i.e. made stronger or weaker) by it – a relationship I depict in the right panel of Figure 1.2. The logic is straightforward: if broad swathes of the population genuinely support an electoral authoritarian regime as their only "savior" from turmoil and dysfunction, they are more likely find its propaganda believable, its repression justified, and to accept its use of clientelism, vote fraud, and other machinations as "necessary evils." And where these regimes enjoy genuine majority support, social pressures to conform might convince even citizens who would otherwise be critical to back the strong-armed policies of incumbents.[16] In all these cases, the degree of social control commonly attributed to pure coercive power is, in fact, largely catalyzed by the overwhelming popularity of strongman incumbents in troubled societies.[17]

This framework improves upon current understandings of electoral authoritarianism in at least two crucial regards. First, it challenges the prevailing view that electoral autocracies are largely sustained by a more sophisticated use of coercive instruments like clientelism, repression, and propaganda, as well as by institutional manipulations. Instead, I highlight the intersection between crises, popular opinion, and the mass appeal of authoritarian rulers as the most basic pillars of electoral authoritarianism. These previously omitted variables not only

---

[16] On this topic, see Noelle-Neumann (1984), Manaev, Manayeva, and Yuran (2010), Kalinin (2016), and Hellmeier and Weidmann (2019).

[17] This moderating effect of popular appeal also operates in the opposite direction. The use of coercion and manipulation by electoral autocracies that are widely despised by their populations is particularly ineffective and prone to backfire (see e.g. Hale 2014 and Tucker 2007).

allow authoritarian incumbents to win and maintain power thorough the ballot box, but also enable them to effectively employ coercive tactics and manipulate institutions to further reinforce their dominance.

Second, accounting for the underlying popular appeal of electoral authoritarian regimes, as well as the circumstances that enable it, allows us to develop an overarching theory of electoral authoritarianism that explains the entire trajectory of these regimes: (1) their origins; (2) their durability; and (3) their demise. Specifically, considering the popular appeal of elected strongmen allows me to address four key unexplained paradoxes of electoral authoritarianism: (1) how electoral autocracies rise and become hegemonic with minimum coercion and manipulation; (2) why many of them persist despite their abysmal performance, exposure to democratization pressures, and diminishing coercive capacity; (3) how electoral autocracies collapse despite their substantial coercive power, isolation, and robust economic performance; and (4) how these regimes are able to engage in blatantly authoritarian behavior without losing domestic support.

Research Design and Chapter Outline

In the chapters that follow, I develop a full theoretical framework which argues that electoral autocracies are, to a large degree, products of popular demands for strong-armed, effective rule, which emerge in the wake of profound political, economic, and security crises. To validate these claims, I employ a three-pronged empirical strategy. First, using an extensive cross-national regime transition and survival analysis, I test the core macro-level implication of this book's analytic framework: that electoral autocracies are the most likely regime type to emerge and persist in the wake of acute crises and decay. Second, to verify whether electoral authoritarian parties and leaders have a distinct and consistent "strongman" appeal, designed to take advantage of the collective traumas and fears of crisis-weary majorities, I perform a comparative content analysis of the campaign rhetoric of incumbents in electoral autocracies and democracies. Third, to show that the strongman appeal of these regimes allows them to achieve dominance at the polls with minimal resort to coercion, I perform a multilayered comparative analysis of popular opinion patterns and voting behavior before and after the rise of electoral autocracies.

This last component of the empirical strategy is a combination of: (1) an in-depth study of mass attitudes and electoral behavior in the Russian electoral authoritarian regime since the 1990s; and (2) a cross-national analysis of the corresponding mass opinion patterns in electoral autocracies and democracies from across the globe. The focus on the Russian case has several unique advantages. First, in the decade since the Soviet collapse, Russia experienced the steepest peacetime decline in history – a socioeconomic cataclysm twice as intense as the Great Depression of the 1930s (Mitra and Selowsky 2002; Eberstadt 2010). Studying the Russian case therefore offers particular leverage to examine how such traumatic crises shape popular sentiments and regime preferences. Second, since Vladimir Putin's rise in 2000, Russia has become an archetype of hegemonic electoral authoritarianism, which many other electoral dictatorships from across the world have strived to emulate (see e.g. Caryl 2015, 2018). Hence, the Russian case not only represents the phenomenon of interest for this book with the greatest conceptual clarity, but the fact that it has served as a global template of robust electoral authoritarianism also implies that its key features are broadly generalizable. Third, due to its size and military and economic power, Russia has been less susceptible to external democratization pressures than most other electoral autocracies. A focus on Russia is thus, in effect, a way to control for these external factors, isolating the endogenous dynamics of systemic crises, popular opinion, and electoral authoritarianism. Finally, compared to other electoral autocracies, Russia offers an unparalleled variety of high-quality popular opinion data and other resources, allowing for a particularly detailed tracing of the interplay between mass opinion and regime trajectories.

Following this research strategy, this book's analysis proceeds in several steps. Chapter 2 fully develops the overarching theoretical framework of the book. It first specifies a comprehensive theory as to why electoral authoritarianism tends to be the most preferred remedy for popular majorities living in troubled societies. It then moves on to define the specific rhetorical template and campaign strategy – what I describe as the elected strongman appeal – that authoritarian incumbents use to press their advantage and win favor among electorates distraught by turmoil. Finally, Chapter 2 develops a full theory of electoral competition in societies that have experienced deep, traumatic crises. This segment traces how justifying electoral authoritarianism as a strong-armed response to a national emergency enables authoritarian parties and leaders to achieve a genuine popularity advantage over their opponents, and to secure power through the ballot box and with minimal coercion.

Chapter 3 provides a detailed empirical test of the central macro-level implication of this book's analytic framework: that electoral autocracies tend to emerge in the wake of deep security, economic, and political crises – circumstances that allow such regimes to compellingly justify their rule as necessary in order to preserve order and stability. Based on a comprehensive cross-national analysis of regime transition and survival patters for 1960–2014, this chapter demonstrates that socioeconomic and security crises are the best predictors of transitions to electoral authoritarianism. The analysis also demonstrates that those electoral autocracies that are preceded by the deepest economic crises, and that subsequently manage to make the greatest progress toward restoring prosperity, have the lowest risk of democratization.

Chapter 4 challenges the prevailing view in the current literature that electoral authoritarian regimes rely on a hodgepodge of inconsistent legitimizing strategies, opportunistically drawn from various disparate platforms and ideologies. Using cross-national data from the Comparative Manifestos Project Dataset (Volkens et al. 2016), this chapter shows that the campaign strategies and rhetoric of electoral autocracies have instead followed a remarkably consistent pattern. Practically without exception, they have embraced the elected strongman appeal, which justifies their rule as a popularly mandated response to a national emergency.

In Chapter 5, I begin to trace the popular opinion patterns in electoral autocracies with a comparative analysis of the paradigmatic case of Russia. The chapter first outlines the scope and consequences of Russia's catastrophic post-Communist cataclysm, and how this traumatic experience prompted ordinary Russians to place an absolute premium on restoring order and stability – outlooks that enabled the rise of Vladimir Putin and made his tough-mannered style of governing incredibly popular. Using a uniquely rich dataset of 418 surveys for the 1993–2011 period produced by the Levada Center – Russia's leading independent polling organization – this chapter demonstrates that in societies traumatized by upheaval, the strongman appeal trumps ideological, programmatic, and value orientations, and aligns mass opinion and political competition along a new cleavage: the choice of accepting or rejecting electoral authoritarianism as a regime that can restore order. I show that the choices imposed by this cleavage inhibit and divide the opposition and highlight its shortcomings, allowing even weakly performing autocracies to retain power through elections.

Chapter 6 tests the generalizability of the book's analytic framework beyond the Russian case. Examining cross-national opinion data from forty-two electoral autocracies in the 1981–2014 period, drawn from the European and World Values Surveys (EVS 2011; WVS 2014) – the broadest available comparative dataset on popular sentiments about politics – I find that just as in Russia, electoral authoritarian incumbents from across the globe have exploited traumas rooted in unmanageable turmoil to reconfigure mass opinion and political competition in their favor. Chapter 6 also shows that this cleavage structure and logic of vote choice differs from the patterns we observe in stable Western democracies, confirming again that the advantages electoral autocracies enjoy at the polls are largely owing to the extraordinarily subversive power of the elected strongman appeal in troubled societies.

Chapter 7 summarizes the book's findings and discusses its implications. It underlines the most essential limitation of the appeal of electoral authoritarianism: these regimes become superfluous both when they succeed and when they fail to deliver stability. To maintain popular consent, electoral autocracies must therefore manufacture the types of crises that justify their existence. This paradoxical dynamic has profound implications for their domestic and international behavior, as recently demonstrated by the aggressive posture of electoral autocracies from across the globe, ranging from Vladimir Putin's Russia, through Recep Tayyip Erdoğan's Turkey, to the Philippines under Rodrigo Duterte.

2 | *Crises, Popular Opinion, and Electoral Authoritarianism*

To suppose that majority rule functions only in a democracy is a fantastic illusion. The king, who is but one solitary individual, stands far more in need of the general support of society than any other form of government.

Bertrand De Jouvenel (1962, 106)

This book is based on a counterintuitive and disturbing premise. It argues that electoral autocracies – the most widespread and persistent form of authoritarianism in the world today – are not sustained by their more subtle capacity to repress, bribe, brainwash, and otherwise manipulate populations into submission. Instead, the rise and resilience of these regimes is largely a product of their ability to convince popular majorities to willingly consent to their rule. Rising in societies traumatized by deep political, socioeconomic and security crises, electoral authoritarian incumbents attract genuine popular support by posing as tough, efficient strongmen, who are uniquely capable of restoring order and addressing injustices. They win elections by representing the existential anxieties of populations beset by turmoil and despair and by persuading voters that their alternatives are worse. The popular legitimacy these regimes secure by prevailing at the ballots does not restrain their authoritarian behavior. It actually enables it. Electoral dictators use their mandate to restore order and stability as a license to remove any checks on their power, and to unleash violence and censorship against their opponents, detractors, and various "undesirable" minorities.

Instead of assuming that electoral autocracies grow out of the barrel of a gun, the slush fund flows of a political machine, or the mouthpiece of propaganda, this book proposes a broader and more nuanced explanation: that to a large extent, societies voluntarily (though often reluctantly) choose to support electoral authoritarian rule because they believe it is best suited to maintain order and offer redress for their grievances. Electoral authoritarianism, to put it differently, rises not just because it is imposed upon its subjects, but to a large degree, because many of its subjects also think it is useful – and indeed necessary – in some circumstances.

A skeptic might ask: why would a society in crisis endorse electoral authoritarianism – an institutionally incoherent and unstable hybrid system, mixing democratic and authoritarian features (Gates et al. 2006)? If the ultimate purpose is to impose a more peaceful or just order, why not support a more forceful, unelected autocracy – perhaps a military or a single-party dictatorship? I argue that counterintuitively, the seemingly unstable institutional dualism of electoral authoritarianism is exactly what makes these regimes so appealing to societies beset by turmoil and dysfunction. For ordinary citizens who live in despair, or believe their country to be tottering on the brink of collapse, electoral autocracy seems the best remedy because it mixes authoritarianism and democracy *in moderation*. To them, a regime that eliminates the destabilizing pluralism of liberal democracy but is still electorally accountable protects against the two great perils that arise in times of political turmoil: (1) the disarray of an unfettered democratic contestation; and (2) the rise of a completely unchecked, tyrannical dictatorship. This is the main reason why the world's longest-lasting electoral autocracy, the seventy-one-year reign of the Institutional Revolutionary Party (PRI) regime in Mexico, was dubbed the "perfect dictatorship." As Oppenheimer (1998, 97) put it:

[i]ts major accomplishment was of a *negative nature* [my emphasis]: preventing the cycles of dictatorships and bloody revolts that had shaken Mexico throughout history. To put an end to politicians' temptations of unlimited power, Mexico's post-revolutionary rulers created a system of elections every six years, with no reelection.

Most other electoral autocracies have retired their dictators less regularly than Mexico but retained the essential advantages of this system. On one hand, electorally endorsed authoritarianism allowed incumbents to wield unchecked executive power, quashing disruptive factionalism, maintaining stability, and pushing through essential reforms. On the other, it prevented them from becoming too entrenched and therefore capable of unleashing an unbridled tyranny.

Because of these traits, electoral authoritarianism is poised to appear as the best, middle-ground remedy to popular majorities in *both* democracies and closed autocracies beset by crises. For majorities seeking change to address unmanageable crises in either democracies or closed autocracies, electoral authoritarianism seems to be the safest bet: a system that does not radically dismantle the current one, thereby risking further instability, but one that is still different enough to address its major flaws. Offering "the best" of both ends of the regime spectrum – a streamlined "democracy-lite" in dysfunctional democracies, and a reformed and more inclusive "authoritarianism-lite" in oppressive, closed dictatorships – electoral authoritarian regimes are, at a minimum, poised to appear as the least bad solution for societies afflicted by crises and instability. Such expectations may be well founded, according to empirical studies. Miller (2015a, 2015b), for instance, shows that even barely competitive electoral autocracies have been much more responsive to popular demands than closed dictatorships, and have produced improvements in health, education, and gender equality that are as strong as in democracies.[1]

This account sheds new light on the proliferation of these regimes over the past two decades. As the failure of closed, completely unchecked dictatorships to deliver stability and prosperity became widely apparent, electoral authoritarianism gained popularity as a far more moderate, majority-pleasing, or "domesticated" form of strong-armed rule for volatile and dysfunctional polities. And the allure of electoral autocracy as a relatively benign dictatorship, fit for troubled societies, does not end there. Once these regimes are established, lingering fears of instability among the population also enable those regimes to cling on to power. This mindset, moored in the collective trauma of unmanageable turmoil or injustice that has preceded electoral authoritarianism, can have perverse consequences. Fearing that a more democratic order might undermine the stabilization and new privileges gained under authoritarian rule, and lead to greater turmoil, popular majorities can prove remarkably unwilling to rise even against electoral autocracies that are highly inefficient, corrupt, and oppressive (on this, see also Morgenstern and Zechmeister (2001)). This dynamic is crucial for understanding the remarkable durability of some of the world's most notoriously ill-performing electoral autocracies – such as Zimbabwe under Robert Mugabe, Venezuela under Hugo Chávez and Nicolás Maduro, and Serbia under Slobodan Milošević.

---

[1] On this, see also Cassani (2017a) and Little (2017).

This argument differs from most existing accounts of the role of crises in regime transitions. First, while most of the current literature suggests that crises play a comparable role in *all* types of regime transitions,[2] I argue that deep, traumatic upheavals tend to disproportionately give rise to electoral autocracies and prolong their rule. Second, most existing works have considered political, security, and socioeconomic upheavals as essential factors in the breakdown of different political regimes, but not as sources of legitimation for the regimes that succeeded them (one exception here is Huntington 1991, 41–42). Crises, in other words, have been considered to mostly play a *delegitimizing* role when it comes to political regimes, rather than a *legitimizing* one. I argue, in contrast, that crises have an essential legitimizing function in electoral autocracies in that they create a broad popular demand for a strong-armed but electorally constrained rule, allowing these regimes to be sustained through the polling booth and with limited coercion.

This book's analytic framework builds upon the insights of several important works that recognize deep systemic crises as essential tools for justifying authoritarian rule. In particular, the idea that societies may willingly accept authoritarian rule to achieve a threshold of order and stability essential for civilized existence traces back to Thomas Hobbes' *Leviathan*. According to Hobbes (1640): "[t]he cause in general which moveth a man to become subject to another, is . . . the fear of not otherwise preserving himself." The authoritarian state Hobbes describes is therefore not based on pure coercion but is formed as a social pact: its subjects willingly submit to this highly unequal social order because it pulls them from anarchic conditions, in which life was nasty, brutish, and short.[3]

---

[2] See for example Linz (1978), O'Donnell, Schmitter, and Whitehead (1986b), Huntington (1991), Haggard and Kaufman (1995), Przeworski et al. (2000), Svolik (2008), and Burke and Leigh (2010).

[3] Olson (1993) vividly captured this logic of the authoritarian social contract with the "roving" versus "stationary" bandit metaphor. In the anarchic state of nature, Olson highlights, societies are devastated by the competitive and utterly ruinous plunder of "roving bandits," who opportunistically ransack the unprotected populations. In such circumstances, people are considerably better off if they voluntarily endorse dictatorial rule by bandits who agree to become "stationary" and provide security from the unrestrained pillaging of their roaming counterparts. Both sides stand to benefit, leading to a stable social order.

More recently, Slater (2010) outlined a contemporary account of the authoritarian social contract, arguing that widely shared beliefs that authoritarian rule is needed to maintain order were the key factor that helped autocracies survive the unprecedented democratization pressures. This is why, according to Slater's study of regime trajectories in Southeast Asia, the most robust contemporary autocracies emerged in countries that had suffered from severe or persistent crises. The trauma from such upheavals, he points out, created a shared perception among key elites that their societies were plagued by latent and unmanageable conflicts, and that authoritarian rule was necessary to maintain order. This backdrop enables autocracies to forge a social contract among constituencies with otherwise opposing interests – a pro-authoritarian *protection pact*, uniting a wide range of elites, interest groups, and state officials to support authoritarian rule in exchange for protection from the greater peril of chaos and anarchy.

Slater's key insight is that this shared fear of unmanageable turmoil provides a far more reliable foundation for authoritarian rule than clientelism and other coercive tools emphasized in the literature. Fear of instability, according to Slater (2010, 49), has a decisive advantage over patronage in particular because: "(1) fear is indivisible, whereas state sponsorship of one elite faction leaves fewer resources for others; (2) fear can generate broad support for authoritarian rule among groups whose interests transcend the material (i.e. religious groups), and among those who are hard to reach with targeted state patronage (i.e. urban middle classes)." Widespread perceptions of an existential threat to social order can, in other words, consistently unite key constituencies behind authoritarian regimes in ways that patronage and other coercive tactics cannot.

I use this *neo-Hobbesian* perspective as a starting point to develop a more comprehensive and realistic theory of contemporary electoral authoritarianism, which incorporates the role of popular opinion and legitimation – variables largely omitted from the existing literature. This analytic framework extends current accounts in two fundamental ways. First, while authors like Slater argue that histories of deep systemic crises promote all kinds of authoritarian regimes, I claim that such experiences make electoral autocracies much more attractive than other forms of dictatorship. I argue that for societies reeling from turmoil, dysfunction, and despair, electoral authoritarianism not only seems to be the safer option – far less likely to deteriorate into an outright tyranny than closed dictatorships – but it is also the only one that provides a direct mechanism to enforce the authoritarian social contract. By holding regular multiparty elections that cannot be entirely falsified, these regimes both verify majority consent to their rule and provide a much more substantial institutional route for popular rebellion if they do not deliver on their promise to restore stability and address grievances.

Second, I claim that the electoral authoritarian social contract is sustained by a bottom-up, *popular demand* for authoritarianism at least as much as by the top-down supply of authoritarianism. This differs from the authoritarian protection pact described by Slater, which is an elite-level contract, maintained with top-down repression. In this regard, Slater assumes that an authoritarian regime is safe from popular uprising as long as it can motivate state officials – particularly the repressive apparatus – to deploy coercive force against its opponents, convince economic elites to pay higher taxes and finance the regime's political machines, and cajole the communal elites and the middle class to bestow it with symbolic legitimacy, and provide "intellectual justification for non-democratic rule (p. 16)."[4] This echoes the long-standing thesis in the literature, articulated by O'Donnell, Schmitter, and Whitehead (1986a, 22) that "no transition can be forced purely by opponents against a regime which maintains the [elite] cohesion, capacity and disposition to apply repression" (O'Donnell, Schmitter, and Whitehead 1986a, 22).[5]

The problem with this approach, as I have suggested in Chapter 1, is that the coercive power of autocracies – electoral ones in particular – is rooted on their preexisting popular support, and thus cannot be viewed as an independent explanatory factor. Regimes that enjoy majority support as guarantors of stability, prosperity, and justice could repress their opponents with relative impunity – and become even more

---

[4] The only broader segment of the population that Slater references as a constitutive element of authoritarian protection pacts is the vague notion of the "middle class," "which refrained from joining popular sectors in anti-regime mobilization, helped provide intellectual justification for non-democratic rule, and formed the social backbone of authoritarian ruling parties (p. 16)." However, the middle classes envisioned in this fashion are conceptually closer to a relatively privileged quasi-elite than to a popular majority that can provide mass support for authoritarian regimes.

[5] On this elite-centric perspective of authoritarian survival and breakdown, see also Geddes (1999), de Mesquita et al. (2003), and Svolik (2012).

popular for doing so. Widely despised autocracies that rely on coercion, on the other hand, tend to swell the ranks of their opponents and hasten their own demise. Due to this structural interdependence between coercive power and popular support, an elite-level authoritarian social contract, imposed on the rest of the population with top-down repression, is unlikely to provide the basis for a stable dictatorship.

An even more fundamental problem of the elite-centric perspective of the authoritarian social contract is that the intra-regime squabbles, splits, and coups which may lead to its demise are not independent of the mass appeal of autocracies. Instead, they tend to be its products. According to a near-universal consensus in the literature of *coups d'état*, the lack of popular legitimacy of incumbent regimes is the most robust predictor of elite defections and military coups.[6] This is because major shifts in popular sentiments – manifested as declining popular approval, disappointing electoral results, greater oppositional activism, and mass protests – are the clearest indicators that a regime is weakening and that a potential coup could muster the necessary support to succeed. Conversely, high incumbent popularity is the best signal that their ouster might be met with mass resistance – the main historical predictor of coup failure (Geddes 2005; Luttwak 2016).[7]

In other words, incumbent popularity (or rather, the lack thereof) is the most reliable coordination device in the hands of coup-plotting elites. It resolves the vexing collective action problem of potential elite conspirators by providing them with a tangible rationale to join a coup coalition.[8] From this standpoint, the most eloquent critique of

---

[6] See e.g. Linz (1978, 17), Belkin and Schofer (2003), Thyne (2010), and Johnson and Thyne (2018).

[7] According to Linz (1978, 17), it is "unlikely that military leaders would turn their arms against the government unless they felt that a significant segment of society shared their lack of belief [in that government's legitimacy]." Also, as Luttwak (2016, xvi, 24) put it, "lack of reaction from the people is all the coup needs to stay in power" and "coups rarely succeed if guns are much used and fail totally if the situation degenerates into civil war."

[8] Unfavorable popular appraisals and real or anticipated popular revolts lurk in the background of palace or military coups for one more reason. As Wintrobe (1998), Svolik (2012), and others argue, the increased threat of a rebellion makes elites within the military or the repressive apparatus indispensable for dictators, and therefore more liable to seize power through coups. Decreasing popularity also has a tendency to make dictatorships less effective, potentially opening them to further challenges and hastening their demise. In this sense, Way (2006) notes

the elite-centric account of authoritarianism was put forth five centuries ago, by none other than the foremost theorist of elite intrigue: Niccolò Machiavelli. According to Machiavelli (1532, 80),

one of the most potent remedies a prince has for conspiracies is not to be hated by the masses, for whoever conspires always believes that he will satisfy the people with the death of the prince, but if he believes he would offend them, he will not pluck up the courage to make such a move.

This dynamic not only protects authoritarian incumbents from elite plots but also gives them special leverage to subordinate the elites in their countries. In electoral autocracies, favorable mass sentiment has allowed leaders such as Russia's Vladimir Putin, Turkey's Recep Tayyip Erdoğan, or Venezuela's Hugo Chávez to subdue powerful oligarchic, regional, bureaucratic, and military elites, and helped some of them (Chávez in 2002 and Erdoğan in 2016) to defeat military coups against their rule (Corrales and Penfold-Becerra 2015; Gel'man 2015; Cagaptay 2017). Thus, rather than being passive and powerless pawns and victims of elite intrigue, mass publics and their attitudes have also played a central role in *policing* the authoritarian elites.

This is why popular consent is part and parcel of every authoritarian social contract. To put it simply, the supply side of opposition politics in autocracies (the emergence of elite challengers to the regime) is highly contingent on the demand side at the mass-level (dissatisfied social strata seeking alternatives to the regime). As result, a growing popular hostility toward a dictatorship is what provides the option to rebel for dissenters within the elite. The lack of widespread popular resentment against such a regime, on the other hand, dramatically boosts the risks associated with defection, and therefore, indirectly helps preserve elite loyalty to the regime. I argue that this pattern is especially pronounced in societies gripped by fears of turmoil, dysfunction, or loss of privilege, where authoritarian social contracts are more likely to emerge. In such circumstances, anxious populations are far more likely to rally against elite challenges and coups in popular

that state and regional officials, military commanders, and the media "have been less likely to follow orders to favor the incumbent if they thought that s/he faces serious challenges" (on this, see also Gehlbach and Simpser 2015; Rundlett and Svolik 2016). Thus, as Hale (2014, 12) observes in his study of post-Soviet authoritarian leaders, "the strongmen who were overthrown just also happened to be among the least popular leaders."

regimes, and to punish the instigators for the turmoil they have introduced. Thus, by being hostile to elite rebellions in such contexts, popular majorities indirectly enable dictators to control the elite.

Electoral authoritarianism greatly strengthens this link between popular dispositions and elite behavior because it provides regular and institutionalized opportunities to both monitor mass opinion shifts and to take advantage of them. As Langston (2006, 61) points out, "[t]he growing willingness on the part of the electorate to vote against the dominant party ... allows the ambitious politician within the dominant coalition to make a new cost-benefit analysis: the payoffs from remaining within the regime fall, while at the same time the benefits from competing outside it rise" (on this, see also Hale 2014). Or to turn the argument around, the absence of anti-regime sentiments among the population leaves no viable option to rancorous elites but to stay loyal, allowing the regime to prevent defections with relatively little resort to repression.

Indeed, the quasi-democratic, electoral nature of these regimes is an especially powerful deterrent against elite challengers. Quite simply, overthrowing a popularly elected government is likely to rally a much stronger opposition than deposing an unelected dictatorship – a dynamic that makes elite coups much more likely to fail, or to be short-lived. This is why electoral authoritarianism is a platform uniquely suited to sustaining authoritarian protection pacts in societies affected by upheaval and dysfunction. As long as widespread traumas from unmanageable crises and a history of injustice under previous political orders make these regimes appear to be the only viable alternative for the majority of the population, they can enjoy an unparalleled degree of safety from both popular revolts and elite coups.[9]

---

[9] Empirical evidence shows that the greater reliance on popular legitimation of authoritarianism, driven by the proliferation of electoral autocracies after the Cold War, played a major protective role against elite coups and infighting. Using the data on authoritarian regime collapses compiled by Svolik (2012), for instance, we can see that after 1989, the share of top-down, elite-driven coups among unconstitutional leadership removals in autocracies dropped to 26 percent from 55–68 percent for 1946–1989, while oustings due to democratic transitions, popular revolts, and civil wars respectively reached a combined total of 53 percent (from just 10–11 percent previously). Crucially, this pattern of bottom-up challenges replacing intra-elite coups also reduced the overall rate of authoritarian regime breakdown. The percentage of unconstitutional leadership replacements in autocracies from both elite and popular revolts was 67 percent for the period before 1991, 58 percent for the 1992–1999 period, and 29 percent for 2000–2008.

Paradoxically, fears of instability and loss of privilege also make common people a more reliable champion of authoritarianism than the elites. There are several reasons for this. First, ordinary citizens will generally be more motivated than elites to seek the protection of authoritarian strongmen if intractable crises and upheavals sweep the nation. The rationale is simple: common people have far fewer resources to protect themselves from turmoil than the elites. In times of conflict and broad social dysfunction, elites generally have access to private security and alternative residences in the country and overseas, where they can take refuge if their physical survival is threatened. The common layperson does not. Elites may lose much of their wealth during economic crises, but unlike the wage-earning masses, they generally do not need to fear the specter of abject poverty. Ordinary people, who are much more dependent on the stability of the state for their safety, economic welfare, and status, therefore stand to lose much more in a crisis. As result, they may be more inclined to endorse an authoritarian Leviathan that guarantees order.

Another, more basic reason why authoritarian protection pacts are likely to be anchored in popular consent is because ordinary citizens can ensure the continued survival of these regimes by just *doing nothing*. To nourish an autocracy, elites, on the other hand, have to actively contribute to it: they have to pay much larger taxes, administer the regime's subjects, justify its rule, repress its opponents, and so on. These are responsibilities that can be shirked for one's own benefit, and in the hope that someone else will pick up the tab. That is to say, elites must overcome the collective action problem in order to cooperate in supporting authoritarian rule. Common folk should merely succumb to it: fail to cooperate in deposing autocracy and fail to support the regime's opponents. For the average citizen, in other words, it is enough to do virtually nothing to act in support of authoritarian rule.

The consent of a popular majority is therefore not only a broader and more potent basis for sustaining an autocracy, but paradoxically, it is also a more reliable one. Compared to cajoling elites to stake their money, effort, pride, and fate in sustaining authoritarian rule, persuading the masses not to get in its way – particularly when they fear this might cause chaos, instability, or new injustices – seems like a much better bet. Again, as Machiavelli had concluded long ago, "the common people will love the prince for whatever benefits he gives them, even just being left in peace to work and prosper, whereas the nobles will always resent having to acknowledge his pre-eminence" (as paraphrased by Newell 2016, 120). And populations can certainly do much more than sit on the sidelines to support their authoritarian rulers. They can vote for the regime, attend its rallies, signal loyalty by reciting its slogans, inform on its opponents, cheer their persecution, or even carry it out by joining vigilante groups (see e.g. Hellmeier and Weidmann 2019). But they do not have to do any of this. All it takes for authoritarianism – particularly of the electoral variety – to survive in one form or another is that its citizens never become willing to mobilize against it.

From the same vantage point, the spread and durability of electoral authoritarianism can also be attributed to the great variety of majority coalitions that can be rallied to support it. Where elite protection pacts are only united by perceived bottom-up threats to the current order, electoral authoritarian social contracts can be spawned by a much more heterogeneous set of legitimizing fears and constituencies. They may be sustained by a broad popular majority that shares the elites' terror of anarchy and the disintegration of the state, as in postrevolutionary Mexico, Singapore after independence, and Russia since the Soviet collapse. But they could equally be propped up by various underprivileged majorities who feel they have been empowered by elected strongmen, as in Venezuela since the rise of Chávez, Turkey under Erdoğan, or Zimbabwe under Mugabe. Whether they are motivated by portents of chaos or fears of exclusion and despair, these very different constituencies still share the same fundamental Hobbesian motive for supporting electoral authoritarianism: the belief that it is the only regime that can use unchecked executive power to impose order or address injustices, while still being held electorally accountable to the popular majority that brought it into power. This has the potential to become a much more insidious, pervasive, and enduring political order than what current understandings of electoral authoritarianism suggest.

Putting these arguments together, the central claim of this book that electoral authoritarianism is formed and sustained as a sort of a broad-based protection pact in troubled societies has two immediate empirical implications. The first is that such regimes have a strong tendency to both emerge *and* to last longer after the most severe kinds of crises, upheavals, and deprivations in the affected societies. Second, if electoral autocracies succeed by convincing stability- and status-seeking majorities that they are the least bad form of government for desperate circumstances, they will emerge in times of crisis at a much higher rate than democracies and closed autocracies.

But what are the kinds of crises and turmoil that can produce such autocracy-sustaining effects? I turn to this issue in the next section.

The Legitimizing Crisis

Without the slump of the 1930s, Hitler would have remained a vociferous fringe ringleader.

Ernesto Laclau (2005, 177)

Just like the concepts of legitimacy (Huntington 1991, 46) and populism (see Müller 2017), crisis is a notoriously vague construct which social scientists have struggled to define in a satisfactory way. In his treatise on social crises, Habermas (1973) defines the essence of this phenomenon in medical terms: as "the phase of an illness in which it is decided whether or not the organism's self-healing powers are sufficient for recovery." One problem here is that just like potentially life-threatening medical conditions, regime-shattering crises have many objective and subjective symptoms that make diagnosis difficult. An economic crisis, for instance, may be identified with empirical indicators – a drop in GDP per capita, rise in unemployment, inflation, and so on – that are relatively undisputed as "objective" measures and inherently comparable across contexts. But what matters more politically are the subjective popular reactions to these circumstances, and these can vary dramatically. The same "objective" indicators of economic decline – or casualty figures from military conflict and terror attacks – can produce discordant reactions among different constituencies living within the same county, and across different time periods, leading some to vote against incumbents, while others remain attached to them.[10] Clearly, what constitutes a politically meaningful crisis is, to a large extent, in the eyes of the beholders (see also Schedler 2018).

---

[10] On the topic of divergent assessments of economic and other circumstances, as well as the political reactions to them, see for example Duch, Palmer, and Anderson (2000), Pei and Adesnik (2000), Evans and Andersen (2006), and Achen and Bartels (2017).

The problem does not seem to become much easier even if we assume away subjectivity and turn to more tangible indicators of crises. In this realm, the empirical literature has produced a vast and ever-expanding list of conditions that have regime-destabilizing effects and increase demand for authoritarian rule.[11] A further challenge is that the present study claims that authoritarianism may be legitimated by different types of crises and of majority coalitions affected by them. While in one setting elected strongmen could be boosted by a cross-cutting coalition gripped by fear of unmanageable turmoil, they may, in another context, draw on the support of aggrieved economic, ethnic or religious majorities. How do we condense this disorienting muddle of contingent, loosely related, and often contradictory "objective" circumstances and subjective reactions into a coherent definition and measure(s) of a systemic crisis?

To avoid concept-stretching and subjectivity while also capturing this heterogeneity, I adopt a *minimalist* measure of autocracy-legitimizing crises, based on the two most tangible macro-level factors: conflict and macroeconomic decline. There are several key advantages to this approach. First, it grounds the concept of crisis in the most

---

[11] Studies have associated regime breakdowns and demand for authoritarian rule with a plethora of security issues, including high crime rates (see e.g. Bermeo 1997, Pérez 2003, Bateson 2012; and Caroline Abadeer, Alexandra Blackman, Lisa Blaydes, and Scott Williamson, "Did Egypt's Post-Uprising Crime Wave Increase Support for Authoritarian Rule?" unpublished working paper, 2019); terrorism (see e.g. Merolla and Zechmeister 2009; Davis and Silver 2004), unmanageable contentious action (see e.g. Bermeo 1997, Gibson 1997, and Slater 2010), and ongoing or potential domestic and international conflicts (S. V. Miller 2015). Different forms of political instability, including polarization (Linz 1978; Sartori 1976; Hetherington and Weiler 2009; Svolik 2020) and institutional inconsistency (Gates et al. 2006) have been found to have similar effects. Among economic factors, economic crises (Linz 1978; O'Donnell, Schmitter, and Whitehead 1986a; Huntington 1991; Gasiorowski 1995; Brancati 2014b); corruption (Seligson 2002; Booth and Seligson 2009); and rapid social modernization (Huntington 1968; Inglehart and Welzel 2009) have all been linked to regime instability in both democracies and autocracies. The spread of authoritarian outlooks among the population, in turn, have been traced to recessions, income inequality, unemployment, and inflation (De Bromhead et al. 2012; Feldman and Stenner 1997; Funke et al. 2016; Miller 2016; Norris and Inglehart 2019; Solt 2011). Researchers have found similar effects for natural and environmental threats and disasters (Fritsche et al. 2012), resource scarcity, and high rates of infectious diseases and population density (Gelfand et al. 2011; Thornhill et al. 2009; Thornhill et al. 2010; Murray et al. 2013; Blickle 2020).

explicit, clearly delimited, and broadly comparable indicators available. A theory built using this definition is readily falsifiable, as it can be directly tested with empirical data cross-nationally and longitudinally. For this purpose, in the empirical analyses of regime transitions in Chapter 3 and beyond, I measure crisis with just two indicators: (1) the rates of GDP decline, calculated as a percentage drop in real GDP per capita over a fixed time period; and (2) armed conflict, identified with the UCDP/PRIO Armed Conflict Dataset (Pettersson and Eck 2018) and the Correlates of War Dataset (Singer and Small 1994) conflict thresholds of 25 and 1,000 annual battle deaths, respectively.

The second key advantage of this minimalist definition based on economic decline and conflict is that it reduces subjectivity in defining crises. Flying bullets and empty pockets (and stomachs) provide a unifying traumatic experience that cuts across all social divides – class, ethnic, sectarian, partisan, educational, and so on – and produce a common sense of impending doom (see e.g. Chzhen, Evans, and Pickup 2014). Hence, in spite of its narrowness, the minimalist conception of a systemic crisis may, paradoxically, best capture the whole gamut of calamities and victims that may push populations to reject their political regimes and embrace electoral authoritarianism. The reason is straightforward: regardless of their origins and nature, crises serious enough to trigger existential anxieties among majorities acquire an economic and/or a security dimension in due course. Sooner or later, all crises with autocracy-legitimizing potential become security and/or economic crises.[12]

This convergence of upheavals ensures that whatever the latent conception of a systemic crisis may be, it will be ultimately captured by the broadest macro-level indicators of economic decline and conflict. To borrow Habermas' medical analogy again, a potentially fatal

---

[12] As a concept, a systemic crisis therefore has the opposite properties from electoral authoritarianism. As I elaborated in detail in Chapter 1, any form of systematic manipulation of democratic institutions is sufficient to identify a regime as an electoral autocracy, but no one form of that manipulation is necessary. Thus, a minimalist definition is *not* appropriate in this case, as focusing on any particular set of manipulative strategies will lead us to miss others and therefore misclassify regimes. In contrast, a crisis that has escalated to systemic, regime-shattering proportions almost always involves economic decline or mass violence. As these, in other words, are necessary conditions, a minimalist definition of systemic crisis centered on them is both appropriate and conveniently parsimonious.

crisis may have many different causes and symptoms, but it is ultimately defined by the failure of the primary life-supporting functions of the organism. As control of violence and economic provision are the primary functions of any social order, armed conflict and economic collapse are, by the same token, the most definitive symptoms that it faces a crisis with a potentially fatal outcome. From this perspective, macro-level indicators of conflict and economic decline have the best chance of reflecting the full scale of the angst, misery, and grievance that might push societies to demand a strong-armed government.

The final advantage of this minimalist definition of a regime-infirming crisis is that it imposes a relatively high standard for empirically validating the theory of the crisis origins of electoral authoritarianism. If disparate majorities may conceive of many different circumstances as crises that call for regime change, a theory narrowly focused just on economic decline and conflict should be harder to support empirically. Given the diversity of circumstances and experiences associated with autocracy-legitimizing crises, strong evidence in support of a theory based on a minimalist conception of crisis should make us more confident of its validity.

Still, for all the grief and despair they create, systemic crises are not enough for electoral authoritarianism to be established as a broad, popularly endorsed "protection pact." To achieve this outcome, authoritarian forces must also have a distinct and compelling popular appeal, which will give them a unique competitive edge in winning the support of the crisis-weary popular majorities. I analyze the structure, origins, and logic of this appeal in the next section.

The "Strongman" Electoral Authoritarian Appeal

Without doubt, the most conspicuous feature of electoral authoritarian regimes from across the world has been their sharp-edged rhetoric. We are exposed to the boastful, offensive, xenophobic, and often violent appeals of their leaders long before we witness their actual use of violence, and before they stage full-scale assaults on democratic institutions and practices. Russia's Vladimir Putin rose to prominence by promising to "waste terrorists in the outhouse" in Chechnya (Judah 2013, 33). Egypt's Abdel-Fatah al-Sisi claimed the country's presidency on the promise to "finish off the Muslim Brotherhood" (BBC 2014). Hugo Chávez called an opposition challenger a "low-life pig" whom he was going to "pulverize" (Naranjo 2012). Turkey's Recep Tayyip Erdoğan pledged to "chop off the heads of traitors," "sign the death sentence" for a Kurdish opposition leader, and to "drown" and "starve" Kurdish rebel groups in Turkey, Syria, and Iraq (Loveluck 2018; Sterling and Beech 2017). All of these and most other electoral autocrats have insisted that their countries are "under siege" as they cast themselves in the role of strongman protectors against enemies foreign and domestic. And at the same time, they have all gone out of their way to emphasize their popular mandates and democratic credentials. Vladimir Putin branded himself as the world's "purest, most absolute democrat since Mahatma Gandhi" (Reuters 2007). The most resonant campaign slogan of Hugo Chávez was "With Chávez, the people rule" (Hawkins 2010, 15). "We are the people!" Recep Tayyip Erdoğan declared at his party's rally, and asked his opponents: "Who are you?" (Müller 2019).

This distinctive popular appeal is one of the few readily discernible traits shared by all electoral autocracies. Yet, it is rarely taken seriously, and almost never considered as an explanatory factor that could shed light on the origins and durability of these regimes. The vulgar and seemingly superficial appeals of elected autocrats have been routinely dismissed as populist "cheap talk," which does not reflect any meaningful policy or governing agenda. Breaking every norm of civilized and substantive political discourse, they have all too often appeared like the incoherent ramblings of unaccountable dictatorships.

But these impressions are wrong. First, "strongmen" electoral authoritarian incumbents have taken their own popular appeal very seriously. They have relentlessly strived to follow through on even their most outlandish threats and promises: they have killed, maimed, and imprisoned the opponents they threatened, vigorously persecuted the minorities they disparaged, and initiated the conflicts they warned about. And whenever they failed to match their rhetoric in these areas, it was not for a lack of trying. Elected autocrats have also toiled long and hard to attract genuine popular support and show that their democratic rhetoric was more than just a cynical façade. They have frequently called snap elections and referenda to showcase their popularity and to legitimize their policies. They have campaigned incessantly and often much harder than their oppositions and counterparts in democracies. They have hosted marathon talk shows and call-in programs, performed elaborate stunts to bolster their ratings, and spent lavishly on welfare and other projects to please popular majorities.

And then, there is another, crucial reason to take the popular appeal of electoral authoritarian incumbents seriously. If we perform a systematic and impassionate analysis of their rhetoric, sweeping aside its shock value and theatrics, we will find that it adheres to a remarkably consistent legitimation formula and governing doctrine, tailored to appeal to societies affected by turmoil and dysfunction. This doctrine has three core principles. The first is that troubled societies can only be successfully governed by tough-minded, effective, and uncompromising parties and leaders, who will impose order and unify the country by any means necessary. The rationale behind this *Rally-Around-the-Strongman* argument is straightforward: in times of danger and tumult, no other form of government is forceful, flexible, and accountable enough to ensure the survival and prosperity of the nation. From this standpoint, the rule-based liberal democratic order is seen as too slow, as unreliable, and as too prone to paralyzing squabbles to deal with existential threats.

To achieve these purposes, strongman electoral autocrats insist they must be allowed to govern completely free of political, administrative, and legal restraints, and unencumbered by the norms of governmental conduct used in normal circumstances. Everyone, including the opposition, must submit to the authority of these regimes, as they pursue the supreme collective interest of national self-preservation. In this sense, the strongman electoral authoritarian doctrine advocates a system of governance that resembles a *state of emergency*, when the normal, rule-based, and pluralist democratic constitutional order is suspended until the executive branch has resolved an existential crisis threatening the nation. Against this backdrop, the coercive and violent behaviors of electoral autocracies are justified as exceptional measures, necessary to ensure the survival and wellbeing of the nation, or its core, constituent majority. At the same time, people are reassured that this arrangement is only temporary – that a democratic constitutional order will be restored as soon as the danger has passed. This legitimation formula was captured in one remarkably candid statement by Russia's Vladimir Putin. Comparing the country's electoral authoritarian "manual regime," which allowed him to personally intervene in every aspect of governing, to the rule-based, democratic "automatic regime," Putin said:

We, emerging from a deep systemic crisis, were forced [my emphasis] to do a lot in a so-called "manual regime." When will that time arrive when most things, or the basic things, can function in an "automatic regime?" ... This demands time ... When the legal, and economic, and social base has grown up and become stable, then we will not need manual steering ... I think that will be in 15–20 years. (cited in Taylor 2018, 311)

This strategy of justifying electoral authoritarianism as a form of emergency rule, suited for troubled societies, has been used by virtually every regime of this sort. Among the first to trace its basic contours was Guillermo O'Donnell (1994),[13] who analyzed the patterns of legitimation of the regimes that emerged in post-crisis contexts in Latin America. While O'Donnell mischaracterized these regimes as largely democratic (calling them "delegative democracies"), he astutely described their efforts to justify themselves as implicitly governing in a state of emergency. According to O'Donnell, in these regimes:

Presidents get elected by promising that they – being strong, courageous, above parties and interests, *machos* – will save the country. Theirs is a "government of saviors" ... Delegative democracies rest on the premise that whoever wins election to the presidency is thereby entitled to govern as he or she sees fit, constrained only by the hard facts of existing power relations and by a constitutionally limited term of office. The president is taken to be the embodiment of the nation and the main custodian and definer of its interests ... [O]ther institutions – courts and legislatures, for instance – are nuisances ... Accountability to such institutions appears as a mere impediment to the full authority that the president has been delegated to exercise.

To achieve this level of political dominance, electoral autocrats rely on the second core tenet of the strongman legitimation formula, which might be called the *Negative Legitimacy* frame. It contends that no other political force apart from the strongman leaders and party leaders has the strength, competence, devotion, and integrity to lead the nation in times of national emergency. This claim takes advantage of the profound popular disillusionment with the political class in countries that have been affected by turmoil. In such contexts, the most

---

[13] The very first author to trace the outlines of the strongman electoral authoritarian legitimation formula in modern times was Max Weber (1918), who labelled these regimes as *Führer democracy*: the popularly endorsed rule of a charismatic individual, promising to promote welfare, security, and equality.

prominent political opponents of electoral authoritarian regimes have often been in power when crises escalated and are thoroughly delegitimized for their perceived incompetence. Others are labeled as too radical, or as too new and untried to be able to govern effectively in a fragile society.

From the standpoint of the strongman doctrine, preventing such political alternatives from seizing power constitutes nine-tenths of good governance. By blocking the rise of supposedly irresponsible, incompetent, and corrupt oppositions, these regimes have justified their purpose – protecting the nation from another calamity – as well as the authoritarian methods used to accomplish it. Mexico during the reign of the Institutional Revolutionary Party (PRI) provides one vivid example of this negative legitimacy rationale. There, regime officials falsifying the ballots regarded their actions as "patriotic fraud": carried out for the good of the country, to prevent "irresponsible" opposition parties from winning power and sowing chaos (Oppenheimer 1998). From a legitimation standpoint, this argument is more than just a cynical excuse for unjustifiable behavior. It is part of a distinct political philosophy and appeal, based on the premise that governing in troubled societies is too important to be left to anyone who can win an election.

The third core principle of the strongman electoral authoritarian governing doctrine – the *Democratic Legitimacy* frame – is also the most important distinguishing feature of these regimes. While most dictatorships since at least the time of Plato's *Republic* have legitimized themselves as protectors of the people and national interests in times of grave danger,[14] only electoral autocracies have validated their authority as national "saviors" with the quintessentially democratic institution of majority rule. The will of popular majorities, expressed at regular elections, is, in this sense, the key enabler of electoral authoritarianism. It allows these regimes to credibly pose as dictatorships in the name of the people, and for the protection of the common good and the constitutional order in times of crisis. It discourages elite coups, allowing electoral autocracies to police their elites better than traditional closed dictatorships. But most importantly, overwhelming

---

[14] As Plato (1985) described this dynamic: "[t]his and no other is the root from which a tyrant springs; when he first appears above ground he is a protector [of the people] ... having a mob entirely at his disposal, he is not restrained from shedding the blood of kinsmen."

popular support, demonstrated at the polls, enables these regimes to become and to remain authoritarian. By winning broad popular support at the ballot box, electoral autocracies enlist what de Tocqueville (1840) called the practically "irresistible" moral and political power of the expressed will of the majority to dismantle, circumvent, and wipe out any rules, institutions, and opponents that inhibit their free rein. Electoral support allows strongmen to claim they are not tyrants.

The foundation of elected authoritarianism, in other words, is not coercion or manipulation, but these regimes' adherence to the core democratic tenet of majoritarianism. It is the reason why popular electoral authoritarian regimes have so easily trampled over long-established norms, institutional safeguards, and other relatively autonomous institutions, such as legislatures, judiciaries, and the media, which could block, challenge, and reverse their actions – effectively bypassing what O'Donnell (1994) called "horizontal accountability." The source of this overwhelming power lies in the appropriation of the majoritarian principle: if the electoral authoritarian mandate is an expression of the sovereign will of the majority, these regimes cannot be checked or challenged by anyone or anything else except through another plebiscite. And given the gravity and urgency of these regimes' mission of national salvation, nothing should stand in their way until the next election – not even the voters who have elected them.[15]

This is key to the success of electoral authoritarianism. An executive that behaves in an authoritarian fashion under the pretense of a supreme emergency can continue to do so practically indefinitely as long as it remains popularly elected. Since victory in nationwide elections is the ultimate standard of legitimate (and presumably democratic) authority, winning elections allows autocrats to justify their behavior and dominate their societies far more effectively – without much reliance on repression, without compelling ideologies or achievements, and even without overwhelming popular support. All it takes to keep even a mediocre electoral autocracy in power, in this context, is to consistently win a majority – or in many cases, just

---

[15] O'Donnell (1994, 60) illustrates this logic by pointing out that: "[in 'delegative democracies'] voters are supposed to choose, irrespective of their identities and affiliations, the individual who is most fit to take responsibility for the destiny of the country ... After the election, voters/delegators are expected to become a passive but cheering audience of what the president does."

a plurality[16] – at the polls. The confirmation of the regime's popularity and democratic legitimacy (however lopsided) obtained in this fashion will defuse opposition among the rest of the electorate far better than any coercive measures. If many people are convinced that the violations of democratic principles in the name of order and stability are acceptable, and signal their beliefs at regular elections, then the regime overseeing this state of affairs cannot be easily resisted, or even be branded as undemocratic. The only real check on emergency power maintained in this fashion, and therefore on authoritarianism, is popular opinion (on this, also see Agamben 2005).

To summarize these arguments, we can distill three core principles of the strongman electoral authoritarian appeal: (1) that a society faced with upheaval must unify behind a strong, capable, and paternalistic leadership (the *Rally-Around-the-Strongman* frame); (2) that no other political alternatives apart from the strongman electoral authoritarian party/leader is able to perform this role and guide the nation through difficult times (the *Negative Legitimacy* frame); and (3) that their mandate and governing style are validated by the ultimate moral authority – the sovereign will of popular majorities, expressed in regular elections (the *Democratic Legitimacy* frame).

To the extent these legitimizing mantras are repeated over time and across different countries ruled by these regimes, electoral autocracies should have a very particular set of *rhetorical fingerprints*. These could be used as a "litmus test"[17] to identify electoral autocracies – as well as parties and leaders who wish to establish such regimes – based on how much their public discourse matches the legitimation formula described in the preceding passages. In particular, if this theory of electoral authoritarian legitimation is correct, we could use this "litmus test" to differentiate electoral autocracies from democracies. This is something which the existing regime indices have struggled to do reliably, as I have emphasized in Chapter 1.

---

[16] For example, the electoral autocracies in Hungary and Malaysia in recent years have been effectively sustained by parties that have secured less than 50 percent of the total vote (*The Economist* 2014, 2018).

[17] On the possibility of putting together an empirical "litmus test" for authoritarian intent and behavior of elected incumbents, see Linz (1978, ch. 2) and Levitsky and Ziblatt (2018, 21).

What kinds of differences should we expect to find between the popular appeals in these two regime types? If electoral authoritarian incumbents do indeed justify their reign as popularly mandated governments of national salvation, their rhetoric will diverge from democratic incumbents in two fundamental ways. First, to a much greater extent than their democratic counterparts, the campaign and other mass appeals of electoral authoritarian parties and leaders will emphasize the need for unity, falling in line with collective national goals in times of trouble, and the need to surrender some freedoms to a strong paternalistic state that will guarantee stability, prosperity, and justice (i.e. the *Rally-Around-the-Strongman* frame). In other words, they will disproportionately appeal to what Inglehart and Welzel (2005, ch. 2) label "survival values": economic and physical security, national unity and cohesion, and intolerance of dissent.

Second, this rhetoric of rallying behind a tough-minded government of national salvation will be strongly counterbalanced by claims of democratic legitimacy. We should, in other words, observe a paradox: in their popular appeals, electoral authoritarian incumbents should place more, not less, emphasis on democracy than their counterparts in liberal democracies. Electoral autocracies will reject the label "undemocratic" with pugnacious indignation, despite their crass trampling over democratic institutions and civil liberties and the persecution of their opponents. Citing their majority-endorsed role as national "saviors" in times of crisis, they will instead portray themselves as the only true democracies and the most perfect embodiment of the will of the people (the *Democratic Legitimacy* frame).

The underlying philosophy here is that in times of crisis, the most democratic system is the one that represents popular demands for restoring stability by any means necessary. To advertise these "virtues," electoral autocracies will therefore tend to turn the volume up on proclamations of their innately democratic nature. Claiming that only they can look after the interests of the "common men and women" in societies beset by turmoil and dysfunction, these regimes will even promote themselves as champions of individual rights and freedoms under such circumstances. Along the same lines, they will also assume the role of "guardians" of the democratic order and constitutions in their countries, and regularly justify their actions in legalistic terms (on this, see Hawkins 2010, 34; Corrales 2015).

Looking at these arguments, one might not be able to help but wonder: how is the strongman savior appeal of electoral authoritarianism any different from the conventional, "garden variety" populism? Indeed, the two share many common features and frequently overlap. Like populism, the strongman savior appeal is, to a large degree, a strategy for winning and maintaining power, not a fully fledged ideology or programmatic platform based around a fixed set of ideals and a vision of the future.[18] Like populism, the strongman appeal relies on people-centrism and majoritarianism to maintain an aura of broad popular legitimacy, and a charismatic bond between the leaders and the masses. Also, both populist and strongman appeals thrive on crises and boast a Manichean, "us versus them" outlook, portraying their political opponents (foreign and domestic) as irreconcilable enemies of "the common people."[19]

Despite this overlap, there are three crucial differences between these legitimation strategies. First, populism is not automatically a threat to the democratic procedural system.[20] The primary motive of electoral authoritarianism, in contrast, is to suspend democracy, even though it is portrayed as an effort to "save" it. Second, populism has an anti-elitist, anti-status-quo orientation (Hawkins 2010, ch. 2). Strongman electoral authoritarianism, on the other hand, has in many cases sought to preserve, and even restore the status quo that was upset by a major crisis. Strongman electoral authoritarian leaders like Russia's Vladimir Putin and Egypt's Abdel Fattah al-Sisi, or parties like Mexico's PRI, do not attract support by promising to tear down the status quo; they do so by promising to safeguard it (Singerman 2002; Hill and Gaddy 2015, ch. 5; *The Economist* 2015a). Finally, unlike populism, strongman electoral authoritarianism is much more than a product of pure charisma, enlisted to address grave crises or injustice. It is also a fully fledged illiberal political doctrine and social contract – with specific

---

[18] On this, see Weyland (2001). Also, as populists and strongman parties and leaders promote themselves as "fixers" in many different contexts, their appeal lacks a stable referential grounding in any single set of ideologies, cleavages, and policies, and appears "formless" Laclau (2005, xi).

[19] On populists exploiting crises, see Moffitt (2014) and Laclau (2005, 177); on the populist Manichean outlook, see Hawkins (2010, 33–34).

[20] On this, see Arditi (2005), Mudde (2007, ch. 6), and Kaltwasser (2012). Populism does, however, have a tendency to erode democracy, particularly of the liberal sort (see e.g. Allred et al. 2015, Houle and Kenny 2016, and Müller 2017).

prescriptions about who should wield political power (and why everyone else should not), and how it should be organized, exercised, and legitimated – that claims to offer better solutions to the problem of good governance in unstable societies than its alternatives.

Thus, on the whole, populism and strongman majoritarianism may have substantial overlap, but they are two distinct concepts. While populist autocrats may be the most common category, there are still non-populist autocrats and nonauthoritarian populists. More importantly, if populism is an attempt to take advantage of democracy to achieve its goals, strongman electoral authoritarianism is a template for a new, completely different political regime, which will eclipse and replace democracy.

This discussion raises a related question: Is there a difference between the popular appeal of electoral authoritarian regimes and the strongmen that lead them? Or to be more specific, is the appeal of electoral autocracies a product of the outsized personal charisma and popularity of their strongman leaders? This book's frequent mention of "strongmen," may indeed give this impression. But this conclusion would be wrong. Electoral authoritarianism, as I elaborated in the preceding passages and in Chapter 1, is much more than a charismatic strongman. It is a fully fledged legitimation strategy and governing doctrine for troubled societies. Strongmen earn their label and become popular by adhering to this legitimation script and doctrine, and not the other way around.

Hence, from this book's standpoint, a "strongman" is a *role*, rather than a person. A particular leader may come to be seen as a good fit for the strongman role by demonstrating he can serve the purpose of imposing order and justice in dysfunctional polities. Russia's Vladimir Putin earned the public's trust to perform this role by crushing the resistance in Chechnya, which epitomized his country's catastrophic decline. Hugo Chávez gained credibility as the protector of Venezuela's urban and rural poor majority by tearing down the old party system, which constituencies believed was driving them into despair, and by using oil wealth to fund massive social programs (Canache 2002; Hawkins 2010; Seawright 2012).

The achievements and charisma of such individual strongmen certainly raise confidence in the electoral autocracies they lead. They contribute to people's positive "running tally" of these regimes' performance relative to the alternatives, bolstering their resilience.

However, the most fundamental pillar of electoral authoritarianism is not the appeal of its leaders, but the broad popular demand for this kind of rule, and the structural conditions that help generate it. As long as majorities fear instability, injustice, and dysfunction, and electoral authoritarianism seems like the least bad safeguard against such dangers, they will support even mediocre strongmen. This is why, as I show in Chapter 5, Russia's electoral autocracy endured under its faltering founder Boris Yeltsin in the late 1990s.

Ultimately, the appeal of electoral authoritarianism as a system, over that of its individual leaders, is confirmed by an old pattern: the tendency of new elected autocrats to spawn in places where old ones were recently removed. All too often, politics in countries that experience electoral authoritarian rule unfolds according to the same predictable cycle: rise of a popular strongman, mass disillusionment and leadership change, soon to be followed by the rise of another leader or party of the same mold (see O'Donnell 1994, Hale 2014, and Loxton 2016). The decline of one elected strongman does not necessarily reduce the appeal of another that might rise soon after. Only addressing the crises, insecurity, and despair that make electoral authoritarianism attractive can break this cycle and reliably diminish popular demand for elected strongmen. What matters over the long run, in other words, is the appeal of electoral authoritarianism as a system, not the appeal of the strongman that runs it.

It will be useful to briefly summarize this section's claims at this point. I have argued that the doctrine of electoral authoritarianism, in essence, calls for the unfettered rule of a leader, party, or government that has secured a broad electoral mandate to address a national emergency. In turn, the "absolute moral imperative" of representing the will of the majority, expressed in this fashion, is used to justify the authoritarian behavior of these regimes – the bypassing or dismantling of checks and balances, and the repression of the opposition. As an ideal, electoral authoritarianism therefore best embodies the concept of a "tyranny of the majority" articulated by James Madison (1787, 1788): the notion that a despotic government can be formed not just by a small power-wielding elite, but also by a popular majority unified in the pursuit of some common purpose. Electoral authoritarianism is, in effect, an effort to harness this potential by offering itself as the conduit for the shared interests of the majority in times of crisis. The desired end product is a "perfect autocracy," as Mario Vargas Llosa shrewdly characterized the Mexican electoral authoritarian regime under the PRI: a dictatorship that majorities willingly endorse as a solution to their common problems (Castañeda 2000, viii). And because of this property, it cannot be easily resisted with democratic means.

The central issue then, is how electoral authoritarian incumbents secure majority support, compelling elites, state officials, and ordinary citizens to collaborate in subverting democracy. The key lies in these regimes' ability to convincingly justify themselves as informal states of emergency, uniquely poised to tackle their countries' troubles. This legitimation strategy enables electoral autocracies to appeal to the most fundamental interest of ordinary people, elites, and bureaucrats alike: self-preservation. But above all, they all fall in line with electoral authoritarian rule because of its uncanny ability to dominate political competition in troubled societies without much resort to coercion. I turn to this issue in the following section.

How Strongmen Win at the Polls

Establishing an electoral autocracy, particularly of the robust, hegemonic variety, is a gargantuan task of social and institutional remodeling that is extremely vulnerable to reversals at every stage. It involves dismantling existing institutions and setting up new ones – an endeavor fraught with setbacks, and relentless pushback from vested interests, hostile constituencies, and external forces. It requires that emergent elected autocrats take control of the state administration, the media, and the commanding heights of the economy – all in the face of fierce resistance, many legal and institutional roadblocks, and outside pressures. Then, once they succeed, authoritarian parties and leaders need to leave many, if not all, of their enemies behind; enemies that can form opposition parties, run for office, and even in the best of times for these regimes, win posts at the regional and local level, or seats in Parliament. And contrary to conventional wisdom, electoral autocracies cannot primarily rely on crude coercive tools, like repression, clientelism, propaganda, and vote fraud, to seize and maintain power. Before they fully take the reins of the state, they simply lack the resources to do so. After consolidating power, too much coercion can backfire. At the very least, it will defeat the purpose of electoral authoritarianism, effectively transforming these regimes into the closed dictatorships they are supposed to upstage.

How do electoral dictatorships manage to rise and persist against such unfavorable odds? I have argued that the most powerful tool in the hands of authoritarian parties and leaders is not violence or corruption, but their ability to redefine the terms of political competition in societies that have experienced turmoil and dysfunction. Taking advantage of people's existential anxieties, authoritarian political forces achieve dominance by introducing a new salient dimension of electoral choice: the option to accept or reject electoral authoritarianism as a solution for their country's problems. This new cleavage allows authoritarian parties and leaders to win genuine popular support as representatives of a pragmatic alternative, aiming to restore and maintain order by combining the "best" features of democracy and dictatorship. Above all, it shifts the agenda of the public away from traditional cleavages and issue stances that favor the programmatic alternatives to electoral authoritarianism. For how can people worry about ideologies and partisan attachments when they believe their most basic interests, or even the survival of the nation is at stake?

The electoral authoritarianism cleavage also enables authoritarian forces to frame the opponents of strongman rule – especially those with liberal views, and the parties and leaders that held power during the country's traumatic crises – as incompetent, irrelevant, out of touch, and dangerous. In this context, even the mere act of opposing electoral authoritarianism – the most vocal proponent of imposing order and justice – can discredit and divide its challengers. Under such circumstances, some opposition forces remain vehemently opposed to elected strongman rule, while others often adopt accommodating stances to avoid being seen as forces of chaos or as traitors. The end result is a watered-down and divided opposition, incapable of staving off an authoritarian takeover.

This remarkable capacity to attract anxious electorates and to discredit and divide its opponents makes the strongman electoral authoritarian appeal a perfect representative of what Riker (1996, 9) called *heresthetics*:[21] "the art of setting up situations – composing alternatives among which political actors must choose – in such a way that even those that do not wish to do so are compelled by the structure of the situation to support the heresthetician's purpose." To put it differently,

---

[21] Riker derived the term "heresthetic" from the root of the Greek word for "choosing," or "deciding." See Riker (1996, 9).

heresthetics is the art of "structuring the world" for an audience of electors, so that the manipulator wins their *genuine* support. A key goal of such maneuvers is to divide one's opponents – a stratagem that even the losing side of political contests can use to turn the tide of public support in their favor. According to Riker (1986, 1):

[f]or a person who expects to lose on some decision, the fundamental here-sthetical device is to divide the majority with a new alternative, one that he prefers to the alternative previously expected to win. If successful, this maneuver produces a new majority coalition composed of the old minority and the portion of the old majority that likes the new alternative better.

The purpose of heresthetics, in other words, is to create "wedge issues," which divide the opposition and lure voters toward one's own position. As I elaborate in the passages that follow, and then demonstrate empirically in Chapters 5 and 6, the simultaneous use of the *Rally-Around-the-Strongman*, *Negative Legitimacy*, and *Democratic Legitimacy* frames of the electoral authoritarian legitimation script achieves precisely this objective.

The great advantage of these heresthetic appeals is that they are based on amplifying or minimizing preexisting mass beliefs. This is a key point. Heresthetics does not involve changing people's opinions – only manipulating the criteria according to which they make their choices. It redefines the situation by increasing the salience of different considerations, leading voters to reach different decisions with the same set of attitudes (Riker 1990, 49). In other words, heresthetic issue manipulation induces individuals to change their minds without revising any of their underlying beliefs: it only alters the priority people give to their different opinions when making political choices. The other crucial strength of this tactic is that people will still be compelled to do the perpetrator's bidding even when they know they are being manipulated. The stakes and interests they have in the issues raised by the manipulator may be so high that they are simply unable to avoid being exploited for agendas they would otherwise oppose.

The use of heresthetics has never been systematically studied in electoral autocracies, but these regimes are their most natural habitat. Above all else, the justification of authoritarian rule as a response to a national emergency in the wake of upheavals is the most quintessential heresthetic maneuver, capable of bestowing genuine electoral legitimacy to a dictatorship. Few other issues can redefine political competition and displace existing cleavages and political competitors like the call for an effective, unrestrained executive power in times of crisis. A strong-armed regime established to address a national emergency rises above ideology and other differences and cleavages. It has no natural substitute around which its opponents – particularly those hailing from the traditional ideological and programmatic political spectrum – could unite.

In fact, attempts to counter this appeal tend to divide rather than unite any programmatically oriented opposition. Take a generic polity where a broad range of nationalist/conservative, liberal, leftist, and right-wing parties dominate the mainstream, for instance. The nationalists might challenge an electoral authoritarian regime's appeal as provider of order and justice by arguing that it is not tough enough in dealing with the crisis, and propose its replacement with an even more repressive dictatorship and a return to traditional values. Liberals, in contrast, may claim the situation is made worse by the regime's brutality and plead for democratization. Leftists, on the other hand, might promote an alternative regime that addresses the needs of the impoverished, while right-leaning oppositions propose austerity measures as a way out of the crisis. Deep systemic crises invite radical solutions, so the appeals of these traditional political groupings are bound to become unusually extreme, pushing their stances further apart.[22]

The upshot is a bitterly divided opposition, unable to come together against the authoritarian alternative it seeks to defeat. Indeed, under these circumstances, it is likely that at least some of these factions will prefer supporting the electoral authoritarian option than uniting with their programmatic rivals who oppose it. Those that agree with the claims that emergency rule by a strongman electoral authoritarian regime is necessary, on the other hand, place an absolute premium on stability by definition. As result, they pay little heed to the programmatic cleavages that divide the opposition and are unified in their support of the elected strongman regime. By justifying their rule as a response to national emergencies, electoral authoritarian forces therefore execute the ultimate heresthetical ploy: they divide their opponents and unite their supporters.

---

[22] On the tendency toward extremism among oppositions in electoral autocracies, see Greene (2007) and Corrales and Penfold-Becerra (2015, 30).

To visualize the effect of the electoral authoritarian heresthetic maneuver, consider a simple simulated scenario in Figure 2.1, based on an
issue-based competition typical for many democracies. The left panel in
this graph portrays electoral competition in a majority-rule system
dominated by two parties, positioned along a single liberal/conserva-
tive cleavage that ranges from strongly liberal at -3 to strongly conservative at 3.[23] The distribution of the voters on this scale is slightly
leaning to the liberal side of the spectrum (the median voter position is
at -0.4) – a common pattern in many societies.[24] With two traditionally
dominant parties, this distribution of preferences would enable the
moderate liberal party to win with 60 percent of the vote.

Now suppose that an electoral authoritarian party, appealing for
a strong-armed, but electorally accountable executive which would
represent the majority's interests and unify the country behind its
leadership, enters the race. Promising to end partisan bickering and
ideological divisions, this party might take a stance at the neutral point
(i.e. zero) on the liberal/conservative scale in Figure 2.1.[25]

The politics-as-"normal" scenario in stable societies does not favor
this kind of contestant. Its electoral authoritarian appeal will remain
marginalized as long as people do not feel sufficiently threatened by

[23] This model captures the logic of electoral competition in the broadest set of
      circumstances. It can accommodate virtually any cleavages along which parties
      and voters may be distributed, including left/right, ethnic, sectarian, social, and
      other politically relevant divisions and identities.
[24] See for example Bobbio (1996), Budge et al. (2010), and Pew (2014). The
      ideological distribution of the electorate in Figure 2.1 is simulated by creating
      four equally sized constituencies (each comprising 25 percent of the total
      electorate), drawn from normal distributions with means of -2, -1, 0, and 1 on
      the liberal/conservative scale, and standard deviations of 1.
[25] While this catch-all, middle-of-the-road, ideologically uncommitted stance is
      a common among strongman parties and candidates, it is not always the
      position they would most benefit from. A similar logic of electoral competition
      applies when the peak of the voter distribution is not near the center, but takes
      on a more radical position on one side of salient cleavages, or if the distribution
      is bimodal, with more voters on one side of ideological spectrum. In this case,
      authoritarian forces would maximize their vote if they took an ideological
      stance that matched the views of this more numerous section of the electorate.
      An example of this is the positioning of Venezuela's electoral authoritarian
      regime under Hugo Chávez. Seeking to ingratiate himself with the more
      numerous poor and pro-left voting bloc in Venezuela's polarized electorate,
      Chávez took a decidedly leftist stance. This put him in a dominant position
      electorally, and split his opposition between the less numerous moderate and
      right-wing constituencies (Corrales 2006).

instability to contemplate such extreme solutions. When the times are good, the issue that this party tries to promote – concentrating power in the hands of a strong popularly mandated executive – simply does not enter the voter calculus. It is therefore forced to compete along the traditional ideological spectrum, where the mainstream programmatic parties enjoy a "home-field" advantage. As I depict in the simulation in the right panel of Figure 2.1, the authoritarian party would be "squeezed out" in this scenario, as the established liberal and conservative parties maximize their votes by moving as close as possible to the median voter.[26] As a result, it would only capture a sliver of the total vote, representing only the most ideologically indifferent or disenchanted portions of the electorate.

This situation reverses, however, in times of deep and persistent crises and dysfunction, which the traditional programmatic parties appear ill-equipped to address. Such contexts allow electoral authoritarian challengers to inject their appeal for strong-armed leadership – unconstrained by checks and balances and unburdened by ideology – into the mainstream. This is because in times of crisis, an additional consideration becomes salient in the minds of most voters: the issue of whether power should be concentrated in the hands of an unrestrained executive, empowered by a popular mandate to address the country's troubles.

I illustrate the effects of this shift in Figure 2.2. Voters and parties in these graphs have the same stances as before on the left/right scale, but now they also align along a second, equally salient dimension:[27] a regime scale, denoting whether they believe their country should be

---

[26] In this scenario, I assume that the traditional liberal and conservative parties could credibly shift their positions only as far as the most moderate left and right positions in the spectrum: -1 and 1 on the scale in Figure 2.1, respectively. This is consistent with adjustments to the classical spatial model equilibrium behavior that account for the partisan and ideological constraints on shifts along the issue space (see e.g. Adams et al. 2005), as well as for the fact that voters will discount appeals that shift too far from a party's traditional stance (see e.g. Grofman 1985). At the very least, parties/candidates will not be able to dramatically change their core stances within one electoral cycle (Enelow and Hinich 1984, 39).

[27] For simplicity, I assume that the voters' preferences along the two dimensions are unrelated (i.e. orthogonal) and that they are weighted equally when deciding which alternative to vote for.

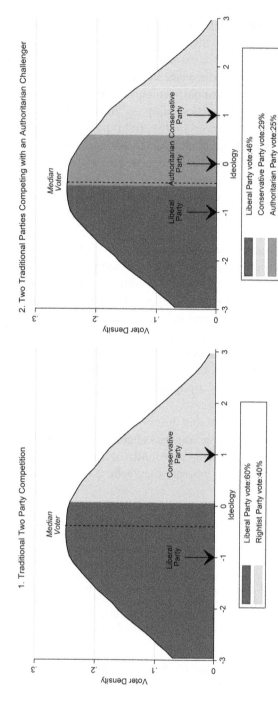

Figure 2.1 Electoral competition in a one-dimensional issue space

governed by a strong-armed but popularly elected executive, empowered to mount a forceful response to the crisis.[28]

The first (top-left) graph in this figure plots the voters' (the small dots) and the parties' (the large dot, triangle, and diamond) stances on both issues, but assumes that *only the left/right cleavage is salient* – the politics-as-"normal" scenario. This, in effect, is a two-dimensional version of the graph in the right panel in Figure 2.1. As only the liberal/conservative cleavage matters to voters in this scenario, the electoral authoritarian party captures just a relatively thin slice of support between the dashed lines at –0.5 and 0.5, which demarcate the midpoints between the stances of the three parties. Squeezed in by the competing appeals of the mainstream left and right parties, the electoral authoritarian contestant is marginalized and pushed to third place.

The tables turn when a major crisis strikes and voters become just as preoccupied with measures for restoring order and addressing griev-ances as with their ideological preferences. I illustrate this in the second (top-right) graph in Figure 2.2. Distraught by hardship and the inability of the current system to deal with the turmoil and dysfunction in the country, most voters in this situation favor a moderate authoritarian shift: a tough-mannered, but popularly elected government that will restore order, while also bowing to the wishes of the majority. That is to say, the median voter under these circumstances is attracted to the elected strongman platform of the authoritarian party/candidate, placed at 1 at the regime scale in the graphs in Figure 2.2.[29]

The great heresthetical power of the strongman electoral authoritar-ian appeal in this context is that it cannot be effectively countered by the mainstream parties. Having served as the cornerstones of the prior, more democratic regime, the established parties of the left and right cannot plausibly take the pro-authoritarian stance that has become

---

[28] Several prominent studies have also indicated that this sort of alignment along a democracy/authoritarianism dimension, in addition to the conventional programmatic cleavages, is a common feature of political competition in electoral autocracies and that it disadvantages oppositions (Moreno 1999; Greene 2007; Magaloni 2006, 179–180). However, these authors have not linked this development with prior experiences of socioeconomic turmoil and bottom-up popular demand for authoritarianism to guarantee stability or to address grievances.

[29] The voter positions on the regime scale are obtained from a simulated normal distribution with a mean of 1 and standard distribution of 1.

fashionable because of the crisis.[30] Even more fundamentally, these mainstream parties controlled government and dominated politics when the crisis struck. Having demonstrated weakness and inability to contain the crisis, their attempts to campaign on a strongman platform will have little credibility among the voters.

Because of this past record of failure, which will be emphasized by the electoral authoritarian party's *Negative Legitimacy* frame during the campaign, it is reasonable to assume that the mainstream parties will be perceived to hold a moderately *anti*-authoritarian stance, represented by -1 on the regime scale, no matter how hard they attempt to appease the median voter on this issue. The authoritarian party, in contrast, leverages its dominance on the newly salient regime issue to redefine the terms of political competition in its favor. If the left/right cleavage allowed the mainstream parties to marginalize the authoritarian party, restricting its support to a sliver of disenchanted and ideologically indifferent voters, the appeal of tougher government in times of crisis allows it to turn the tables on its competitors – to corner and divide them in the emerging issue space.[31]

By being the only alternative that can plausibly offer a tougher, more efficient regime to the crisis-weary electorate, the authoritarian party peels away votes from across the ideological spectrum, pushing its competitors' support toward the bottom quadrants of the now two-dimensional issue space. Thus, even if we assume, as in this simulation, that voters put equal weight to their preferences on the left/right and the regime scales – a quite generous assumption about the importance of this traditional cleavage in times of crisis – the electoral authoritarian party wins the election with 41 percent of the vote in the scenario in

---

[30] A similar logic applies to competition between an electoral authoritarian and liberal parties in a country emerging from a closed dictatorship. Where such transitions have occurred in the wake of profound crises, the appeals of electoral authoritarian forces as guarantors of order may seem more credible than those of their democratic counterparts, as well as those of the proponents of a return to a closed dictatorship.

[31] These constraints on the appeals of the three parties/candidates in the strongman heresthetic model can be related to the concept of issue ownership, whereby voters trust (or distrust) certain political actors to better "handle" particular issues based on their previous performance and reputation in that area (Petrocik 1996). While perceptions of issue ownership are dynamic and can change with relative performance in office (Sides 2006, 2007), catastrophic failures in handling a crisis might entrench these perceived party/candidate competences for longer periods of time (see Achen and Bartels 2017).

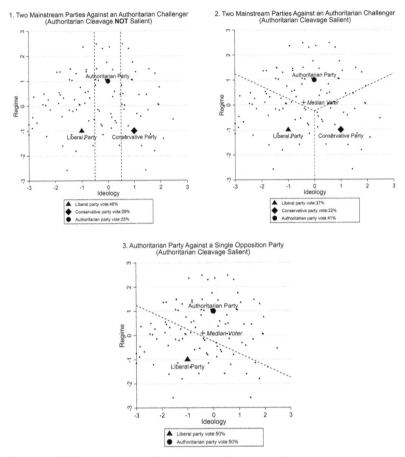

Figure 2.2 Electoral competition in a two-dimensional issue space

the second graph in Figure 2.2. On the other hand, the liberal and conservative parties garner 37 and 22 percent, respectively.

This is a stunning result. The electoral authoritarian forces win the popular vote without any resort to coercion and manipulation, and even without capturing a simple majority. The root cause of this exceptional political coup is the programmatic division among the mainstream political forces. Taken together, the traditional liberal and conservative parties in the simulation in the second graph of Figure 2.2 attract 59 percent of the vote. Thus, if they combine their forces, they will solidly defeat the authoritarian challenger. They could even block an authoritarian takeover even without uniting. All it takes to match the authoritarian challenge is for one of the mainstream parties to drop out of the race. I illustrate this in the bottom graph in Figure 2.2, which depicts a scenario where the electoral authoritarian party competes only against the stronger, liberal party. The result is a draw: both the mainstream democratic option and the electoral authoritarian challenger win 50 percent of the vote.

Thus, the strongman heresthetic wins in times of crisis not just because of the strength of its appeal, but because it allows the electoral authoritarian party or candidate to exploit the divisions among its opponents. As I show in the simulations in Figure 2.2 and empirically in Chapter 5, when the electoral authoritarian challenger brings forth the new salient strongman regime cleavage, on which it is a clear favorite of the electorate, it cannot be effectively checked by a divided political spectrum. And the other ideological cleavages most main-stream parties and candidates identify with create precisely these sorts of divisions. By appealing to divergent constituencies with anti-authoritarian and moderate outlooks, the traditional liberal and con-servative parties in the second graph of Figure 2.2 split the opposition vote and enable the authoritarian challenger to win. Indeed, the general effect of any salient cleavages in troubled societies is to divide the opponents of strong-armed rule, while its supporters, who are indiffer-ent about these cleavages and primarily care about restoring order or addressing their grievances, remain unified.

The heresthetic model therefore provides a crucial insight into why multiparty electoral systems are particularly vulnerable to authoritar-ian dominance in times of crisis. Quite simply, the pluralism and diversity of programmatic choices that makes political competition vibrant and its outcomes relatively unpredictable in times of peace and prosperity exposes electoral systems to a sustained authoritarian takeover in the wake of major upheavals. The call for strong-armed rule in times of crisis is the perfect "wedge issue" which turns ideo-logical pluralism into a weapon wielded by its opponents.

These results also highlight the explanatory power of the elected strongman appeal and its heresthetic effect. By resolving one of the most enduring puzzles of electoral authoritarianism – the question of why the oppositions to such regimes are so often divided – this model provides a single integrated account that captures the logic of electoral authoritarianism in *all stages* of its trajectory: how these regimes emerge, how they maintain power, and how they collapse. First, it shows how previously marginal authoritarian forces can rise to power in times of national emergency without winning even a simple majority of the votes, let alone attracting broad membership. This paradox has led some scholars to conclude that the idiosyncratic behavior and mistakes of the established political elites, rather than popular electoral choices, have played a decisive role in cases of democratic collapse (see e.g. Bermeo 2003). However, this interpretation requires a rather heroic assumption that the two can be separated and ignores the ways in which a strongman appeal reshapes electoral competition in times of crisis.

According to the elected strongman heresthetic model, authoritarian forces win elections precisely because the mainstream political elites *can do very little* to prevent this outcome when the median voter prefers a tougher leadership, geared to restore stability or to deal with grievances. All it takes for an electoral authoritarian alternative to win in such circumstances is for their diverse opponents to take part in the elections. When they do, their preexisting programmatic identities and appeals along traditional cleavages divide the opposition to the electoral authoritarian alternative, clearing its way to power – sometimes without having won a simple majority of the vote. Indeed, the more divided the electorate is along salient cleavages represented by various parties, the fewer votes the electoral authoritarian party requires to win.

From this perspective, the weak resistance mainstream elites have put up against authoritarian challengers in periods of national emergency is not a simple product of idiosyncratic factors, like leader personalities or miscalculations. Instead, it is largely driven by a systematic feature of running for office in such contexts: the constraints that opposition parties face in competing with electoral authoritarian alternatives. To prevent an electoral authoritarian force from winning in these circumstances, its opponents must do one of the following: (1) form a coalition against it; or (2) withdraw from the electoral race in favor of the strongest party/candidate among them. In other words, to resist an authoritarian takeover, the mainstream political actors have to either overcome a massive collective action problem, amplified by their divergent platforms and identities, or to abolish themselves in favor of their ideological rivals for at least one electoral cycle. It is not difficult to see why self-interested, vote-maximizing politicians find it very hard to act coherently when faced with these alternatives. Hence, the problem that allows electoral authoritarianism to rise is less a result of its opponents' choices than their *lack of satisfactory choices*.[32]

Second, this same dynamic also helps explain why electoral authoritarian regimes so easily maintain power after they become established. Quite simply, voters' choices along the regime cleavage become far more consequential after a regime promising to restore stability and address injustices consolidates power. Should they reject the elected strongman regime, risking renewed turmoil and despair, or play it safe by endorsing it? The high stakes involved, as Dominguez and McCann (1998) astutely observed in the case of Mexico under the PRI, compel voters to make their vote choices sequentially, in two stages. First, they decide whether to support or reject the elected strongman regime based on the consequences this might have for the country's stability. Then, those voters "brave enough" to reject the regime need to choose an opposition alternative they want to replace it with.

This sequential decision-making logic not only deters voters from turning against the electoral authoritarian system, but also structures electoral choice in starkly asymmetric terms: as an option to preserve the elected strongman regime, or to replace it with one of its *many* conceivable alternatives. This encourages a proliferation of challengers with diverse and incongruent appeals, all vying against each other to replace the current system. Even among groups favoring nondemocratic substitutes, opposition to electoral authoritarian incumbents has, for this reason, been regularly split among supporters of nationalist, religious, leftist, personalistic, or military dictatorships (see e.g. Rose, Mishler, and Munro 2006, 95–97). The fundamental problem of the opposition in this cleavage structure is not that there are not enough voters with anti-regime outlooks, but that they cannot agree on which alternative to replace it with. In stark contrast, the elected strongman regime has a much easier time pooling together its side of the political spectrum, given the unifying motive of its supporters to

---

[32] This is not to say that cross-cutting party alliances against authoritarian forces cannot arise; indeed, there were several such cases in interwar and contemporary Europe, as Linz (1978, 13), Bermeo (2003), and Levitsky and Ziblatt (2018, ch. 1) point out. However, such coalitions are rare precisely because the logic of electoral competition outlined here works against them.

preserve the status quo, as well as the purported stability and privileges that come with it.

Finally, the strongman heresthetic model implies that electoral authoritarian regimes are defeated when these patterns are reversed. Specifically, it points to two crucial mechanisms through which electoral autocracies lose popular and electoral support. First, voters might turn against these regimes because the situation in the country has stabilized to such an extent that most voters come to believe that strongman rule is no longer necessary. Paradoxically, by achieving its purpose of restoring stability, an elected strongman regime loses its purpose (on this dynamic, see also Huntington 1991, 55), and the logic of electoral competition begins to drift back toward the politics-as-"normal" scenario depicted in Figure 2.1. When the existential danger passes, citizens become naturally preoccupied with more conventional issues and concerns, and as result, the elected strongman appeal gets gradually "crowded out" by the programmatic parties. In the second scenario implicit in the strongman heresthetic model, voters withdraw their support for the electoral authoritarian regime by shifting to the oppositional, anti-authoritarian side of the regime cleavage. They may be prompted to do this due to a blatant failure of the elected strongman regime to deliver on its promise of restoring stability and overcoming indignities – perhaps because it has suffered a catastrophic military defeat or a withering economic crisis, or simply because it has proven itself to be even more corrupt and dysfunctional than its predecessors.

The strongman heresthetic model, in other words, suggests that electoral authoritarian regimes legitimized as vital purveyors of security and justice in times of crisis lose popular support both when they succeed and when they fail in their missions of restoring stability or addressing grievances. We might call this phenomenon the *crisis legitimation paradox*. From this perspective, electoral autocracies are inherently unstable (though not necessarily short-lived) because they have to balance two contradictory demands to sustain their strongman appeal: they must supply enough stability and other improvements to be perceived as the indispensable guarantors of order and justice, while also maintaining a sense of a genuine existential threat to justify their reign.

This is a crucial insight, which pinpoints the roots of the aggressive behavior of many strongman electoral authoritarian regimes at home and abroad. Faced with the danger of becoming seen as irrelevant and needlessly repressive, these regimes are often compelled to sustain and even manufacture the crises and threats that vindicate their rule. The conflicts in which electoral autocracies engage during their reign are therefore not just diversionary, but also "revitalizing": their purpose is to renew these regimes' core legitimacy as the essential protectors of order, stability, fairness, and the general national interest. This resembles the "gambling for survival" (or "resurrection") mechanism described in the diversionary conflict literature: the pursuit of high-stakes conflict to demonstrate competence in an effort to maintain popular support and to survive politically.[33]

The need to both sustain and tackle the crises that justify elected strongman rule is also a crucial vulnerability, which creates opportunities for oppositional mobilization. This is why electoral autocracies have been particularly sensitive to what Lyall (2006) called "rhetorical entrapment": the highlighting of the inconsistencies between the regime's promises and achievements, particularly in the realms of maintaining order, security, and basic socioeconomic stability and equity. By taunting regimes to live up to their own promises of rooting out threats, conflicts, and deprivation, even severely weakened or previously nonexistent oppositions may be able to mobilize contentious movements and dissent against seemingly robust electoral authoritarian regimes. By the same token, contentious action against elected autocracies not only mobilizes people's grievances, but also poses a direct challenge to these regimes' auras of invincibility and promises to maintain order. From the standpoint of an ordinary citizen, how can a regime ensure stability and claim that it represents the most basic interests of society if it is unable to keep its population off the streets?

Putting the Argument Together

What can we conclude from this discussion? If this book's theory is valid and electoral authoritarian regimes are indeed legitimized with a strongman appeal that exploits their populations' heightened sense of insecurity or despair, we should observe three interrelated patterns. First, electoral autocracies will tend to disproportionately emerge in societies plagued by deep and persistent systemic crises and

---

[33] On this mechanism, see for example Downs and Rocke (1994), Goemans and Fey (2009), Chiozza and Goemans (2011), and Haynes (2017).

dysfunction. This is because such backgrounds provide the broadly shared traumatic experiences that give credibility to claims that a hybrid system – neither too democratic nor too authoritarian – is best poised to avoid the shortcomings of these two "pure" regime alternatives and to guarantee order and stability.

The second key claim of this book's theoretical framework is that the impact of crises and other structural factors on the rise and persistence of electoral authoritarianism is not direct but channeled through the ability of these regimes to attract genuine popular support. As I have argued in this chapter, popular consent is the ultimate arbiter of politics in electoral dictatorships because it simultaneously shields these regimes from rebellions from below,[34] justifies their coercive and manipulative tactics, and enables them to better control their elites. From this perspective, experiences of deep systemic crises matter mainly because they can be used to motivate societies to willingly endorse electoral autocracy.[35] Specifically, the emergence of stable electoral authoritarianism has hinged on these regimes' ability to compellingly justify themselves as the safest and most pragmatic governing system for troubled societies.

I claim that for this reason, successful electoral autocracies from across the globe have adopted a distinct and consistent legitimation formula – a "strongman" appeal that consists of three core arguments: (1) that societies faced with instability can survive only if they unify under the protection of a strong, competent, and uncompromising leadership (the *Rally-Around-the-Strongman* frame); (2) that no other political alternative except the strongman electoral authoritarian party or leader is qualified to guide the nation in times of crisis (the *Negative Legitimacy* frame); and (3) that their mandate as strongman "saviors" is endorsed by popular majorities in regular elections (the *Democratic Legitimacy* frame). To the extent these propositions are true, electoral authoritarian incumbents should leave a clear set of "rhetorical fingerprints" in their legitimizing appeals, which reflect this strongman

---

[34] Acemoglu and Robinson (2006) make a similar argument by claiming that the threat of popular rebellion is the key constraint and driver of authoritarian politics.

[35] This argument follows Dahl's (1971) broader observation that "[t]o the extent that [structural factors like economic development, inequalities, cleavages, government effectiveness and so on] ... propel a country toward a hegemonic regime or toward public contestation and polyarchy, they must operate, somehow, through the beliefs of the people."

doctrine and clearly set them apart from their counterparts in established democracies.

The third key argument of this book is that traumatic experiences of unmanageable crises make ordinary people extraordinarily receptive to this strongman appeal. They redefine the ways in which voters perceive their political choices, allowing autocrats to cajole them to willingly – if reluctantly – consent to authoritarian rule. Structural conditions and the strongman appeal are therefore necessary, but insufficient conditions for the rise of electoral autocracy, according to this book's analytic framework. To enable electoral authoritarianism, structural decline and authoritarian overtures must be matched by profound shifts in political outlooks, which allow manipulative incumbents to eliminate other alternatives in people's minds.

Can these sentiments be manufactured by authoritarian propaganda? This is a valid concern. Even in democracies, there is a long-standing claim that the political beliefs of the public are largely produced by elites, who supply the interpretations, the ideologies, and the alternatives with which people operate (Zaller 1992; Converse 2006). However, I argue that such concerns do not contradict the theory I outlined above. First, this theoretical framework also explains the rise and consolidation of electoral autocracies – processes that take place before many such regimes establish dominance over the media and elite discourse. This limits the one-sidedness of political appeals and media coverage, and thus the possibility that the public will uncritically commit to supporting electoral authoritarianism. Second, I argue that electoral autocracies rise by exploiting traumas from deep systemic crises – predispositions that cannot be manufactured by propaganda, as they both precede it and are beyond its capabilities. Also, people's assessments of the ability of electoral autocracies to serve their legitimizing purpose – restoring stability – are difficult to manipulate. Deep crises of the sort that legitimize authoritarianism are felt by everyone, and so is the success or failure of these regimes in addressing them. So, to paraphrase Lincoln, one-sided communications and propaganda can fool some people some of the time, but not most people most of the time, about whether their leadership is losing wars and insurgencies, overcoming economic slumps, addressing endemic crime, and so on.

Finally, unlike in closed dictatorships, citizens of electoral autocracies have far more opportunities to sample alternative viewpoints and information sources. Electoral autocracies do not exert full media dominance, so there are always some alternative, even pro-oppositional information sources available (Gehlbach 2010; Walker and Orttung 2014). For these reasons, the primary purpose of authoritarian media control is not to manufacture reality, but to undermine the credibility of its alternatives (Walker and Orttung 2014, 72) – to convince people that things will be worse if the opposition takes power. In other words, propaganda does not create, but only amplifies the popular appeal of electoral autocracies, as well as the general disrepute of their alternatives.

I test this chapter's propositions in the remainder of this book. In the next chapter, I investigate the link between security and economic crises, and the rise and persistence of electoral authoritarianism. In Chapter 4, I assess whether electoral autocracies from across the world have adhered to the strongman legitimizing appeal – emphasizing the need for a strong-armed, but popularly elected governing system which will protect their societies in times of crisis. In Chapter 5, I explore the thesis that the justification of electoral authoritarian rule as a response to a national emergency has indeed allowed Russia's archetypal electoral authoritarian regime to marginalize and divide its opponents. In Chapter 6, I examine the extent to which these mechanisms extend beyond the Russian case.

3 | *The Crisis Roots of Electoral Authoritarianism: A Macro-Level Analysis*

> [T]he desire for a strong leader who can identify domestic enemies and who promises to do something about them without worrying overmuch about legalities ... [is] latent in every democratic electorate, waiting for sufficiently widespread human suffering to provide conditions for their explosive spread.
>
> Christopher Achen and Larry Bartels (2017, 316)

The most basic empirical implication of this book's analytic framework is that electoral authoritarian regimes have a strong tendency to emerge in the wake of sustained, traumatic and seemingly unmanageable crises – particularly conflicts and socioeconomic collapse. Such upheavals compel the affected societies to prioritize stability and effective, strong-armed governance. They also erode the appeal of political forces that can resist the rise of authoritarianism. This interplay of distinct background circumstances and shifts in mass attitudes enables leaders and political forces with reputations for strong-armed, effective leadership to gain decisive and persistent advantages over their alternatives, and establish authoritarian rule with relatively little resort to repression and largely through the ballot box.

I claim that the secret of the success of electoral authoritarian regimes in times of turmoil lies in their hybrid nature. By combining authoritarian and democratic features, electoral authoritarianism has a broad appeal as the best (or least bad), middle-of-the-road remedy in both democracies and closed autocracies beset by crises. To those seeking change in both troubled democracies and decaying dictatorships, electoral authoritarianism is poised to appear like the safest, most benign solution: a system that does not completely dismantle the current one, thereby risking further instability, but one that is still different enough to address its major flaws.

If these propositions are true, we should observe three clear macro-level patterns. First, in the wake of deep systemic crises, electoral authoritarian regimes should emerge at a significantly greater rate than any other regime alternative. Democracies plagued by unmanageable conflicts and socioeconomic decay should be much more prone to backsliding into electoral authoritarianism than to collapsing into military, single-party, or other forms of dictatorship. Similarly, military dictatorships, single-party regimes, and other closed autocracies faced with profound security, economic, or social crises should be much more likely to transition to electoral authoritarianism than to democratize. We should, in other words, observe a single converging pattern: regardless of whether the collapsing regime is democratic or authoritarian, transitions preceded by deep, unmanageable crises will disproportionately result in the rise of electoral authoritarianism.

The second key macro-level implication of this book's theoretical framework is that major political, socioeconomic, and security crises play a disproportionate role not just in the rise of electoral autocracies, but also in their ability to stay in power. This is because traumas from the crises that preceded electoral authoritarianism make the affected societies reluctant to push for full democratization or the imposition of a full dictatorship, particularly if electoral autocracies have managed to restore stability and bring some improvements.

The third key implication of this book's theory is that histories of deep, traumatic upheavals also enable electoral autocracies to more effectively use the traditional authoritarian tools, like repression, propaganda, clientelism, vote fraud, and so on. By allowing electoral authoritarianism to compellingly justify itself as a form of emergency rule in troubled societies, systemic crises not only make these regimes more popular than the alternatives, but also legitimize their coercive and manipulative tactics as measures that are necessary for restoring and maintaining order. Traumatic experiences of turmoil under alternative orders also shield these regimes from external democratization pressures and popular revolts that may come about as a result of poor economic performance.

Taken together, these macro-level implications of the book's theoretical framework can be summarized in the following hypotheses:

H1 Regime transitions leading to the rise of electoral autocracies are most strongly and consistently predicted by deep economic and security crises;

H2 Deep economic and security crises in both democracies and closed dictatorships are more likely to trigger transitions to electoral autocracies than to any other regime type;

H3 Electoral autocracies will be particularly resistant to regime change if they have been preceded by major economic and security crises, and if they have managed to deliver tangible improvements in stability;

H4 The experience of deep socioeconomic, political, and security crises moderates the effects of coercive power, economic performance, external influences, and other structural factors.

What kind of macro-level evidence would invalidate this theory? If electoral autocracies are primarily sustained through the more proficient use of clientelism, repression, and other manipulative tactics, as emphasized in the existing literature, then structural factors and conditions that are conducive to the use of such coercive tools should be the most robust predictors of transitions to these regimes. Electoral authoritarianism would tend to emerge in poorer societies, which are more dependent on state largesse and patronage, and in states with strong repressive apparatuses and access to significant natural resource rents. The breakdown of democracies and closed autocracies should be at least as likely to produce regimes like military dictatorships as electoral autocracies, because the former would be more reliant on raw coercive power and less restrained in its use. Similarly, electoral autocracies that have better records of economic achievement, or are less exposed to external democratization pressures and influences would be both more likely to emerge and more resistant to democratization once established.

These alternative accounts of the rise and persistence of electoral autocracy, representing the prevalent views in the current literature, can be summarized in the following hypotheses:

H5 The rise and the resilience of electoral authoritarianism are best predicted by conditions favorable for societal control through patronage, repression, and other authoritarian tools, as well as by their economic performance and exposure to external democratization pressures;

H6 Regimes with large coercive and patronage endowments, better economic performance, and less exposure to democratization pressures will be at least as prone to transitions to closed autocracies like military dictatorships as to breakdowns resulting with electoral authoritarianism.

Data Used in the Analyses

As dependent variable for this chapter's analyses, I use the regime indicator from the Authoritarian Regimes Dataset (ver. 6.0) of Wahman, Teorell, and Hadenius (2013), covering the 1960–2014 period. As I elaborated in detail in Chapter 1, this measure best matches the conceptualization of electoral authoritarian regimes as political systems that rule within a democratic constitutional framework, but subvert it informally, by using many different combinations of manipulative tactics. To check if this indicator's threshold separating democracies and electoral autocracies drives the results, I also perform robustness tests with a higher, 7.5 average combined Freedom House and Polity IV score threshold for democracies. Apart from identifying democracies and electoral autocracies, I also use the Authoritarian Regimes Dataset regime to define military regimes and single-party regimes – the other relevant authoritarian regime types used in this analysis.[1]

For the key independent variable, I use only the most tangible and widely accepted indicators for major crises: economic decline and conflict. As I discussed in Chapter 2, this minimalist definition of crisis avoids the noise and subjectivity that might afflict more wide-ranging measures. It also sets a high evidentiary standard for confirming this book's theoretical propositions. Given the narrowness of these measures, significant findings in favor of the theory of crisis origins of electoral authoritarianism should bolster our confidence in its validity.

I measure economic crises using an indicator of GDP per capita percentage decline over a three-year period, derived from the Institute for Health Metrics and Evaluation (IHME) comprehensive GDP per capita series (James et al. 2012). This dataset combines the five most commonly used sources of GDP per capita data to produce the most comprehensive and robust series of GDP per capita data currently

---

[1] This dataset defines military regimes as autocracies where the military either directly or indirectly controls the executive, and single-party regimes as polities where only one party is allowed to contest power. The classification of these regimes in the Authoritarian Regimes Dataset of Wahman, Teorell, and Hadenius (2013) closely matches other prominent datasets that cover these closed authoritarian regimes, such as the dataset compiled by Barbara Geddes, Joseph Wright, and Erica Frantz, "Autocratic Breakdown and Regime Transitions: New Data" (unpublished manuscript, 2013).

available.[2] I measure economic crises using GDP per capita percentage *decline* over a three-year interval, which takes a value of zero when economic growth is positive and registers percentage decline in GDP when it is not. This measure is better suited for this purpose than the standard annual GDP change indicators, as major economic crises tend to unfold over several years. The three-year interval indicator is also more appropriate than longer-term measures of economic performance (e.g. GDP change over five or ten years) as these tend to include the post-crisis recoveries.[3] As economic expansion may have the opposite, regime-strengthening effects, preventing collapses and transitions to other regimes, I also employ a separate indicator of the extent of GDP growth over a three-year period. Analogous to the GDP decline indicator, this measure takes a value of zero when GDP growth is negative and registers the percentage growth otherwise.[4]

To measure conflict – the second macro-level indicator of systemic crisis – I employ two complementary indicators. The primary measure I use captures higher-intensity conflicts. Derived from the Correlates of War dataset (COW), it tags conflict as episodes of violence that

---

[2] The data sources used for the IHME estimates include GDP per capita data from World Bank World Development Indicators, the United Nations Statistics Division National Accounts, the IMF World Economic Outlook Database List, the Maddison Project (Bolt and van Zanden 2019), and the Penn World Tables (Heston, Summers, and Aten 2012). The comprehensive GDP scale estimated in this fashion addresses the inconsistencies, errors, and gaps that have plagued each of the existing individual measures of GDP per capita. For a discussion of the reliability and the comparative performance of this composite scale, see James et al. (2012).

[3] Specifically, the mean duration of recessions in the IHME dataset is slightly above 2 years and its standard deviation is about 1.6 years, making the 3-year GDP decline indicator most suitable for this analysis.

[4] To check the robustness of these measures, I perform analyses with alternative economic development data (from the Maddison Project and Penn World Tables), with alternative indicators (using infant mortality and electricity consumption per capita) and using different time intervals (one, five, and ten-year periods). The advantage of the infant mortality indicator of development is that it is less correlated with resource rents and better captures how broadly the benefits of development are distributed (Ulfelder 2007, 1004; Kapstein and Converse 2008). In turn, electricity-consumption-based measures of national wealth provide a better measure of the informal economy and tend to reduce biases in standard government reporting-based measures of GDP in many developing nations (see e.g. S. Johnson et al. 1997). These alternative model specifications, presented in the Online Appendix to this chapter, produce very similar results to the three-year growth and recession indicators presented here.

produce more than 1,000 battle deaths per year (Singer and Small 1994). The second measure I employ is from the UCDP/PRIO Armed Conflict Dataset (N. P. Gleditsch et al. 2002) and uses a lower-intensity conflict threshold of twenty-five annual battle deaths.[5] For both measures, I operationalize the conflict indicators used in the analyses as the rates of conflict over the preceding three-year period. The conflict indicators used in this chapter's analyses therefore represent the number of years of conflict that a country has experienced over the past 3-year period. Similar to the economic crisis indicator, this interval captures the somewhat more persistent patterns of conflict.[6]

There are several broader advantages to using *both* the COW and PRIO measures of conflict in this chapter's analyses. On one hand, the higher-threshold COW indicator is unlikely to record the typically low-casualty coercive tactics employed by regimes, providing a cleaner measure of conflicts with autocracy-legitimizing potential. Using the lower-threshold PRIO measure, on the other hand, provides better coverage of low-intensity conflicts that are also regularly used to justify authoritarian rule. Ultimately, using both measures allows me to also verify a key proposition of the crisis theory of electoral authoritarianism. Namely, if this theory is valid, higher-intensity conflicts, captured by the COW conflict variable, should, on average, lead to much greater increase in the likelihood of transition to electoral authoritarianism than the lower-intensity ones, captured by the PRIO indicator. As for the economic growth and decline indicators, I perform a wide range of robustness tests in the Online Appendix to this chapter, to validate the effects of the COW and PRIO conflict measures.[7]

---

[5] For both the COW and PRIO indicators, I employ a fairly restrictive coding for the participants in conflicts, which marks countries as affected by conflict only if it takes place on their territory, or if they are the primary or secondary side in the conflict. This coding generally avoids tagging great powers and their allies involved in proxy wars outside their borders as conflict participants – an approach more in line with the book's conceptualization of security crises as calamities in which a country's population is directly affected.

[6] This is also the empirically most appropriate time interval for measuring major conflicts, because the mean duration of high-intensity conflicts in the dataset used for this analysis is 3.9 years and the median is 2 years.

[7] These include indicators that record conflict rates over different intervals (one, five, and ten years) and the cumulative number of years a country has been in conflict, as well as expanded measures that include extraterritorial and proxy conflicts, in which a country is not a primary or secondary participant. In addition, in the Online Appendix for this chapter, I estimate models with

To test hypothesis 3, that the electoral autocracies most resistant to collapse are those that were preceded by more turmoil, and that have made greater progress in restoring stability and prosperity, I use two sets of additional indicators in the models of the duration of electoral authoritarian regimes, presented in the last empirical section of this chapter. First, I employ indicators of conflict and economic decline in the three-year periods *before* the emergence of electoral autocracies. Second, I measure the percentage change in real GDP *throughout the tenure* of electoral authoritarian regimes. These indicators capture the intuition that overcoming the crises that have justified electoral authoritarianism serves as the key standard by which these regimes will be evaluated by their societies.

The regime survival and transition analyses in this chapter also include a range of variables accounting for alternative explanations and controlling for potential confounders. For these purposes, I use several indicators of the capacity of autocracies to subdue their societies with coercion and manipulation. As the most general proxy of a country's susceptibility to authoritarian pressure, I use the level of economic development, captured by a GDP per capita measure from the IHME dataset. I employ this measure because it represents a mechanism on which the literatures on democracy, modernization, and electoral authoritarianism appear to be in agreement: that relative poverty is the essential precondition for authoritarian forces to establish clientelistic and coercive strangleholds over their societies.

Apart from GDP per capita, I include two more specific measures of coercive and clientelistic power. First, I measure state repressive capacity using the number of military personnel per thousand inhabitants, calculated from the National Material Capabilities Dataset (Singer 1988). One key reason for using this indicator is that a large share of repression may be carried out in secret (Davenport 2007), which means it is better captured by the scale of the repressive apparatus than by observed acts of repression.[8] Second, to measure the scale of

a number of alternative indicators of security threats that could be construed as crises justifying authoritarianism: assassinations, government crises, protests, riots and revolutions (contained in the Banks dataset conflict index), conflicts in neighboring states, the presence of discriminated groups, natural disaster risks, and terrorism.

[8] The best available measures of directly observed repression, such as the Political Terror Scale (Gibney et al. 2017) and the CIRI Human Rights Data Project (Cingranelli, Richards, and Clay 2014), record acts of violence that overlap with

clientelistic resources available to political regimes across the world, I include the World Bank indicator of total natural resource rents as percent of GDP – the source of patronage most consistently associated with the consolidation and survival of authoritarian rule in the empirical literature (Gassebner, Lamla, and Vreeland 2013; Ross 2015).[9]

Finally, the regime survival and transition analyses in this chapter include controls for a range of relevant institutional and contextual variables. These represent factors that could influence both the countries' propensity to experience systemic crises and the ability of authoritarian forces to win elections, potentially confounding the link between the two. For this reason, I include controls for membership in the European Union, the North Atlantic Treaty Organization (NATO), and the Organisation for Economic Co-operation and Development (OECD), as the economic and security guarantees and the institutional incentives of the members of these organizations may prevent and ameliorate crises and act as deterrents against the rise of authoritarian forces (see e.g. Gassebner, Lamla, and Vreeland 2013). As external democratization pressures and "contagion" effects may exert a similar influence, I also include an indicator calculating the proportion of other democracies that share a land or river border with each given country, derived from the COW Direct Contiguity Dataset version 3.1 (see Stinnett et al. 2002). Additionally, as democracies with presidential systems have been highlighted as potentially more unstable and conflict-prone compared to parliamentary ones, I include a type-of-political-system variable from the Database of Political Institutions (Beck et al. 2001) in the analyses of transitions from

the measures of conflict. For this reason, using state repressive capacity as a proxy for coercive behavior allows me to better separate it from conflict. Furthermore, because internal repression is a very manpower-intensive task, the number of military personnel per thousand inhabitants is the best macro-level proxy of repressive capacity (see Albertus and Menaldo 2012). To check the robustness of this measure, I also perform auxiliary analyses with an alternative, resource-based measure of state repressive capacity: the Composite Index of Military Capacity form the National Material Capabilities Dataset.

[9] This measure represents the total sum of oil, natural gas, coal, mineral, and forest rents as a percentage of a country's GDP. In the Online Appendix to this chapter, I also perform auxiliary analyses with an alternative, more specific indicator of the total value of oil and gas production from the Oil and Gas Dataset (Ross and Mahdavi 2015), which also provides somewhat better data coverage than the natural resource rents measure.

democracies.[10] Similarly, as newly founded countries may have a greater tendency to decay into turmoil, I include an indicator denoting the number of years since each country has gained independence. Finally, all analyses include a Cold War dummy marking the 1960–1989 period, as well as regional dummies for Africa, the Americas, Asia, Europe, the Middle East, Oceania, and the post-Soviet area, to control for time period and regional effects. I provide a detailed description of the dataset and the variables used in the analyses in the Online Appendix to this chapter.

To reduce problems with reverse causality and endogeneity, I use one-year lags for all the independent variables in the models, except the indicators for the number of years since independence and the Cold War and region dummies. Also, because of the considerable skewness in their distributions, I use natural logs of the GDP per capita, military personnel per capita, and total natural resources rents as a percentage of GDP variables.

Crises and Electoral Authoritarianism: Aggregate Patterns

The two most basic empirical implications of this book's theoretical framework, summarized by hypotheses 1 and 2 in this chapter, are that electoral autocracies will disproportionately emerge in the wake of national crises and upheavals, and at a significantly greater rate than other regime types. As a first step toward evaluating these claims, I explore the aggregate patterns of conflict and economic decline across different regime types, and in particular, among electoral autocracies, democracies, and military dictatorships: the regimes that account for the overwhelming majority of transitions in the 1960–2014 period,[11] and which have been the main competing outcomes in processes of regime change (see Bermeo 2016). I depict these aggregate trends graphically in Figures 3.1 and 3.2 below.

The patterns that emerge strongly support the claim that electoral autocracies have crisis origins. Looking at the right panel of Figure 3.1,

---

[10] See e.g. Linz (1990) and O'Donnell (1994); for a critique of this view, see Cheibub (2007). This indicator denotes whether the country has a parliamentary, presidential, or assembly-elected president system for the selection of the chief executive.

[11] If we exclude transitional regimes lasting up to three years, electoral autocracies, democracies, and military dictatorships have accounted for almost 90 percent of all transitions for the 1960–2014 period (or 41, 31, and 17 percent, respectively), according to data from the Authoritarian Regimes Dataset ver. 6.

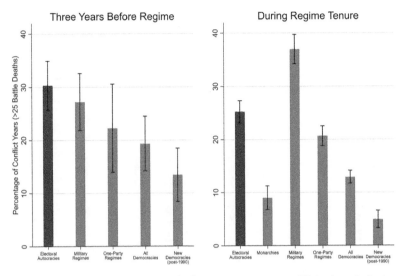

Figure 3.1 Conflict three years before a regime is established and during a regime's tenure (1960–2014)
Note: bars presented with 95 percent confidence intervals

we see that between 1960 and 2014, electoral autocracies have, on average, engaged in internal or international conflicts 25 percent of the time *during their tenures* – a rate of conflict that is five times greater than in new democracies established after 1990, and is only surpassed by military dictatorships. But the crucial difference between these different regime types is shown in the <u>left panel</u> of Figure 3.1, which displays the aggregate rates of conflict in the immediate three-year periods *before their rise*. Here, we see that the three-year periods preceding the rise of electoral autocracies exhibit the highest propensity for conflict of *all* regime types. Indeed, these regimes seem to have even more violent origins than military dictatorships, which are considered to be especially likely to emerge as a result of violent upheavals (Geddes, Frantz, and Wright 2014, 157). Specifically, countries that eventually transition into electoral authoritarianism are, on average, at conflict for about a full year in the three-year period before the rise of the regime. This is twice the rate of conflict of the immediate periods that precede new democracies, a third more than the period before the rise of all democracies, and 3 percentage points above the average amount of conflict that precedes military dictatorships.

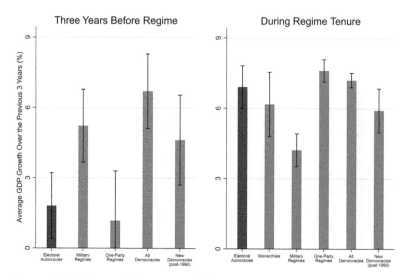

Figure 3.2 GDP growth three years before a regime is established and during a regime's tenure (1960–2014)

*Note: bars presented with 95 percent confidence intervals

The relationship between economic performance and political regimes exhibits the same behavior. A comparison of three-year GDP growth rates by regime type, displayed in Figure 3.2, shows that economic performance was *much lower* in periods preceding electoral autocracies than ahead of the rise of all other regime types apart from single-party regimes. Again, the contrast with new democracies and military dictatorships – the main competing outcomes to the rise of electoral authoritarianism – is telling. During their tenure, electoral autocracies perform somewhat better economically than new democracies (by an average of about 1 percentage point over a three-year period) and much better than military dictatorships (by about 2.7 percentage points). However, in the three-year periods before their establishment, electoral autocracies display a much weaker economic performance than both new democracies and military dictatorships – 3.5 and 2.5 times lower than these competing regime outcomes, respectively. This suggests that electoral autocracies emerge not only from the most conflictual but also from the most economically stagnant backgrounds – a pattern consistent with this book's crisis-origins theory of electoral authoritarianism.

Perhaps most compellingly, this data shows that electoral autocracies do not simply emerge in more conflict-prone and economically

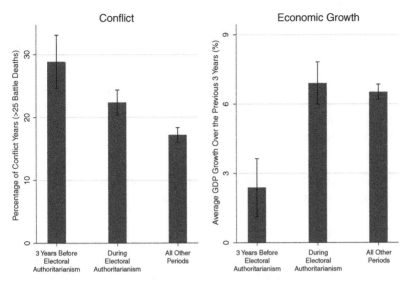

Figure 3.3 Conflict and GDP growth in countries that have experienced electoral authoritarian rule (1960–2014)
Note: bars presented with 95 percent confidence intervals

backward countries. Instead, they tend to follow the worst periods in *any* country that has had spells of electoral authoritarianism. I illustrate this in Figure 3.3, which depicts the rates of conflict and economic growth *only* for countries that have experienced electoral authoritarian rule. It displays these patterns across three distinct periods: (1) the three-year intervals *before* these regimes are established; (2) the periods *during* their tenure; (3) *all other periods* when electoral authoritarianism is not the governing system. Again, a clear pattern emerges: periods right before the rise of electoral autocracies have been the most conflict-prone and economically stagnant for countries that experienced this type of regime. In particular, countries that have had electoral authoritarian rule since 1960 have, on average, experienced conflict 29 percent of the time in the three-year periods before the rise of these regimes, as opposed to 23 percent during the reign of these regimes, and 17 percent in all other periods. Similarly, these countries registered GDP growth rates of just 2.4 percent on average in the three-year periods before the rise of electoral authoritarianism, and about 6–7 percent otherwise.

Taken together, these aggregate patterns of conflict and economic stagnation – the two most tangible indicators of acute systemic crises – are highly consistent with this book's theory of the crisis origins of electoral authoritarianism. They not only support the thesis that electoral authoritarian regimes have the most violent and economically stagnant backgrounds of all, but that they follow the most troubled periods in the histories of the countries they have governed.

But do these aggregate patterns hold up in a multivariate setting, after accounting for other, potentially confounding factors? I examine this in the sections that follow.

The Structural Correlates of Electoral Authoritarianism: A Regime Survival and Transition Analysis

Methodology

The complexity of regime transitions creates at least four important methodological challenges for testing this book's theory of the crisis roots of electoral authoritarianism. First, there are competing risks of regime failure. Each regime has many possible alternatives, so it can "fail" or transition not only to electoral autocracy, but also into other regime types – democracies, other types of dictatorships, or simply collapse into a failed state. As the baseline risks of regime transition and the impact of the key structural factors are likely very different for transitions between various regime types, we must use a methodology that takes this into account. Second, some countries are "repeat offenders" in terms of some types of regime breakdowns and transitions. As each additional transition may alter the likelihood of another one, the modeling strategy must incorporate the repeatable nature of regime failures to avoid potential biases. Third, due to the complexity of these processes, some sources of variability across countries are bound to remain unobserved and unaccounted for in models of regime transitions. Some strategies for assessing the impact of such country-level heterogeneity are therefore necessary.

I account for all of these peculiarities by performing analyses of regime transitions with two types of Cox proportional hazards event-history models: (1) the conditional risk-set model and (2) the conditional frailty model with country-level random effects. Event-history models (also called survival models) analyze the factors affecting the length of time until an event (in this analysis, a regime transition) occurs. Cox survival models provide a very flexible estimation framework that can also be modified to deal with repeated and competing events

(B. S. Jones and Branton 2005; Box-Steffensmeier and Jones 2004). Their fundamental advantage is that they do not impose a parametric specification of the baseline hazard (in this analysis, the regimes' risk of transition when all the variables included in the analysis equal zero), or the duration dependency function (which determines how the risk of transition changes over time), but allow these to take any form suggested by the underlying data.

In addition, this modeling strategy has three key benefits for the present analysis. First, both the conditional risk-set and frailty Cox models allow me to stratify the estimates by the number of prior transitions, or "failures." Intuitively, this approach allows the experience of prior transitions to increase or decrease the chances that a particular regime will succumb to another one. Second, I estimate all the models in this analysis using the partitioned likelihood approach, where a separate estimate is produced for each type of transition. Thus, for instance, I obtain separate estimates for transitions from democracies to electoral autocracies and from democracies to military dictatorships. This allows for both baseline hazards and estimated variable effects to be different for these two types of regime transition, capturing their key substantive distinctions. Third, the conditional frailty Cox model allows me to account for any unmeasured risk factors that could produce heterogeneity in the risk of regime failure across countries – the fact that some countries might be prone to experience regime transitions for reasons that are not accounted for in the model (see Box-Steffensmeier, De Boef, and Joyce 2007). Hence, estimating both the conditional risk-set and frailty Cox models enables me to leverage their advantages and offset their disadvantages.[12] Quite

---

[12] The conditional risk set model's strength is that it accounts for correlation in event times due to unobserved subject-specific (here, country-specific) heterogeneity and repeated events by adjusting the variance-covariance matrix. But it does not directly incorporate the heterogeneity in the estimation process, producing potentially biased (though consistent) estimates of the covariate effects. The conditional frailty model, on the other hand, directly incorporates the subject-level heterogeneity in the estimates as random effects, producing unbiased estimates of covariate effects and a generally superior performance over other estimators (Box-Steffensmeier, Linn, and Smidt 2014). However, conditional frailty estimates are sensitive to the correct parametric specification of the distribution of the random effect term, which is generally unknown. Also, these individual frailty terms must be independent of the model's covariates – an often untenable assumption that can produce severely biased and inconsistent results if violated (Box-Steffensmeier, De Boef, and Joyce 2007, 240).

simply, if the results from these two types of models match, we can be more confident they reflect empirical realities.

Using this versatile methodological approach, I perform two groups of analyses. First, I test this chapter's hypotheses 1 and 2, that regimes plagued by severe crises will disproportionately transition to electoral autocracies by estimating models of seven types of transitions: *from democracy* to (1) electoral authoritarianism and (2) military dictatorships; *from military dictatorship* to (3) electoral authoritarianism and (4) democracy; and *from single-party regimes* to (5) electoral authoritarianism, (6) democracy and (7) military dictatorship. The reasons for focusing on these transition types are both substantive and methodological. From a substantive standpoint, they represent the two distinct paths through which electoral autocracies emerge – the breakdown of democracy and the liberalization of closed autocracies. Methodologically, these transition types account for the great majority of the regime changes in the period under study, which ensures that I both examine the key competing outcomes and that I have sufficient data for consistent estimates and a full range of robustness tests.[13]

The second set of analyses I perform evaluate hypothesis 3, that experiences of deep systemic crises make electoral autocracies more durable and less prone to collapse. For this purpose, in the last empirical section of this chapter, I estimate models of transitions from electoral authoritarianism to: (1) democracy and (2) military dictatorship. Again, these types of transitions represent the vast majority of breakdowns of electoral authoritarian regimes, which ensures that the key substantive outcomes are accounted for in the analysis, and that it has sufficient data for consistent estimates and robustness tests.

---

[13] According to the Authoritarian Regimes dataset, forty-eight electoral autocracies emerged as result of the collapse of democracies, while another thirty-nine and thirty-two emerged through transitions from military dictatorships and one-party regimes, respectively. Together, these transitions account for about 82 percent of all transitions to electoral authoritarian regimes. Another twenty-six, or about 18 percent of electoral authoritarian regimes emerged from civil wars, regimes labeled as transitional, from monarchies, and from regimes that are unclassified. As there are too few regimes in each of these residual categories, or they do not represent coherent regime types, I omit them from the analysis.

Transitions from Democracies

Democracy is a child of peace and cannot live apart from its mother.

William E. Rappard (1938)

The data on democratic breakdowns consist of 3,683 country-year obser-vations, covering 128 countries in the period between 1960 and 2014. These observations record whether a democracy experienced a transition to another regime type in a given year. There are sixty-four democratic collapses in the data, the great majority of which (forty-eight) produced electoral autocracies, giving rise to about a third of the electoral authori-tarian regimes since 1960. In turn, thirteen democratic breakdowns gave rise to military dictatorships. I describe this data in more detail in Part 1 of the Online Appendix to this chapter.

Using this data, I estimate separate Cox models for the two key types of democratic collapse: transitions from democracies to electoral autocracies and to military dictatorships. I present the results of these analyses in Table 3.1. For both types of transitions, Models (1)–(3) and (5)–(7) represent conditional gap time Cox estimates, and Models (4) and (8) provide conditional frailty Cox estimates. All of these models are stratified by the number of prior democratic spells. The baseline Models (1) and (5) include the indicators for conflict, GDP growth and decline, the level of GDP per capita, country memberships in EU, NATO, and OECD, the share of a country's neighbors that are democratic, and the number of years that have elapsed since a country's independence. Models (2)–(3) and (6)–(7) include three additional variables: the measure of military size, which captures the state's repressive capacity, resource rents as share of GDP, and two indicators for the type of political system.[14] These variables reduce the number of observations in the estimates because of missing values,[15] so I estimate Models (1) and (5) without them as a check for biases due to the constrained sample size.

Models (3) and (6), in turn, use an alternative indicator of conflict, based on the twenty-five annual battle-deaths threshold. As I highlighted before, this measure not only captures the impact of many lower-intensity con-flicts on regime transitions, but contrasting its effects with the higher,

---

[14] I include dummy variables for assembly-elected president and parliamentary system, with presidential systems serving as the baseline category.

[15] The military size indicator has data until 2012, while the resource rents and political system indicators do not cover the period before 1970 and 1976, respectively.

1,000 annual battle-deaths indicator in Models (1)–(2) and (5)–(6) allows us to test a key premise of this book's theory: that higher-intensity security crises increase the likelihood of transition to electoral authoritarianism more that lower intensity conflicts. Finally, all models in Table 3.1 include region and Cold War dummies to control for possible regional and historical period influences.

All estimates in Table 3.1 are expressed as hazard ratios, which represent the increase or decrease in the chance of failure – or in this case, regime transition – per one-unit change in a given variable, when all other factors are kept constant. The advantage of hazard ratio estimates from survival models is that they are easier to interpret. A hazard ratio equal to one indicates that the predictor is *not* associated with an increase or decrease in the chances of a regime transition. A hazard ratio that is greater or lower than one, on the other hand, indicates that an increase in that predictor is associated with an increase or decrease in the likelihood of transition, respectively. The size of this increase or decrease is a simple multiple of the estimated hazard ratio. For example, an estimated hazard ratio of 0.5 indicates that a one-unit increase in the predictor reduces the risk of transition by half. In turn, a hazard ratio of 2 suggests that the same change in the predictor doubles the odds of transition.

If this book's theory is valid, security and economic crises should more strongly and consistently predict transitions from democracy to electoral authoritarianism than to military dictatorships. This is because electoral autocracies can better exploit these upheavals to secure broad societal consent to their rule. If, on the other hand, the alternative theories that electoral autocracies are products of their special ability to more effectively employ repression and clientelist practices are correct, then structural factors that facilitate the use of these manipulative practices should be most strongly associated with the rise of these regimes. Specifically, lower economic development, and greater repressive capacity and access to resource rents should be the strongest predictors of transitions to electoral authoritarianism. By the same token, military takeovers should be even more closely predicted by high repressive capacity and resource rents, and low, clientelism-enabling income levels, as these regimes are presumably more reliant on brute coercion.

The results of the analysis presented in the left panel of Table 3.1 strongly support the former, crisis-origins theory of electoral autocracy. The estimates from all models in the left panel of Table 3.1 suggest armed conflicts in the preceding three years are associated with a significantly increased risk of democratic collapse leading to electoral authoritarianism. Based on the estimates from Model (2), a single year of high-intensity conflict (>1,000 battle deaths) in the preceding 3-year period is associated with an increase in the risk of transition from democracy to electoral authoritarianism of 261 percent,[16] or by about 2.6 times, all else being equal. Thus, a democracy that has experienced nonstop conflict in the 3 preceding years will face a risk of collapsing into an electoral autocracy increased by a whopping 4,626 percent, or 46 times greater, compared to a democracy with the same values on all other variables that has not experienced conflict in this period.

To see how large this estimated effect is, consider a hypothetical case of a democratic country with a small, 5 percent probability of transitioning into an electoral autocracy. If this democracy experiences one year of high-intensity conflict over a three-year period, its probability of backsliding into electoral authoritarianism will more than triple to 16 percent. For two years of conflict, this probability will rise to about 41 percent, and after three years, it will reach 71 percent. In other words, a relatively short, three-year conflict has the capacity to transform a democracy with a minuscule probability of backsliding into electoral authoritarianism into a high-risk case. These results are robust to an exhaustive range of alternative specifications and measures of conflict and violence, which I present in the Online Appendix to this chapter (see Part 1 of the Appendix).

The results in the left panel of Table 3.1 also seem to provide support for the alternative hypothesis 5, that electoral autocracies emerge and thrive in environments that allow them to coerce and manipulate their societies into submission. In particular, they suggest that higher per capita income significantly diminishes the risk of democratic backsliding toward electoral authoritarianism: a potential indication that societies in low-income, economically vulnerable democracies are more easily subdued by repression, clientelism, and other coercive pressures. Based on estimates in Model (2), a one standard-deviation increase in log GDP per capita in an average democracy is associated with about an 82 percent decrease in the relative hazard of backsliding into electoral authoritarianism, when all else is equal. To translate this into a more concrete scenario, a hypothetical democracy that has a 50 percent probability of transitioning to electoral authoritarianism would see

---

[16] Calculated as $100 \times (\beta[\text{Conflict over the Past 3 years}] - 1)$ from the estimates in Table 3.1.

Table 3.1 *Repeated events history models of democratic breakdowns, 1960–2014*

| | Democracy → Electoral autocracy | | | | Democracy → Military dictatorship | | | |
| | Conditional gap time | | | Cond. frailty | Conditional gap time | | Cond. frailty | |
	(1)	(2)	(3)	(4)	(5)	(6)	(7)	(8)
Conflict with >1,000 casualties in the past 3 years	3.25 (0.92)**	3.62 (1.09)**		3.61 (0.86)**	0.00 (.)	0.00 (0.00)**		
Conflict with >25 casualties in the past 3 years			1.53 (0.29)*				1.51 (0.67)	1.55 (0.41)
Extent of GDP growth over 3-yrs	1.01 (0.03)	1.01 (0.04)	1.00 (0.04)	1.01 (0.03)	0.96 (0.06)	0.96 (0.06)	0.97 (0.05)	0.98 (0.05)
Extent of GDP decline over 3-yrs	1.00 (0.02)	0.99 (0.02)	0.99 (0.03)	0.99 (0.02)	0.97 (0.08)	0.89 (0.08)	0.88 (0.07)	0.9 (0.09)
Log per capita income	0.30 (0.10)**	0.19 (0.08)**	0.19 (0.08)**	0.19 (0.05)**	0.45 (0.26)	0.55 (0.29)	0.63 (0.40)	0.45 (0.15)
Log military size		1.54 (0.88)	1.69 (1.06)	1.54 (0.49)		2.07 (1.54)	1.90 (1.44)	1.69 (0.6)
Log resource rents		0.97 (0.25)	0.97 (0.26)	0.97 (0.2)		1.54 (0.44)	1.76 (0.61)	1.94 (0.5)+
EU or NATO membership	0.27 (0.17)*	0.38 (0.22)+	0.53 (0.34)	0.38 (0.19)				

	(1)	(2)	(3)	(4)	(5)	(6)	(7)	(8)
OECD membership	0.46 (0.36)	0.52 (0.40)	0.36 (0.34)	0.52 (0.25)	0.07 (0.11)+	0.05 (0.08)*	0.03 (0.06)+	0.02 (0.01)*
Democratic neighbors share	1.45 (0.63)	1.56 (0.87)	1.92 (1.10)	1.56 (0.57)				
Parliamentary system		1.62 (0.84)	1.36 (0.70)	1.62 (0.56)				
Assembly-elected President		1.00 (0.71)	0.88 (0.54)	1 (0.38)				
Years since independence	1.00 (0.00)	1.00 (0.00)	1.00 (0.00)	1 (0)	1.01 (0.01)	1.00 (0.01)	1.00 (0.01)	1 (0.01)
Cold War dummy	0.23 (0.12)**	0.21 (0.15)*	0.51 (0.33)	0.21 (0.08)*	6.40 (5.74)*	8.79 (8.09)*	7.68 (6.70)*	6.79 (2.79)*
Region dummies	YES	YES	YES	YES	YES	YES	YES	YES†
Variance of the random effect (θ)				0.00				0.00**
N	3619	2447	2447	2447	3619	2805	2805	2804
Number of failures	48	39	39	39	13	13	13	13
Likelihood ratio for θ				0				161.56
l-likelihood		−107.711		−107.71	−42.5127			−37.83
Log-likelihood for model	−159.427	−107.711	−112.39	−107.71	−42.5127	−36.7498	−36.946	−37.83

Note: Estimates represent hazard ratios. Robust standard errors provided in parentheses.

† The conditional frailty model (8) does not include the region dummies for Europe and the post-Soviet region, as their strong negative correlation with the outcome creates convergence problems for this model.

+p<0.10 *p<0.05 **p<0.01

this risk reduced to 15 percent if its GDP per capita is higher by one standard deviation (or by about 9,500 US 2005 constant international dollars). And as I show in Part I of the Online Appendix to this chapter, the effect of economic development is robust to a wide variety of alternative specifications, including different GDP measures from different sources as well as alternative development indicators. Clearly, rising per capita income has a strong impact on the stability of democracies – as Przeworski and Limongi (1997) have noted, these regimes tend not to break down after they reach a certain income level.[17]

However, a closer scrutiny of the results in Table 3.1 indicates that the theory of the crisis origins of electoral authoritarianism better explains democratic collapse into electoral authoritarianism. First, a direct comparison between the effects of these two variables shows that keeping the peace plays a more important role in preserving democracy than economic development when it comes to transitions to electoral autocracy. To demonstrate this, I re-estimated Model (2) in the left panel of Table 3.1, replacing the conflict indicator with a simple dummy variable indicating the *absence* of high-intensity conflict just in the previous year. The results show that the absence of conflict only in the year prior to the observed outcome is associated with a decrease in the risk of transition to electoral authoritarianism by more than 96 percent.

For a more intuitive representation of the size of this effect relative to the impact of economic development, consider again the hypothetical scenario involving an average democracy, which faces a 50 percent probability of backsliding into electoral authoritarianism. If this democracy has managed to avoid conflict in just the past year, its probability of collapsing into electoral authoritarianism is diminished from 50 percent to less than 4 percent. This democracy would not be able to match this reduction in the risk of electoral authoritarian takeover even if it increased its log GDP per capita by a full standard deviation in the sample of democracies for 1960–2014. If it somehow did manage to pull off this incredible developmental leap, it would see its chances of transitioning to electoral authoritarianism reduce to 15 percent – an impressive decline in the risk of democratic backsliding, but still one that is far less reassuring than avoiding conflict. Thus, in line with the quote from William E. Rappard at the

---

[17] In this sample, the development level beyond which there are no democratic breakdowns is about 16,300 US 2005 international dollars, which is in the 65th percentile of the distribution of this variable.

beginning of the section, maintaining peace seems to play a greater role than economic development in preventing the rise of electoral authoritarianism in democracies.

The second reason why this is the case relates to the size and timing of the developmental leaps required to prevent democratic backsliding toward an electoral authoritarian regime. A one-standard-deviation increase in GDP per capita is roughly equivalent to a jump from the 25th percentile to the 60th percentile of GDP per capita, of from about 5,000 to 14,500 US 2005 international dollars per person. In more tangible terms, this represents a leap from a third-world country income in the late 1960s/ early 1970s to a first-world country income in the same period: from that of Chile or Turkey in 1973 to that of the United Kingdom, France, or Germany in 1967, for instance. Such improvements in national income bring clear benefits for the stability of democracies – only two out of the sixty-six democratic collapses have occurred in countries at or above the 60th percentile of GDP per capita. However, the latter are exceedingly rare. Just five low-income democracies have made the developmental leap from the 25th to the 60th percentile of GDP per capita in the period covered by this dataset. On average, it took these countries more than twenty-four years to achieve this rise in per capita income.[18]

In stark contrast, just a few years of conflict can lead a democracy to ruin. To illustrate with the same hypothetical scenario as before, an average democracy in the 25th income percentile that has a 50 percent probability of transitioning to an electoral autocracy would see reduction in its risk to about 15 percent if it maintains a steady developmental path and manages to reach median income levels, with all else being equal. However, the probability that this newly minted middle-income democracy will fall to electoral authoritarianism would soar back up almost 90 percent if it experiences three consecutive years of high-intensity conflict. And such rates of conflict are a far more common occurrence among low-income countries than big developmental leaps. Almost half of all the conflict for the 1960–2014 period have occurred in democracies in the bottom quartile of the per capita income distribution.

[18] The countries that made this progress in income are the relatively small nations of Botswana, Malta, Cyprus, and Saint Kitts and Nevis, as well as Chile. Malta achieved this wealth increase in the shortest period of time (seventeen years), while Chile took the longest (thirty-eight years).

The key takeaway here is that economic development helps explain the different rates of democratic backsliding into electoral authoritarianism across low- and high-income democracies, but does not account for much of the within-country variation in this outcome over time. It may take a generation, at best, for the democracies most at risk to reach income levels high enough to preclude democratic breakdown, and very few of them achieve that feat. A short conflict, in contrast, can push even medium-income democracies toward electoral authoritarianism. Also, economic progress is not easily manufactured by a set of political actors; for the most part, it is driven by the decisions of consecutive administrations and impersonal market forces. Conflict, on the other hand, is far more readily incited, exported across borders, and generally exploited by authoritarian political forces.

But there is a third, and even more compelling bit of evidence that conflict has primacy over economic development as a key correlate of transitions from democracies to electoral autocracies. Consistent with hypothesis 4, the protective effect of higher economic development against democratic backsliding into electoral authoritarianism appears to be conditioned by conflict. To show this, I estimate an alternative specification of Model (2) from Table 3.1 that contains an interaction term between the conflict and log per capita income variables. According to the results, which I provide in full in Table A.1.11 of the Online Appendix, log per capita income has a significant negative (i.e. lower than 1 in hazard ratios) association with the risk of transition to electoral authoritarianism, while its interaction with conflict has a strong and significant positive (i.e. greater than 1) connection with this outcome. This suggests that the protective influence of economic development diminishes as the rates of conflict increase. I portray this relationship visually in Figure 3.4 below.

The estimates in this graph show that the impact of a one-standard-deviation increase in log per capita income is significant *only in the absence of conflict*; even a single year of high-intensity violence completely curtails this effect. This is a crucial finding, and a qualification of one of the long-standing empirical relationships in the literature – that between economic development and the stability of democracy. The estimates in Figure 3.4 and Table A.1.11 in the Online Appendix show that the democracy-preserving impact of development is not unconditional but is predicated on the absence of major episodes of violence. If,

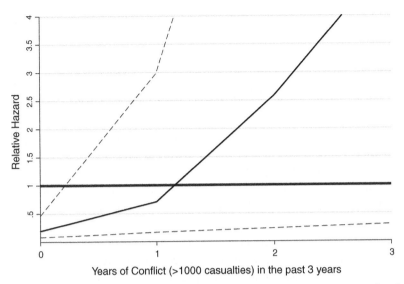

Figure 3.4 The marginal effect of GDP per capita on the relative risk of democratic backsliding to electoral authoritarianism, conditional on the levels of conflict
Note: Relative hazard estimated for a one-standard-deviation increase in log per capita income. The dashed lines indicate 95 percent confidence intervals.

as the previous results have confirmed, democracy is a "child of peace," so are the protective effects of high economic development.

The fourth and final indication that security crises are better predictors of democratic collapse into electoral authoritarianism than coercive and manipulative capacity lies in the fact that the two more specific measures of coercive power than economic (under)development – log military personnel per capita and log resource rents per capita – do not reach substantive or statistical significance in any of the models in the left panel of Table 3.1. This also includes the conditional frailty model (4), which accounts for individual idiosyncratic outcomes in individual countries, as well as the models in Table A.1.9 in the Online Appendix to this chapter, which use alternative indicators of repressive capacity and resource rents.

But how do these patterns compare to transitions from democracies to military dictatorships? If the crisis theory of electoral authoritarianism is correct, these regimes should rise in the wake of deep systemic crises at a much higher rate than other types of dictatorship, as summarized in hypothesis 2. In particular, a leap from democracy to a closed military dictatorship may be seen as too radical by many, especially in times of crisis. Why risk the tyranny of an unbridled dictatorship when an equally tough, yet more representative and restrained electoral authoritarian regime might be just as effective in addressing or preventing another crisis?

The analysis of democratic breakdowns leading to military dictatorship in Table 3.1 strongly confirms these expectations. Across all models in the right panel of the table, the estimated relationship between conflict and military takeovers is exactly the *opposite* of that for democratic breakdowns resulting in electoral autocracies. According to the results from Model (6) in the right panel of Table 3.1, a single year of high-intensity conflict in the previous three-year period is associated with a virtually 100 percent *reduction* in the odds of a military takeover in a democracy. In other words, while conflict strongly increases the odds of democratic backsliding to electoral authoritarianism, it all but precludes the rise of a military junta.[19] This is consistent with the raw aggregate patterns observed in Figure 3.1 in the previous section: on average, military regimes tend to be preceded by lower rates of conflict, which then escalate during their tenure. Electoral autocracies display the opposite pattern: they emerge in the wake of some of the most intense episodes of violence and experience less conflict during their reign – just as the crisis theory about the origins of these regimes would predict.

The alternative hypothesis 6, which suggests that democracies with greater coercive and clientelist resources will be at least as prone to military takeovers as to transition to electoral autocracy, is not supported by these estimates. The effects of low development, higher repressive capacity, and access to resource rents on the risk of democratic breakdowns into military dictatorship do not approach substantive or statistical significance at any level in Models (5)–(8). The same is true for a variety of alternative indicators for these factors, which I include as part of robustness tests in Part I of the Online Appendix.

The most reliable predictors of military takeovers in democracies, according to these estimates, are the percentage of democracies in a country's neighborhood and the conditions of the Cold War period.

---

[19] In turn, the broader conflict measure that includes low-intensity conflicts has a positive (i.e. above 1 in terms of hazard ratios) association with military takeovers in democracies, according to the estimates in Model (7), but this effect does not achieve substantive or statistical significance.

The results of model (6) in the left panel of Table 3.1 indicate the average post–Cold War increase in the share of neighboring democracies (from about 40 to 49 percent), is associated with a 22 percent decrease in the risk of a military takeover. The coefficient on the Cold War dummy, in turn, suggests that the risk of military takeover in democracies was almost eight times higher in the period before 1989, all else being equal.

Taken together, these results indicate that military takeovers in democracies have not been driven by escalating security and economic crises. Quite the contrary, high-intensity conflicts in democracies have all but precluded the rise of military juntas. What the estimates in Table 3.1 do suggest is that democratic breakdowns resulting in military dictatorships have been, to a large extent, products of the peculiarities of the Cold War era, and were later stymied by the diffusion of democracy and democratic norms in the post–Cold War period.

This raises an important question: did the post–Cold War era play a crucial role in the rise electoral authoritarianism, potentially overshadowing the role of crises? Indeed, the estimates from models (1), (2), and (4) in Table 3.1 indicate that the Cold War period had a significant negative association (i.e. below one in terms of hazard ratios) with democratic backsliding into electoral autocracy. Specifically, the estimates of Model (2) indicate that the Cold War period is associated with an almost 80 percent drop in the odds of transition from democracy to electoral authoritarianism, after the effects of all other variables are accounted for. Or, if we re-estimate the same model with a dummy variable marking the years after 1989, the period *after* the Cold War is associated with an *increase* in the risk of a transition from democracy to electoral autocracy by 373 percent, or by almost four times the baseline risk, when all else is held constant. In comparative terms, this is nearly 1.5 times the estimated effect of 1 year of high-intensity conflict in the preceding 3-year period.

This may be seen as an indication that democratic backsliding into electoral authoritarianism is an essentially post–Cold War phenomena, induced by the spread of democratic norms and pressures to democratize more than it is driven by conflicts and security crises. But this conclusion is wrong. Upon closer scrutiny, we find that although electoral autocracies did indeed proliferate after 1989, this effect of the Cold War era is closely intertwined with conflict. Namely, the rate of electoral authoritarian takeovers in democracies has increased in the post–Cold War period because much of the Third Wave of democratization has occurred in countries affected by conflict.[20] As this chapter's analysis primarily relies on a quite narrow indicator of high-intensity conflict, much of the effect of this instability in democracies established after 1989 is absorbed by the Cold War indicator. As a result, when we use alternative specifications with a more comprehensive measure of systemic violence, the estimated effects of the Cold War diminish and become insignificant.

We observe this behavior in Model (3) in the left panel of Table 3.1, which employs a broader conflict measure that also incorporates low-intensity conflicts at the twenty-five battle-deaths threshold. Here, the estimated effect of the Cold War is much smaller (i.e. closer to 1) and statistically insignificant at the conventional levels. We obtain the same results if we use an indicator of high-intensity conflict over a longer, ten-year period, or some of the alternative measures of violence and security threats (see the grayed-out estimates in Models (3)–(8) in Table A.1.5 in the Online Appendix to this chapter). In all these models, the substantive and statistical significance of the Cold War dummy greatly diminishes, while the estimated effects of conflicts and other security threats remain consistently strong. This indicates that democratic backsliding into electoral authoritarianism became much more common after 1989 not because this process is somehow an exclusively "post–Cold War phenomenon," but because many more conflict-prone countries joined the ranks of democracies in this period (on this dynamic, see also Levitsky and Way (2015)).

On the whole, the results in this section closely match the predictions of the crisis origins theory of electoral authoritarianism. Democratic backsliding to electoral authoritarianism is most strongly and consistently predicted by conflicts and security crises, a pattern we do not observe with the competing outcome – military takeovers. Furthermore, in line with hypothesis 4, security crises seem to moderate the effect of coercive and manipulative capacity on transitions from democracies to electoral autocracies. In particular, according to this section's estimates, economic development – the standard proxy for

---

[20] While the average number of democracies that had experienced low- or high-intensity conflict in the preceding decade was about ten during the 1960–1989 period, it almost doubled in the post–Cold War era, rising to about nineteen.

a society's vulnerability to clientelistic pressures – has a strong protective influence against democratic backsliding into electoral autocracy *only* in the absence of conflict.

Transitions from Military Dictatorships

Turning to transitions from military dictatorships, this section analyzes a dataset with 1,268 observations for 68 countries which have experienced military rule between 1960 and 2014. The majority of military-regime breakdowns (thirty-nine) in this data resulted with the rise of electoral autocracies, producing about 30 percent of all the electoral authoritarian regimes since 1960. In turn, sixteen military dictatorships transitioned into democracies, ten into single-party regimes, fifteen were followed by regimes designated as transitional, and four and two collapsed into a state of civil war or foreign occupation, respectively. I provide a more detailed description of this data in Part 2 of the Online Appendix to this chapter.

As for democratic breakdowns, I estimate conditional gap time and frailty Cox models of the two most substantively significant types of transitions from military dictatorships: to electoral autocracies and democracies.[21] These specifications differ from the models of democratic failure in two ways. First, all models omit the type-of-political-system variable, as it is substantively less relevant for the dynamics of military dictatorships. Also excluded are the indicators for membership in NATO, the EU, and the OECD, and some regional dummies,[22] as practically no military dictatorships have emerged in these regions or have been part of these organizations. Second, I estimate the effects of resource rents on regime stability using the indicator for the log total value of oil and gas production per capita, developed by Ross and Mahdavi (2015), because it provides much better data coverage of

---

[21] I exclude transitions from military dictatorships to one-party regimes from this analysis for a simple reason: in the Authoritarian Regimes Dataset, most communist/Marxist armed guerilla movements that later established single-party regimes (e.g. Cuba, Angola, Mozambique, Nicaragua, and Cambodia) were initially coded as military regimes. As this creates a largely artificial distinction between the armed guerilla and single-party stages of these regimes, the analysis of these transitions is not substantively warranted.

[22] In particular, I exclude the regional dummy for Oceania, and in some specifications, the Middle East and Europe.

military dictatorships than the World Bank resource rents indicator used in the previous section.

The results from these analyses, summarized in Table 3.2 below, also closely conform to the predictions of the crisis origins theory of electoral authoritarianism. Across all models in this table, *economic crises* emerge as the strongest predictors of transitions from military dictatorships to electoral authoritarianism. According to the estimates of Model (2), each additional percent of negative GDP growth over the previous three-year period increased the odds of military-regime transition into electoral authoritarianism by more than 11 percent. Or to put this in more concrete terms, the average GDP decline of 8.2 percent over a 3-year period for military dictatorships that existed in the 1960–2014 period is associated with an increase in the risk of transition to electoral authoritarianism of 138 percent, or of almost 1.4 times. This effect is stable across various specifications, including the conditional frailty model (4), as well as across the full range of robustness tests in Part 2 of the Online Appendix. Such economic crises among military regimes were also quite common: a full 78 percent of military dictatorships (seventy-seven out of ninety-nine regimes) in the dataset have experienced economic downturns of this scale or larger during their tenures.

Hence, if the findings of the previous section suggest that democratic backsliding toward electoral authoritarianism is best predicted by conflicts and security crises, these estimates suggest that transitions from military dictatorships to electoral autocracies are closely associated with economic woes. Crucially, they also suggest that security or economic crises do not push military regimes toward the competing outcome – full liberalization. On the contrary, they seem to prevent it. The results of the baseline model (5) in the right panel of Table 3.2 indicate that just a single year of conflict above the 1,000-battle-deaths threshold all but precludes a democratization of military regimes. Indeed, this effect is so strong that the full conditional gap time model (6) and the frailty model (8) have difficulties in extracting coefficient and standard error estimates for this variable. Consistent with the crisis-origins theory of electoral authoritarianism, economic and security troubles seem to promote the partial liberalization of military dictatorships to electoral autocracies but preclude their full democratization.

Table 3.2 *Repeated events history models of military-regime breakdowns, 1960–2014*

	Military dictatorship → Electoral autocracy				Military dictatorship → Democracy			
	Conditional gap time			Cond. frailty	Conditional gap time			cond. frailty
	(1)	(2)	(3)	(4)	(5)	(6)	(7)	(8)
Conflict with >1,000 casualties in the past 3 years	0.74 (0.15)	0.81 (0.19)		0.88 (0.19)	0.00 (0.00)**	0.00 (.)		
Conflict with >25 casualties in the past 3 years			1.02 (0.15)				0.61 (0.20)	0.66 (0.17)
Extent of GDP growth over 3 yrs	0.99 (0.02)	1.00 (0.03)	1.00 (0.03)	1 (0.03)	0.94 (0.03)+	0.96 (0.04)	0.95 (0.03)	0.95 (0.04)
Extent of GDP decline over 3 yrs	1.09 (0.04)*	1.11 (0.04)**	1.11 (0.04)**	1.11 (0.04)**	0.98 (0.07)	1.00 (0.07)	1.00 (0.07)	0.99 (0.08)
Log per capita income	1.73 (0.30)**	2.97 (0.86)**	3.07 (0.89)**	3.2 (0.81)**	2.21 (0.70)*	2.34 (0.91)*	2.25 (0.91)*	2.08 (0.64)
Log military size		0.68 (0.27)	0.64 (0.25)	0.55 (0.14)+		0.65 (0.20)	0.54 (0.21)	0.65 (0.21)
Log value of oil and gas production		0.95 (0.02)*	0.94 (0.03)*	0.94 (0.02)*		1.03 (0.03)	1.04 (0.03)	1.04 (0.03)
Democratic neighbors share	4.07 (3.13)+	6.06 (5.08)*	6.60 (5.62)*	4.89 (2.03)+	2.58 (2.17)	2.26 (1.85)	2.10 (1.78)	2.17 (0.95)

Table 3.2 (*cont.*)

	Military dictatorship → Electoral autocracy				Military dictatorship → Democracy			
	Conditional gap time			Cond. frailty	Conditional gap time			cond. frailty
	(1)	(2)	(3)	(4)	(5)	(6)	(7)	(8)
Years since independence	1.01 (0.00)*	1.01 (0.00)*	1.01 (0.00)*	1.01 (0)*	1.01 (0.00)	1.01 (0.00)	1.01 (0.00)	1.01 (0.01)
Cold War dummy	0.08 (0.04)**	0.08 (0.04)**	0.08 (0.04)**	0.07 (0.02)**	0.33 (0.45)	0.35 (0.50)	0.43 (0.69)	0.4 (0.18)
Region dummies	YES†	YES†	YES†	YES††	YES†	YES†	YES†	YES†††
Variance of the random effect (θ)				0				0
N	1251	1220	1220	1219	1251	1220	1220	1219
Number of failures	39	35	35	35	16	16	16	16
Likelihood ratio for θ				0				0
l-likelihood				-70.5				-42.86
Log-likelihood for model	-85.7817	-68.6759	-68.9476	-70.5	-42.5912	-41.6309	-42.4306	-42.86

Estimates represent hazard ratios. Robust standard errors provided in parentheses.

† To ensure convergence, the model omits the regional dummy for Oceania.

†† To ensure convergence, model omits the regional dummies for the Middle East and Oceania.

††† To ensure convergence, model omits the regional dummies for Europe, the Middle East, and Oceania.

* $p < 0.10$, * $p < 0.05$, ** $p < 0.01$

The estimates in Table 3.2 indicate that resources for patronage and repression – factors emphasized in existing accounts of authoritarian durability – have a weaker and less consistent relation to the tendencies of military dictatorships to transition to electoral authoritarianism. In particular, poverty and access to resource rents do not seem to encourage military dictators to liberalize their regimes into electoral autocracies. Indeed, the opposite seems to be true. For one, richer countries governed by military juntas appear to be considerably more, not less, likely to transition to electoral authoritarianism. Based on Model (2), GDP per capita of one standard deviation higher (or about 3,165 2005 US international dollars) is associated with a 183 percent increase in the odds that a military dictatorship will transition to an electoral autocracy.

One might be tempted to interpret this as evidence that greater poverty enables greater authoritarianism, as the shift to a closed, military dictatorship to an electoral one in richer societies still represents a considerable liberalization. But then, we should observe an even greater effect of economic development on the odds of full democratization. This is not the case, according to the estimates in Table 3.2. Based on Model (6), a one-standard-deviation rise in log GDP per capita would increase the risk of democratization of military dictatorships by 125 percent – an effect that is only about two-thirds the size of the impact of the same GDP leap on the risk of transition to electoral authoritarianism in Model (2). This discrepancy holds across all but the baseline models (1) and (5) in Table 3.2, which exclude many of the key variables. Developmental leaps make transitions from military dictatorship to electoral authoritarianism more likely than the democratization of these regimes.[23]

Even if we ignore this discrepancy and assume that log GDP per capita has the same impact on the risks of transition to electoral authoritarianism and democracy, the fundamental problem remains: economic development does not help explain why military

---

[23] The conditional frailty estimates, which account for unobserved heterogeneity in the risks for these types of regime transitions across countries, suggest an even larger gap in the impact of economic development. While the association of log GDP per capita and the risk of transition to electoral autocracy becomes stronger in the conditional frailty model (4), its link to the democratization of military regimes weakens and becomes statistically insignificant in the conditional frailty model (8).

dictatorships transition to electoral autocracies instead of democracies – the key interest of this book. If we reverse the effect of this variable, by *decreasing* their levels of development, military dictatorships reduce the chances of transitioning to *either* electoral authoritarianism or democracy to a comparable degree. The same is true for state repressive capacity, proxied by military personnel per capita. The effect of this variable does not reach statistical significance in most models in the table. But even if we ignore this, we observe that it has a very similar negative (i.e. lower than one in hazard ratios) impact on *both* the risks of democratization and transition to electoral authoritarianism. It therefore cannot explain why transitions from military dictatorships follow along these divergent paths.

In stark contrast, the two crisis indicators – recession and conflict – do a far better job in differentiating between these outcomes. Even moderate recessions, according to this analysis, would raise the prospects of a transition to electoral authoritarianism more than a full standard deviation increase in GDP per capita. And just a single year of conflict in the immediate past would all but preclude the competing outcome of democratization of military dictatorships. Economic development, in contrast, has a similar effect on both the risk of democratization of military regimes and their transitions to electoral authoritarianism. It therefore cannot serve as a useful explanatory factor for these divergent outcomes.

Among the coercive resources, only rents from oil and gas resources, which provide access to direct, nontaxable income that military dictatorships can use as patronage, or to sustain a robust repressive and propaganda apparatus, are associated with diminished chances of transition to electoral authoritarianism. In particular, the results of Model (2) suggest that an increase from zero to the mean level of oil and gas production is associated with a 43 percent *decrease* in the risk of transition to electoral authoritarianism. To illustrate this effect, a hypothetical military dictatorship that has a 50 percent chance of transitioning to electoral autocracy and no access to resource rents would see this probability reduced to about 36 percent if it gained access to an average level of resource rents. In comparison, a shift from positive economic growth to an average recession (an 8.2 percent drop in GDP in the preceding three-year period), would raise the probability of transition to electoral authoritarianism from 50 to about 70 percent (or by 20 percentage points). This suggests that oil and gas rents have a somewhat smaller, but still roughly equivalent impact on transitions from military dictatorships to electoral autocracies as economic crises.

We might assume, based on this comparison, that military dictatorships with large resource endowments may be less prone to liberalize, as they have the means to keep their societies under control through patronage. But this interpretation is somewhat contradicted by the estimated relation between resource rents and the democratization of military dictatorships. According to the estimates in the right panel of Table 3.2, the relationship between resource rents and democratization is positive, and consistently nonsignificant – a counterintuitive result that goes against most current theories of this factor's effect on authoritarian survival. Why would access to resource rents have no impact on the propensity of military regimes to fully democratize, while deterring them from controlled liberalization to electoral authoritarianism?

To investigate this behavior, I perform a range of specification tests, and it turns out that consistent with hypothesis 4, the effect of resource rents is conditioned by one of the crisis variables – the presence of economic downturns. I show this by estimating the models of military-regime transitions to electoral autocracies and democracies with an interaction term between the log value of oil and gas production and GDP change over a three-year period.[24] I provide the full details of these estimates in Table A.2.11 of the Online Appendix and depict the main interaction effects in Figure 3.5 below. These graphs indicate that oil and gas resources have a significant impact only during economic crises. Specifically, as economic downturns intensify, higher oil and gas income significantly *reduces* the risk of a controlled liberalization to electoral authoritarianism and *boosts* the odds of democratization of military dictatorships. According to the results in Figure 3.5, a one standard deviation higher oil and gas revenue in a military dictatorship that is experiencing an average, 8.2 percent economic contraction over a three-year period, is associated with about a 17 percent decrease in the risk of transition to electoral authoritarianism, and a 37 percent increase in the relative hazard of democratization.

---

[24] I use this variable instead of the separate indicators for GDP decline and growth in the models in Table 3.2 to be able to see the behavior of the log value of oil and gas production across the full range of economic performance.

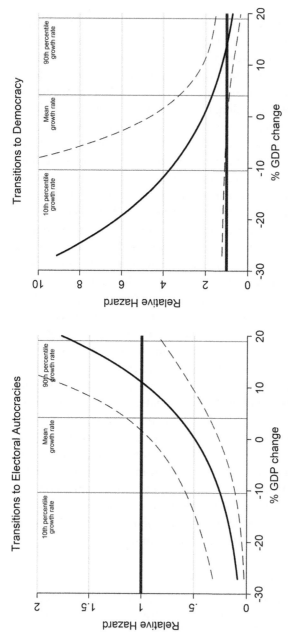

Figure 3.5 The marginal effect of oil and gas production on the relative risk of military-regime transitions, conditional on GDP growth

Note: Relative hazard estimated for a one standard deviation increase in log per capita income. The dashed lines indicate 95 percent confidence intervals.

One way to interpret this result is that oil and gas wealth in military juntas facing economic malaise helps prevent controlled liberalization leading to electoral authoritarianism, but promotes the uncontrolled breakdown and democratization of these regimes – a paradoxical finding that does not appear to align with any existing theory of clientelism and resource-fueled authoritarianism. The reasons behind this behavior are certainly intriguing and warrant further scrutiny. But from the standpoint of the present study, the estimated impact of resource rents provides less clear guidance about the emergence of electoral autocracies than the crisis origins theory. Not only does the effect of oil and gas income on the stability of military dictatorships appear inconsistent with the alternative theories of authoritarian emergence and stability, but this effect is only significant during an economic crisis.

Apart from crises, and coercive and clientelistic resources, the last set of factors that seems to be strongly associated with transitions from military dictatorships to electoral authoritarianism is (geo)political. Based on the estimates in Model (2), a one standard deviation (or 23 percent) increase in the share of a military regime's neighbors that are democracies is associated with a 26 percent increase in the odds that it will transition to electoral authoritarianism, when the other variables are held constant. In turn, the coefficient on the Cold War dummy suggests that *ceteris paribus*, the odds of transition from military dictatorships to electoral autocracies were lower by 92 percent before 1989, compared to the period after.

But the crucial thing to note here is that a rising share of democratic neighbors and the Cold War period are *not* associated with the democratization of military dictatorships – only with their transitions to electoral authoritarianism. We can see this from the consistently nonsignificant impact of these variables on transitions from military regimes to democracies across all model specifications in the right panel of Table 3.2.

This pattern also does not seem to conform with the existing theories about how democratic diffusion and leverage has shaped the liberalization of closed autocracies. Instead, it is consistent with the thesis that electoral autocracies are intended to preserve authoritarianism, while also imposing some constraints on executive power and a degree of liberalization. Regional waves of democratization and post–Cold War democratization pressures, in this sense, may have primarily affected military dictatorships by triggering crises of legitimacy that pushed authoritarian forces to preemptively adopt nominally democratic institutions, which they can still subvert in practice (on this, see e.g. Miller 2017).[25] From this perspective, the findings above support the crisis-origins hypothesis of electoral authoritarianism at least as much as any alternative theory about the effects of democratic diffusion on closed autocracies.

But if transitions to electoral autocracy are calculated attempts to avoid genuine democratization, what prevents these liberalizations from failing in their original purpose and inadvertently sliding toward democracy? In other words, how do military dictators avoid the "liberalizers' curse" (Przeworski 1991, 58) of unintentionally allowing the floodgates of democratization to burst open as they attempt to create a "managed democracy?" The answer, according to the results of this analysis, again points to crises – this time, the presence of security and economic upheavals. The estimates in the right panel of Table 3.2 show that practically no democratizations of military dictatorships have occurred in the wake of conflicts. Yet, conflicts have not precluded such regimes from pursuing "managed liberalization" by transitioning to electoral authoritarianism. Similarly, economic slumps and pressures for democratization have pushed military dictatorships to transition into electoral autocracies, but not to espouse genuine democratization. As predicted by this book's theory, security and economic crises may have allowed electoral autocracy to be compellingly legitimized as the best, "middle-of-the-road" solution for its country's woes – providing some liberalization as a remedy for the failings and rigidity of military dictatorship, but avoiding the potentially destabilizing effects of full democratization.

As in the previous section, I have examined the results of these analysis with an exhaustive set of robustness checks. All of these auxiliary analyses, some of which are presented in Part 2 of the Online Appendix to this chapter, yield results that closely match the ones presented here.

---

[25] This line of reasoning would also correspond with Schedler's (2010) thesis that electoral autocracy emerged as "authoritarianism's last line of defense" after democratic institutions became the norm following the Cold War.

Transitions from Single-Party Dictatorships

The collapse of single-party regimes has been the last major contributor to the rise of electoral authoritarianism. Out of the total of sixty-four transitions from single-party dictatorships, one half (thirty-two regimes) resulted in the rise of electoral autocracies, producing about one fifth of all electoral authoritarian regimes that have come into existence since the 1960s. Another 40 percent of the transitions from single-party regimes produced an equal share of democracies and military dictatorships (thirteen regimes each). The dataset I use to analyze the factors associated with these transitions and their competing outcomes contains 1,848 observations for 68 countries that have experienced single-party rule between 1960 and 2014. I provide a more detailed description of this data in Part 3 of the Online Appendix for this chapter.

Analyzing transitions from single-party dictatorships presents several special challenges because of the unique pattern of rise and fall of these regimes. For one, almost two thirds of all single-party regime breakdowns have occurred in a very narrow three-year period (1990–1992), creating many "ties" in the regime duration data, whereby multiple transitions have occurred in the same year.[26] This extreme clustering of single-party regime breakdowns makes some of the Cox model estimates more variable. It also induces very high collinearity between some variables (e.g. the Cold War indicator) and the outcome, necessitating their removal from some specifications.

More importantly, 34 percent of all transitions from single-party regimes (or twenty-two transitions) were products not only of regime collapse but also of state collapse, as they have taken place in the successor states of the former Soviet Union, Yugoslavia, and Czechoslovakia. As these successor states shared many common features, studying the divergent outcomes of their transitions provides a unique opportunity to isolate the driving factors behind them. But at the same time, including these cases in the analyses requires several adjustments to accommodate for the unique structure of the data and to check for biases. Specifically, while I analyze each of the Soviet, Yugoslav, and Czechoslovak republics as separate cases of single-party failure, all models include dummy variables that capture the effects of their membership in these federations. All analyses also include a separate dummy variable denoting the non-core

---

[26] Specifically, there were thirteen single-party regime collapses in 1990, eighteen in 1991, and nine in 1992.

republics in these federative states in order to account for their specific administrative positions.[27] Finally, all analyses include a dummy variable indicator for communist single-party dictatorships,[28] which captures the unique traits of the communist regime legitimation and its crisis.

The subnational nature of the data for the Soviet, Yugoslav, and Czechoslovak republics presents another set of challenges. First, the GDP per capita data for these cases are, in large part, based on estimates that tend to be less precise (see James et al. 2012). As this could misplace the cutoff point between economic growth and decline, using the separate indicators of economic growth and recession, as in the previous sections, is not appropriate in this analysis. In their place, I use a simple indicator of overall *GDP change* over the preceding three-year period. Second, some key variables are missing data for the Soviet, Yugoslav, and Czechoslovak republics. For the conflict variables, I address this issue by using conflict location data from the PRIO dataset to localize episodes of violence prior to 1991 in the specific republic they took place in. To measure the impact of resource rents on regime survival, I use the alternative total value of oil and gas indicator, as it has fewer missing values for the successor states. Finally, as data on repressive capacity are completely absent for the Soviet, Yugoslav, and Czechoslovak republics, I copy the values of the military personnel per capita indicator from the respective federal state to each of its constituents. This assumes that the repressive apparatuses of these states were all-pervasive and fairly equally distributed across their territory – an idea that has support in the literature (see e.g. Beissinger 2002, ch. 7 and Greitens 2016, ch. 1). While this coding may be less precise, the analysis has several safeguards against any potential biases that might be introduced by it.[29]

---

[27] This dummy variable equals one for the USSR, Yugoslav, and Czechoslovak republics apart from Russia, Serbia, and the Czech Republic, respectively.

[28] Roughly half of all single-party regimes in this dataset (or thirty-five out of seventy-two regimes) were classified as communist under this strict categorization, borrowed from Cheibub, Gandhi, and Vreeland (2010). However, many of the single-party regimes that were not tagged as communist by this indicator, such as those in Cambodia, Angola, Benin, Mozambique, and many other countries, also professed communist/Marxist ideologies and had close relations with the Soviet Union and China.

[29] First, the baseline models for all transition types exclude the military personnel indicator coded in this fashion, eliminating its potential confounding influence on other variables. Second, as the conditional frailty models estimate the unmeasured heterogeneity across cases, they may capture any significant differences in repressive capacity not accounted for with this coding.

Using these adjustments, I estimate Cox survival models of transitions from single-party regimes to: (1) electoral autocracies; (2) military dictatorships; and (3) democracies. The results of this analysis, which are presented in Table 3.3 below, reveal a pattern very similar to the one for transitions from military dictatorships in the previous section. Most importantly, positive GDP change appears to significantly lower the risk of transition from single-party regimes to both authoritarian alternatives – electoral autocracies and military dictatorships – while it does not affect the chances of democratization. Specifically, based on Model (2), a one standard deviation increase in the rate of GDP growth over a three-year period in this dataset (or 10.3 percent growth) is associated with a 55 percent *decrease* in the risk of transition to electoral authoritarianism. This same growth rate would diminish the odds of a military takeover in a single-party regime by almost 69 percent, according to the results in Model (6), when all other variables are held constant.

To contextualize, this 10-percentage-point difference in the GDP growth rate is approximately equal to the gap between the low growth rates of the Soviet Union just before its collapse in 1991, and the period of its greatest economic expansion in the mid-to-late 1960s.[30] This sort of economic stagnation over time was precisely the sort of crisis that fatally undermined the legitimacy of single-party regimes in the late 1980s. As the historical evidence suggests, the consequences of economic failure were particularly acute for the Marxist/communist single-party dictatorships that justified their reign as a more just and prosperous alternative to Western-style capitalism and democracy. Kotkin (2008, 19) succinctly summarized the predicament: "[i]f socialism was not superior to capitalism, its existence could not be justified." Hence, even though many of these single-party regimes were technically not in recession, they were experiencing full-blown crises of legitimacy because of their inferior economic performance. Against this backdrop, the close association between meager economic growth rates in single-party regimes and their increased risk of transition to electoral

---

[30] The three-year growth rate of the Soviet Union in 1990 was 3.6 percent. In turn, its average three-year growth rate for 1965–1970 was about 13 percent, and it was considered to be catching up with the West economically (Saxonberg 2013).

authoritarianism can be seen as evidence in favor of this book's theory of the crisis origins of electoral authoritarianism.

But perhaps the most relevant metric for our analysis is the difference in growth rates between communist regimes at the end of the Cold War. Here, the gap between the growth rates of communist China – the most notable economic high performer and survivor of the "great extinction" of single-party regimes in the late 1980s – and the Soviet Union was much greater. In 1990, the Chinese three-year economic growth rate was about 20 percent, compared to the Soviet rate of 3.6 percent. Based on the estimates from Model (3) in Table 3.3, this 16 percentage-points gap in economic growth is associated with a 73 percent reduction in the risk that communist China would transition to electoral authoritarianism, relative to the Soviet Union. These results suggest that the economic vitality of the Chinese regime at the end of the Cold War may have played a major role in its survival. The deep economic malaise of the Soviet regime, on the other hand, did not contribute to its democratization, but catalyzed the rise of electoral authoritarianism in 10 of its 15 Soviet successor states, including Russia.

This highlights a key pattern: just as with military dictatorships, economic crises consistently predict transitions from single-party regimes to electoral autocracies but are not meaningfully associated with democratization. Conflicts, in turn, are strongly and negatively connected to the latter outcome: they virtually preclude the democratization of single-party dictatorships. According to Models (7)–(9) in the right panel of Table 3.3, even a single year of conflict at the lower, twenty-five-battle-deaths threshold is associated with a 100 percent reduction in the odds of democratization of single-party regimes – an effect that is highly robust to the use of alternative measures and specifications that I present in the Online Appendix.

Transitions from single-party regimes to military dictatorships, on the other hand, have a less straightforward relationship with security or economic crises. While lackluster economic performance appears to promote military takeovers in single-party regimes, high-intensity conflicts appear to discourage it, according to the estimates in the middle panel of Table 3.3. The latter effect is highly statistically significant in Model (6) and hovers around a 10-percent significance level in most other specifications in this table and the Online Appendix. But on the whole, the estimates from these alternative specifications suggest that a single year of conflict in the preceding three-year period is consistently

Table 3.3 *Repeated events history models of single-party-regime breakdowns, 1960–2014*

	Single party → Electoral autocracy				Single party → Military dictatorship				Single party → Democracy			
	Conditional gap time			Cond. frailty	Conditional gap time			Cond. frailty	Conditional gap time			Cond. frailty
	(1)	(2)	(3)	(4)	(5)	(6)	(7)	(8)	(9)	(10)	(11)	(12)
Conflict with >1,000 casualties in the past 3 years	0.78 (0.23)	1.37 (0.74)		2.06 (0.76)	0.37 (0.24)	0.13 (0.09)**		0.67 (0.22)	0.00 (0.00)**	0.00 (0.00)**		
Conflict with >25 casualties in the past 3 years			0.84 (0.26)				0.73 (0.54)				0.00 (0.00)**	
% GDP change over 3-yrs (IHME)	0.94 (0.02)**	0.93 (0.02)**	0.93 (0.02)**	0.92 (0.02)**	0.94 (0.03)*	0.89 (0.04)**	0.93 (0.03)*	0.91 (0.04)*	0.98 (0.03)	1.00 (0.05)	1.00 (0.05)	1.01 (0.04)
Log per capita income	1.26 (0.35)	2.14 (0.89)+	1.83 (0.71)	3 (0.99)*	0.24 (0.21)	0.08 (0.09)*	0.36 (0.41)	0.49 (0.19)	1.44 (0.86)	2.81 (2.40)	2.08 (1.61)	3.99 (1.77)
Log military size		0.88 (0.33)	1.01 (0.36)	0.62 (0.18)		7.16 (4.24)**	3.61 (1.85)*	3.6 (1.28)*		0.47 (0.80)	0.59 (1.23)	0.88 (0.42)
Log value of oil and gas production		0.95 (0.05)	0.96 (0.04)	0.92 (0.04)+		1.05 (0.09)	0.99 (0.11)	0.86 (0.08)		0.82 (0.05)**	0.85 (0.05)*	0.84 (0.07)+
Democratic neighbors share	0.13 (0.19)	0.01 (0.03)*	0.01 (0.03)*	0.06 (0.03)+	0.00 (.)	0.00 (.)	0.00 (.)	2.62 (1.33)	121.86 (256.95)*	1398.69 (5263.17)+	897.07 (3460.12)+	47.89 (24.34)

Table 3.3 (*cont.*)

	Single party → Electoral autocracy				Single party → Military dictatorship				Single party → Democracy			
	Conditional gap time			Cond. frailty	Conditional gap time			Cond. frailty	Conditional gap time			Cond. frailty
	(1)	(2)	(3)	(4)	(5)	(6)	(7)	(8)	(9)	(10)	(11)	(12)
Cold War dummy	0.09 (0.06)**	0.12 (0.09)**	0.11 (0.08)**		0.55 (0.36)	0.52 (0.47)	0.85 (1.02)					
Communist dictatorship	0.00 (.)	0.00 (.)	0.00 (.)		0.00 (0.00)**	0.00 (0.00)**	0.00 (.)		0.00 (0.00)**	0.00 (0.00)**	0.00 (0.00)**	
Nonprincipal successor state	0.32 (0.25)	0.15 (0.16)+	0.12 (0.16)		0.00 (0.00)**	0.00 (.)	0.00 (.)		6.29 (4.63)*	5.06 (2.68)**	3.31 (1.42)**	
Region dummies	YES†	YES†	YES†	YES	YES†	YES†	YES†	YES	YES†	YES†	YES†	YES
Variance of the random effect (θ)				0				0				0.9
N	1732	1227	1227	1242	1732	1227	1227	1242	1732	1227	1227	1242
Number of failures	32	26	26	26	13	13	13	13	13	8	8	8
Likelihood ratio for θ				0				0				0
l-likelihood				-58.52				-34.23				-19.73
Log-likelihood	-60.3096	-40.8496	-40.8382	-58.52	-29.2818	-24.2996	-27.3711	-34.23	-26.2744	-10.5676	-10.221	-14.62

Exponentiated coefficients; Standard errors in parentheses.
† To ensure convergence, the model omits the regional dummy for Oceania, but includes separate region dummies for Europe (without Yugoslavia and Czechoslovakia), former Yugoslavia, and former Czechoslovakia.
+ p < 0.10, * p < 0.05, ** p < 0.01

associated with a 63–87 percent decrease in the odds of a military takeover in single-party regimes. This once again supports this book's theory that only transitions to electoral authoritarian regimes are always strongly and positively associated with economic and security crises. The effect of these upheavals on democratic transitions, as this section's estimates confirm, are always negative, while different kinds of crises have contradictory influences on military takeovers.

Unlike the crisis variables, predictors representing clientelist, repressive, and manipulative resources appear to play a less consistent role in promoting transitions to electoral authoritarianism and preventing the competing regime outcomes, according to the estimates in Table 3.3. In particular, while the level of economic development, captured by log GDP per capita, has a negative association with military takeovers in single-party regimes, and a positive one with their democratizations and transitions to electoral authoritarianism, these effects do not reach statistical significance at conventional levels across most of these models. On the other hand, resource rents, represented by the log value of oil and gas production, have a significant negative effect only on democratization, but do not appear to have a consistent influence on transitions to electoral autocracies and military regimes. Finally, state repressive capacity, proxied by military personnel per capita, has a strong positive effect on military takeovers, but does not seem to reliably predict the democratization of single-party regimes, or their transitions to electoral authoritarianism.

The only predictor associated with an alternative theory of democratization and electoral authoritarianism that has a strong and consistent association with the outcomes of interest in Table 3.3 is the share of a country's neighbors that are democracies. To see the scope of this effect, consider a hypothetical scenario of a single-party regime that has an equal, 50 percent probability of transitioning to either electoral authoritarianism or democracy, and experiences a one standard deviation increase in the share of its neighbors that are democratic. This is equivalent to a surge of 16 percent in a country's neighbors that are democracies, or roughly the difference between Slovenia – the westernmost republic of former Yugoslavia, half of whose neighbors were democratic in 1989 – and the former Soviet Republic of Armenia, a quarter of whose neighbors were democracies in 1989. If such a geopolitical shift occurred, the probability that this single-party regime will transition to electoral authoritarianism would decline from 50 to 33 percent, while its probability of democratization would shoot up from 50 to 77 percent, according to the estimates for Models (2) and (10), respectively.

However, this democratizing influence would be completely offset by comparable shifts in the crisis variables. Thus, a one standard deviation–sized drop in this regime's GDP (or a 10.3 percent economic downturn over the preceding three-year period), would reverse the probability of transition to electoral authoritarianism back to 52 percent, or two percentage points above the starting point. Even more compellingly, just a single year of conflict at the low, twenty-five-battle-deaths threshold would decisively quash this regime's odds of democratization – shrinking its probability of democratization from 77 percent to zero, despite the increased exposure to democratic influences in the neighborhood. Hence, once again, crises seem to condition the effects of other factors related to transitions to electoral authoritarianism or their competing outcomes. In this case, democratic diffusion seems to prevent transitions from single-party regimes to electoral autocracies and to promote their democratization only in the absence of economic downturns and conflicts.

On the whole, this section's findings conform to the distinct pattern we observed earlier: even though poverty, clientelistic and coercive resources, and democratization pressures have had a significant influence on transitions to electoral authoritarian regimes, their effects have generally been overshadowed, and often moderated, by the presence of economic and security crises. As in the previous two sections, these results showcase economic and security upheavals as the most reliable predictors of transitions to electoral authoritarianism. While economic decline is the variable most closely associated with transitions from single-party dictatorships to electoral autocracies, conflicts most strongly and consistently thwart its competing outcomes – military takeovers and the democratization of these regimes. As before, these conclusions hold across the models in Table 3.3 and the extensive battery of robustness tests presented in Part 3 of the Online Appendix to this chapter.

Transitions from Electoral Autocracies

A core premise of this book's analytic framework, summarized in this chapter's hypothesis 3, is that experiences of political, economic, and security crises under previous regimes not only make electoral authoritarian rule more likely, but also make the resulting electoral autocracies more robust and durable. In particular, deep traumas from unmanageable upheavals make societies and elites reluctant to embrace other regime alternatives – both full democracy and closed dictatorship – for fear that these political orders might lead to renewed turmoil and cataclysms. Such outlooks are likely to become particularly entrenched if electoral autocracies score notable successes in restoring order, stability, and prosperity during their reign.

To examine this proposition, I estimate conditional gap time and frailty Cox models of transitions *from* electoral autocracies to other regime types. The data I use for this purpose has 1,768 country-year observations for 108 distinct countries that have experienced electoral authoritarianism in the period 1960–2014. Of the 109 transitions from electoral autocracies in this period, the great majority (73) resulted in democratization, and 22 electoral autocracies transitioned to military dictatorships. I provide a more detailed description of this data in Part 4 of the Online Appendix for this chapter.

The model specifications I use for this analysis differ in two regards from the models of democratic failure. First, I omit the membership of EU, NATO, and OECD and the type-of-political-system variables, as they are less relevant for the dynamics of electoral autocracies.[31] Second, to test hypothesis 3, I employ three measures of the degree to which electoral autocracies were preceded by crises, and the success of these regimes in restoring stability. The first two are indicators of the degree of conflict and economic decline in the last three years of the regimes *preceding* electoral authoritarianism. The third variable captures the extent to which electoral autocracies managed to bring about improvements, measured with an indicator of the GDP change since the

---

[31] First, very few electoral autocracies have been members of these organizations, so adding indicators for membership of them causes estimation problems in the analyses. Second, regarding the political system variable, previous studies have shown that electoral autocracies have strategically embraced institutional ambiguity, such as frequent constitutional changes and high executive turnover, to keep their opponents off balance (Magaloni 2006; Schedler 2013). This sort of manipulation makes the differences between presidential and parliamentary systems in electoral autocracies relatively moot. To check whether the omission of these institutional variables bias the analysis, I also estimate models that include them as controls (results available on demand); the results are virtually the same as those presented in Table 3.4 below.

first year of their reign. As before, the use of these temporally and substantively restrictive indicators of upheaval and economic improvements sets a relatively high threshold for producing estimates that will support this book's theory of the crisis roots of electoral authoritarianism.

Despite this stringent standard of evidence, the results of this section's analyses, presented in Table 3.4 below, closely align with the crisis-origins theory. In particular, the ability of electoral autocracies to improve economic conditions during their tenure, and in some specifications, recessions occurring within the three years preceding the rise of electoral authoritarianism, are strongly and negatively associated with chances of democratization of these regimes. According to the estimates in the left panel of Table 3.4, the cumulative economic growth under electoral authoritarianism is highly significant across all model specifications and consistently diminishes these regimes' vulnerability to democratization. Substantively, the estimates in Model (2) suggest that each additional percent increase in GDP during the tenure of electoral autocracies is associated with a 1.2 percent *decrease* in the chances of liberalization.

To put this in perspective, an electoral autocracy that increases a country's GDP by 50 percent – the mean growth rate of all electoral authoritarian regimes during the period 1960–2014 – is estimated to cut its baseline odds of transitioning to democracy by 45 percent, when all else is equal. In turn, electoral autocracies that increased their country's GDP by one standard deviation of this variable's distribution in the dataset (or by 164 percent) saw their risk of democratization diminished by a whopping 87 percent. Exploring the data shows that some of the most robust and durable electoral autocracies, such as Mexico and Singapore, have achieved growth rates on this scale. Crucially, only the cumulative economic growth across the entire reign of electoral authoritarian regimes has this "democracy-prevention" effect; the short-term, three-year-growth, and recession indicators are nonsignificant across all model specifications in Table 3.4. This is another indication that electoral autocracies may be primarily endorsed for their ability to overcome the deep crises they have inherited, and not for their more recent economic performance.

The link between economic crises that immediately precede the rise of electoral autocracies and the resilience of these regimes is more directly confirmed by the behavior of another variable: the percentage

Table 3.4 *Repeated events history models of electoral authoritarian regime breakdowns, 1960–2014*

	Electoral autocracy → Democracy				Electoral autocracy → Military dictatorship			
	Conditional gap time			Cond. frailty	Conditional gap time			Cond. frailty
	(1)	(2)	(3)	(4)	(5)	(6)	(7)	(8)
Conflict in the last 3 years of the prior regime (>25 battle deaths)	0.99 (0.13)	0.95 (0.14)	1.03 (0.17)	0.96 (0.13)	0.81 (0.19)	0.62 (0.15)[+]	0.56 (0.14)[*]	0.62 (0.16)
% GDP decline in the last 3 years of the prior regime	0.97 (0.02)	0.97 (0.02)	0.97 (0.02)[+]	0.97 (0.02)	1.01 (0.03)	1.02 (0.05)	1.03 (0.05)	1.03 (0.05)
Total % change in GDP under current regime	0.99 (0.00)[**]	0.99 (0.00)[**]	0.99 (0.00)[**]	0.99 (0.01)[*]	0.97 (0.01)[*]	0.98 (0.02)	0.97 (0.02)	0.97 (0.02)
Conflict with >1,000 casualties in the past 3 years	1.13 (0.21)	1.14 (0.22)		1.14 (0.21)	1.33 (0.39)	1.67 (0.53)		1.59 (0.44)

Table 3.4 (*cont.*)

	Electoral autocracy → Democracy				Electoral autocracy → Military dictatorship			
	Conditional gap time			Cond. frailty	Conditional gap time			Cond. frailty
	(1)	(2)	(3)	(4)	(5)	(6)	(7)	(8)
Conflict with >25 casualties in the past 3 years			0.93 (0.14)				1.52 (0.40)	
Extent of GDP growth over 3 yrs	0.98 (0.01)+	0.97 (0.02)	0.97 (0.02)	0.97 (0.02)	1.00 (0.02)	1.01 (0.05)	1.01 (0.04)	1.02 (0.05)
Extent of GDP decline over 3 yrs	0.99 (0.02)	0.99 (0.02)	1.00 (0.02)	0.99 (0.02)	1.00 (0.05)	0.99 (0.05)	0.99 (0.05)	1 (0.04)
Log per capita income	1.28 (0.26)	1.04 (0.22)	1.07 (0.23)	1.04 (0.2)	0.54 (0.17)+	0.47 (0.15)*	0.45 (0.15)*	0.44 (0.14)
Log military size		0.90 (0.20)	0.94 (0.22)	0.9 (0.17)		2.22 (0.76)*	2.09 (0.79)+	2.04 (0.64)
Log resource rents		0.70 (0.13)+	0.69 (0.13)*	0.71 (0.11)+		1.12 (0.37)	1.10 (0.39)	1.09 (0.28)
Democratic neighbors share	1.08 (0.50)	1.30 (0.76)	1.33 (0.76)	1.25 (0.42)	0.80 (0.85)	0.55 (0.90)	0.56 (0.97)	0.5 (0.24)
Years since independence	1.00 (0.00)	1.00 (0.00)	1.00 (0.00)	1 (0)	1.01 (0.00)	1.01 (0.00)*	1.01 (0.00)+	1.01 (0.00)*

Cold War dummy	0.68 (0.25)	0.86 (0.34)	0.90 (0.36)	0.86 (0.24)	2.02 (0.96)	2.69 (1.47)$^+$	2.87 (1.49)*	2.81 (1.09)
Region dummies	YES	YES	YES	YES	YES	YES	YES	YES
Variance of the random effect (θ)				0				0.82
N	1741	1371	1371	1371	1741	1371	1371	1371
Number of failures	73	57	57	57	22	18	18	18
Likelihood ratio for θ				0				0
l-likelihood				−158.36				−47.14
Log-likelihood for model	−224.391	−158.356	−158.421	−158.36	−70.6361	−47.3397	−46.9556	−37.61

Estimates represent hazard ratios. Robust standard errors provided in parentheses.

$^+$ $p < 0.10$, * $p < 0.05$, ** $p < 0.01$

GDP decline in the last three years of the prior regime. This effect falls just below the 10 percent statistical significance level across most models in the left panels of Table 3.4 and in Part 4 of the Online Appendix to this chapter. However, size and significance of this variable are robust to this very broad range of alternative specifications. As such, the estimates for this variable have a consistent and substantively important conclusion: electoral autocracies that were preceded by economic crises have been less likely to democratize.

Specifically, the results in Model (3) suggest that each additional percentage drop in GDP in the last three years of the previous regime decreases the chances of democratization in the electoral autocracy that follows by 3 percent. To put it in more tangible terms, an electoral autocracy that takes over from a regime that experienced about an 11 percent drop in GDP in its last three years (the average GDP decline before the rise of electoral authoritarianism in the dataset) faces a 28 percent lower risk of democratization when compared to an electoral autocracy that was preceded by zero growth over the same period. Importantly, model diagnostics suggest that this effect is *not* time-dependent – the protective, democratization-proofing influence of economic crises before the rise of electoral authoritarianism does not seem to fade as these regimes age. Seen through the lens of the crisis theory of electoral authoritarianism, the trauma from the economic turmoil that preceded these regimes – and the resultant reluctance to democratize – are quite persistent.[32]

According to the estimates in Table 3.4, crises preceding the rise of electoral authoritarianism – this time in the form of conflict – also play a protective role against military takeovers in these regimes. Specifically, the results in Model (6) indicate that one year of conflict at the lower, twenty-five-battle-deaths threshold in the three-year period immediately before the rise of electoral authoritarian regimes is associated with a 38 percent *decrease* in the risk of transition to a military dictatorship. In turn, a three-year high-intensity conflict in the period immediately before the rise of electoral authoritarian rule is associated with a 76 percent decline in the risk of military takeover.

---

[32] It is still possible that the traumas of the crises preceding electoral authoritarian rule recede with generational replacement, which may not be fully captured in these analyses because of the insufficiently long time span of available data on most electoral autocracies. On the generational replacement dynamics of regime support, see Rose and Mishler (2007).

This effect is relatively stable in terms of size and is statistically significant at around the 10 percent level across the models in the left panel of Table 3.4 and the alternative specifications in the Online Appendix.[33]

On the whole, these findings indicate that the crises and failures of the *anciens régimes*, as well as the success of their electoral authoritarian successors in addressing them, protect the latter both from democratization and from the threat of degenerating into closed dictatorships. But could the same be said of all regime types, and not just electoral autocracies? Indeed, the literature has long stressed that economic and security crises induce the collapse of *all* types of regimes, while success in addressing these crises legitimizes and stabilizes the systems that succeed them.[34] Electoral autocracies, from this standpoint, may not be unique in drawing legitimacy from the chaos that preceded them, and from their role in restoring order and prosperity: a proposition that runs counter to the key tenets of the crisis-origins theory of electoral authoritarianism.

To assess this possibility, I perform auxiliary analyses of the factors affecting regime durability in democracies and military dictatorships,[35] using the three key variables from Table 3.4 – conflict and GDP decline in the last three years of the regimes that preceded them, and the rate of GDP change throughout their tenure. The results of this analysis, which I present in Table A.4.3 of the Online Appendix, are unequivocal: economic and security crises before the rise of democracies and military dictatorships, as well as their capacity to remedy their consequences, have no bearing on the survival of such regimes. The effects of these variables are substantively small and/or statistically nonsignificant for all modes of transition from democracies and from military regimes. These results provide clear support for another key tenet of the crisis theory of electoral authoritarianism, summarized in hypothesis 3: that compared to other regime types, electoral autocracies that were preceded by deep economic and security crises, and which have managed

---

[33] The greater noisiness of the estimates in the left panel of Table 3.4 is likely owing to the substantially smaller number of transitions from electoral autocracies to military dictatorships.

[34] See e.g. Linz (1978), O'Donnell, Schmitter, and Whitehead (1986b), Huntington (1991), Przeworski (1991), and Haggard and Kaufman (1995), Gasiorowski (1995), and Brancati (2014a).

[35] As most single-party regimes were formed before the start of this dataset in 1960, data limitations prevent a comparable survival analysis for this regime type.

to deliver tangible improvements in restoring stability, are uniquely resistant to regime change.

But what do the results in Table 3.4 tell us about the alternative theories of electoral authoritarian regime endurance? Among the other predictors in the Table 3.4, access to resource rents – the staple of resource theories of authoritarian durability – appears to be significantly related with a lower risk of democratization of electoral autocracies. The coefficient on lag resource rents is significant across all specifications in the left panel of the table; substantively, using the estimates of Model (2), we can calculate that a one standard deviation increase in the share of resource rents in the GDP of an electoral authoritarian regime is associated with a 33 percent decrease in the risk of its democratization. This is consistent with the alternative hypothesis 5, that access to substantial resource rents, which can be leveraged to control societies through clientelism and repression, greatly increases the robustness of electoral authoritarian regimes.

However, the other results from the analysis help us put this effect in proper perspective. While resource rents certainly make electoral autocracies more resilient to democratization, the traumas from the crises that preceded them, as well these regimes' ability to restore stability, have a much stronger and considerably broader protective effect. First, the crisis and recovery variables have larger relative effects on the risk of democratization of electoral autocracies. Consider again a hypothetical electoral autocracy that has a 50 percent baseline probability of democratizing. Based on the estimates of Model (2) in Table 3.2, if this regime were preceded by an average, 11 percent drop in GDP in the three-year period before its rise, this probability would decrease to 42 percent – almost as much as a full standard deviation increase in the share of resource rents (which would bring the likelihood of democratization down to 40 percent). But let us assume this electoral autocracy has no access to resource rents, and its chances of democratization declines to 42 percent just because its predecessors presided over an average-sized recession for periods before the rise of electoral authoritarianism. If this regime achieves just the mean level of GDP recovery that electoral autocracies achieve during their tenure, its probability of democratization will further diminish to about 28 percent. Therefore, a combination of an average-sized economic crisis under the *ancien régime* and an average-sized recovery would reduce the probability of democratization by more than double one standard deviation increase in the share of resource rents in the economy.[36]

The second key reason why resource rents play a secondary role in the durability of electoral autocracies, according to the results of this analysis, is because they protect these regimes only against democratization. The estimated impact of this variable on the risk of transition to military dictatorships across all models in the right panel of Table 3.4 is positive (i.e. greater than 1 in hazard ratios) and not statistically significant, suggesting that resource rents do not act as deterrents against military takeovers in these regimes. In contrast, prior regime crises and stabilization efforts protect electoral autocracies from *both* democratization and transition to military dictatorship. While deeper recessions under the previous regime and bigger subsequent recoveries during electoral authoritarianism diminish the chances of democratization, conflicts preceding the rise of these regimes protect them from military takeovers, according to these results.

The primacy of the crisis factors is also confirmed by the fact that other alternative theories of survival of electoral autocracies find only partial support in these analyses. Among the other substantively important variables, the log military personnel per capita indicator is associated with increased risk of transition to military dictatorships,[37] but this proxy for the size of the repressive apparatus does not approach statistical significance in any of the models of democratization of electoral autocracies. On the other hand, higher levels of development, proxied by log GDP per capita, are associated with significant decreases in the odds of military takeovers,[38] but appear to have no statistically and substantively significant impact on the risk of transitions to democracy. Hence, the behavior of these variables is consistent with the predictions of the alternative coercive/manipulative power

---

[36] Based on the same simulation, a one standard deviation increase in GDP during the tenure of this hypothetical electoral autocracy – the kind of recovery carried out by high-achieving electoral autocracies like Singapore or Mexico – would, in turn, shrink its probability of democratization to below 9 percent.

[37] To illustrate using the specification in Model (6), a one standard deviation increase in log military personnel per capita is associated with an increase in the hazard rate of a military takeover in electoral autocracies by 86 percent.

[38] Using the specification in Model (6), a one standard deviation increase in GDP per capita is associated with a 54 percent decrease in the risk of transition to military dictatorship.

theories of electoral authoritarianism, summarized in hypothesis 5, but only in models of transitions to military dictatorships. Contrary to the predictions of these theories, repressive capacity and development/poverty have no discernible impact on the democratization of electoral autocracies.

This analysis also finds weak support for the thesis that democratic diffusion significantly affects the survival of electoral autocracies. While the estimated effects of the share of democracies in a country's neighborhood are aligned in the right directions (i.e. they are positively associated with the odds of democratization and negatively correlated with the risk of military takeovers), they do not approach statistical significance at any conventional level across all models in Table 3.4. In turn, the nonsignificance of the Cold War dummy across all models in the left panel of this table implies that there were no meaningful differences between electoral autocracies in the level of risk that they would transition to democracy before and after 1989. This suggests that the electoral autocracies' resilience to democratization is not a relic of the post–Cold War era. The Cold War period did, however, have a meaningful impact on the risk of military takeovers in these regimes, according to these estimates. Based on Model (6), the Cold War was associated with an increase in the risk of an electoral autocracy transitioning to a military dictatorship of 170 percent. This offers partial support for the idea that post–Cold War norms of democratic legitimation did indeed promote the stability of electoral autocracies by preventing their degeneration into military juntas.

Taken together, the findings in this section are highly consistent with the thesis that the experience of crisis under alternative regimes, as well as the ability of electoral autocracies to remedy their consequences, make societies reluctant to dismantle these regimes in favor of democracy or military dictatorship. The alternative explanations that electoral autocracies primarily sustain their rule by leveraging substantial clientelistic and coercive resources, or by avoiding external democratization pressures, find more limited support when the crisis factors are accounted for. The cumulative evidence from this chapter's analyses therefore paints a remarkably consistent picture: the crises and failures of their predecessors not only help these electoral autocracies to win power, but also provide the primary basis on which they maintain their rule.

Conclusion

Based on comparative data on transitions from democracy and military dictatorships, this chapter provides a "high altitude" test of the theory that more than any other form of undemocratic regime, electoral autocracies tend to be products of deep systemic crises. The core premise of this analysis is simple: if electoral autocracies are indeed legitimized by acute crises, transitions to this regime type from both democracies and closed autocracies should be closely predicted by macro-level indicators of crisis.

The cross-national analyses of transitions from democracies, military dictatorships, and single-party regimes presented in this chapter strongly confirm this expectation. As these findings indicate, security and economic crises are the strongest structural correlates of the rise of electoral authoritarianism *across all transition types*: ranging from those resulting from democratic breakdowns to those resulting from liberalizations of military and single-party regimes. Democratic failures leading to electoral authoritarianism, according to this chapter's analysis, have been closely associated with acute conflicts and security crises. Military and one-party dictatorships, in turn, were more likely to pursue "managed" liberalizations to electoral authoritarianism after economic crises.

Moreover, security and economic crises do not only increase the likelihood that an electoral authoritarian regime will emerge – they also diminish the attractiveness of its competing regime alternatives, according to this chapter's analysis. Acute security crises in particular seem to preclude the full democratization of closed autocracies: practically no democratizations of military dictatorships and single-party regimes have occurred in the wake of conflict. In democracies, on the other hand, economic and security crises are much stronger predictors of transitions to electoral authoritarianism than military takeovers. These findings are consistent with this book's theory that in democracies and closed autocracies plagued by unmanageable or existential crises, electoral authoritarianism emerges as a compelling middle-ground remedy. The rise of an effective, strong-armed incumbent, capable of curbing disruptive pluralism without imposing a naked dictatorship, may seem to be the most attractive choice to many citizens living in democracies torn by conflict or socioeconomic collapse. And in closed dictatorships beset by acute problems, a tightly controlled liberalization to electoral autocracy would be preferable to an uncertain and potentially highly destabilizing democratization. For democracies and autocracies alike, the shortest and surest escape route from uncontrollable crises seems to point toward electoral autocracy.

The central role of crises in the rise of electoral autocracies is captured in another set of findings: that conflicts and economic crises moderate the impact of the other key macro-level contributors to electoral authoritarianism emphasized in the literature. In this sense, this chapter's analyses reveal that higher levels of economic development protect democracies from backsliding into electoral authoritarianism only in the absence of conflict. Resource rents, in turn, have significant effects on the survival of military dictatorships only during economic downturns; protecting these regimes from transitions to electoral authoritarianism, but also promoting their democratization. And democratic neighborhoods encourage the democratization of single-party regimes and prevent their controlled liberalization to electoral authoritarianism only in the absence of economic and security crises.

But perhaps the most compelling evidence of the link between economic and security crises and the rise of electoral authoritarianism is provided by the lasting influence of such crises on the stability of these regimes. This chapter's empirical results confirm that histories of deep economic crises before the rise of electoral authoritarianism, and these regimes' success in restoring prosperity, have been associated with a much lower risk of collapse for electoral autocracies – either through democratization or as a result of military takeovers. The experience of traumatic crises under alternative regimes – as well as the ability of electoral autocracies to remedy their consequences – appear to make societies particularly reluctant to turn against their electoral authoritarian rulers.

Still, these macro-level analyses only provide a "high altitude" view of the processes leading to the rise of electoral autocracies. In particular, they cannot verify the crucial mechanisms through which electoral authoritarianism emerges as the preferred, if reluctant, choice among broad popular majorities in the wake of acute crises. These can only be resolved by exploring the patterns of regime legitimation, as well as popular opinion and political choice at the micro-level – tasks I turn to in the next chapters.

4 | The "Strongman" Electoral Authoritarian Appeal: A Comparative Analysis

[T]he tyrant's point of entry into the society ... [lies in his appeal as] the people's protector.

Plato (1985, 257)

A man is not a dictator when he is given a commission from the people and carries it out.

Huey Long, Louisiana Governor (cited
in Williams 1981, 762)

A central premise of this book is that deep systemic crises empower electoral authoritarian political forces by allowing them to win the support and votes of anxious populations. I argue that the key to the rise and endurance of these regimes – as well as their ability to employ coercive tactics – lies in their broad appeal as a remedy for societal disorder and crisis. Autocracies can secure genuine consent because they cater to a core popular demand and instinct – the demand for order when survival is at stake, and the instinct to secure it by any means possible. As summarized by Inglehart (2018, 1): "People's values and behavior are shaped by the degree to which survival is secure ... When survival is insecure, people tend to close ranks behind a strong leader, forming a united front against outsiders – a strategy that can be called the Authoritarian Reflex."

I claim that electoral authoritarianism is based on the appeal to these underlying attitudes at least as much as it is rooted in its coercive methods and machinations. The most successful dictators (in terms of their ability to win and retain power) are not the ones with the most coercive power and patronage resources at their disposal, but those who appear best suited to play the role of the "people's protector" in times of trouble.

Electoral authoritarianism occupies a particular niche in this strategy for legitimizing authoritarian power. Unlike closed dictatorships, these regimes appeal to people's authoritarian instinct in times of existential threat in order to win power by nominally democratic means: by securing majority support in regular multiparty elections. And then, by acting in the name of popular demands to restore order, stability, and justice by any means necessary, they claim to effectuate the democratically expressed will of the majority that elected them.

This stratagem gives electoral autocracies an unparalleled ability to legitimize their rule. As suggested in this chapter's quote from Governor Huey Long of Louisiana – who established "the closest thing to a dictatorship that America has ever known" in the 1930s (Kennedy 2003) – a government carrying out a mandate from a popular majority cannot easily be labeled as a dictatorship. On the contrary, this justification allows the ruling parties and leaders of such regimes to portray themselves as the most quintessential democrats. Touting themselves as popularly ordained national "saviors" in times of social decay and crisis, elected autocrats claim to be the indispensable "guardians" of the democratic constitutional order, which will collapse without their tough, uncompromising, and strong-armed response.

In this sense, electoral authoritarianism represents the apex of the "Trojan horse" authoritarian legitimation strategy, which has served as the dictators' point of entry into their societies as far back as Plato's (1985, 257) *Republic*. As I have outlined in detail in Chapter 2, despite the great differences between electoral autocracies from across the globe, they share an unmistakable common thread in their popular appeal – a set of clearly identifiable "rhetorical fingerprints," that follow this strategy of posing as democracy's "guardian angels."

First, seizing the mantle of savior of democracy in crisis and of their popular mandate won at the polls, elected autocrats spend *more* time talking about the virtues of democratic rule – and in particular, the democratic nature of their own rule – than their counterparts in established democracies. Their public statements are flooded with references to democracy and democratic values. They obsessively justify their every act that subverts democracy as a measure that is necessary to save it. They constantly reference the democratic constitutional order and rule of law when they repress their opponents. They espouse folksy language and demeanor, seeking to project a special connection with the "common man."[1] And they showcase themselves as champions of the individual

---

[1] Venezuela's electoral authoritarian regime, for instance, even projected a bond of "divine kinship" between its founder Hugo Chávez and the common people (Michelutti 2017b). During his massive rallies, Chávez famously coined the catchphrase "I am Chávez, you are Chávez, we are all Chávez" (cited in Mazepus

rights and freedoms of ordinary citizens – claiming that in societies beset by turmoil, these values can only be protected under their tough, uncompromising leadership. Like impersonators trying to deceive a skeptical audience that they are, in fact, their alter ego, electoral authoritarian parties and leaders act out a greatly exaggerated version of the rhetoric and demeanor of their democratic counterparts. They make up with democratic rhetoric for what they lack in substance.

The second component of the electoral authoritarian legitimation formula appeals to the authoritarian reflex of societies traumatized by upheaval. But it does so in a subtle and indirect manner. Electoral authoritarian parties and leaders do not call people to submit to some grand ideology; they make a commonsensical appeal for "national unity" under (their) firm leadership in times of grave threat. They divert blame for their own failures and brutality onto foreign enemies and domestic traitors. They do not overtly reject liberal values, but emphasize collective identities, traditional values, national pride, and the need for a strong, effective state in troubled times. Highlighting these primeval values and priorities, authoritarian forces defuse the appeal of liberalism by tapping into people's instincts for individual and collective self-preservation.

This sets the stage for the third trademark feature of the electoral authoritarian appeal: its excessively negative tone. While strongmen like Hugo Chávez and Vladimir Putin pose as *machos* and tireless problem-solvers in daily media appearances, televised physical stunts, and marathon call-in shows, they constantly disparage their opponents as puny, faint-hearted, incompetent, corrupt, and treasonous. Their regime-controlled media aggressively pushes horror stories of the chaos and misery engulfing societies that have given up the protection of strongmen regimes for vague promises of freedom.[2] The aim of these tactics is to sow fear of the alternatives – a tactic that works best when targeted at anxious electorates living in tumultuous circumstances – so

---

et al. 2016). After his death, the regime sought to perpetuate this mythical bond by embracing the slogan "I am Chávez! We are all Chávez!"

[2] To cite one of many such examples, Mexico's regime-dominated news media coverage during the tumultuous 1994 presidential election was obsessively focused on the war in former Yugoslavia, framing these events as a consequence of the country's backsliding to violence after the tenure of its strongman leader Josip Broz Tito. The underlying message, as one regime insider has directly admitted to Oppenheimer (1998), was that something similar could happen to Mexico if it abandoned the "steady-handed" leadership of the PRI regime.

that these regimes can establish themselves as the indispensable protectors of the nation.[3]

Taken together, these observations suggest that at the most basic level, the popular appeals of electoral authoritarian incumbents are characterized by the same three points of emphasis. Summarizing these as hypotheses, we can say that in their platforms and appeals, electoral authoritarian regimes will place particular stress on:

H1 Democracy, democratic values, and the innately democratic nature of their rule (*Democratic Legitimacy* frame).

H2 Nationalism, collective identities, and the need to unify behind a strong, paternalistic state and leadership in the face of foreign and domestic threats (*Rally-Around-the-Strongman* frame).

H3 Their governing competence, strength, and integrity, and the absence of these qualities among their opposition (*Negative Legitimacy* frame).

This legitimation script of electoral authoritarian regimes has been extensively documented in case studies and journalistic coverage, and will be readily familiar to readers who have followed the behavior of these regimes for any length of time. But save from a few notable exceptions (e.g. O'Donnell 1994; Levitsky and Ziblatt 2018), the political science literature has not systematically explored this pattern of political communication as a defining characteristic of electoral authoritarianism. Could it be the backbone of the narratives that justify electoral authoritarian rule in countries as diverse as Russia and Venezuela, Turkey and Nigeria, and Singapore and Zimbabwe? I examine this in the sections that follow.

The Campaign Appeals of Electoral Authoritarian Regimes: Cross-National Analysis of Party Manifesto Data

Data and Measurement

Studying the systematic patterns of legitimation of electoral autocracies presents two key methodological and empirical challenges. First, to

---

[3] In the Russian case, this fearmongering strategy has been captured in a particularly explicit way in a famous statement from the Speaker of the Russian Parliament Vyacheslav Volodin: "While Putin is there, so is Russia; once Putin is gone, so is Russia" (TASS 2017).

pinpoint the essential similarities and differences of popular appeals across electoral autocracies, as well as between electoral autocracies and democracies, we need to identify an appropriate unit of analysis – in particular, a set of public pronouncements, legitimizing documents, or platforms that have comparable significance across these regimes. Second, to measure the amount of stress these regimes place on different frames and issues in their legitimizing rhetoric, we require a valid, reliable, and broadly comparable metric.

To address both of these challenges, I rely on data from the Comparative Manifestos Project (CMP), which provides the largest and most extensive content analysis of political platforms from across the world (Volkens et al. 2016). Covering the electoral programs of over 1,000 political parties in 50 countries on 5 continents since 1945, the CMP dataset classifies each issue stance in these programs into 56 predefined issue categories that are divided into 5 domains,[4] and are "designed to be comparable between parties, countries, elections, and across time" (Volkens et al. 2016). It then quantifies the *number of mentions* each issue category has received in a party's electoral platform, providing a measure of substantive emphasis.

These traits make this dataset uniquely suited to performing this chapter's analysis. In particular, by virtue of its focus on electoral platforms, the CMP dataset enables us to compare the legitimation strategies of electoral autocracies and democracies at the primary site of political competition in both regime types. Also, by measuring the number of mentions for the same set of substantive issues, this dataset's indicators allow us to systematically identify the fundamental differences in emphasis across parties, elections, countries, regime types, and time. Finally, the CMP dataset is one of the most widely used datasets in comparative politics (see e.g. McDonald and Budge 2014), allowing additional validity checks to be carried out through comparison to a wide array of different approaches to issue-emphasis scale construction, comparison, and analysis.

The cross-national analysis of electoral authoritarian regime legitimation strategies that I perform with this data covers 3,030 electoral manifestos from 937 parties, competing in 456 elections in 54 counties

---

[4] The five substantive issue domains in the CMP dataset are: (1) External Relations; (2) Freedom and Democracy; (3) Political System; (4) Economy, Welfare, and Quality of Life; (5) Fabric of Society and Social Groups.

throughout the 1975–2014 period.[5] Most of this data covers party programs in stable OECD democracies and Eastern European countries. However, the CMP dataset also contains data on the electoral manifestos of 212 parties that have participated in 55 elections in 16 countries that experienced spells of electoral authoritarian rule. The great majority of these electoral autocracies are from Europe and the former Soviet Union (fourteen), and two are from the Middle East and Latin America, respectively (Turkey and Mexico). I provide the full list of these countries in the Online Appendix to this chapter.

The overrepresentation of European electoral autocracies (and particularly Eastern European countries) in this sample raises the prospect of a potential regional bias in the analysis. For this reason, as a robustness check, I perform separate empirical analyses of the appeals of the electoral autocracy in Mexico under the rule of the PRI party. Although this is a single case, the Mexican regime under the PRI has been the longest lasting, and by many accounts, the prototypical regime of this type, as well as historically the most prominent electoral autocracy in Latin America. From a comparative perspective, the Mexican case both precedes most of the other electoral autocracies in the dataset, which were largely established after the Cold War,[6] and has emerged in an entirely different region and under very different historical circumstances from most of the European electoral autocracies in the CMP dataset. Thus, the analysis of incumbent appeals in the Mexican electoral autocracy serves as a check of the robustness of this chapter's empirical findings, as well as of their generalizability.

Turning to the measurement of incumbent appeals, the CMP dataset analyzes party manifestos by counting the number of issue statements in the form of "quasi-statements" that parties devote to each of its fifty-six predefined categories. This raises the issue of how to quantify the relative issue emphasis without introducing potential biases due to the

---

[5] Although the CMP data coverage stretches back to 1945, this analysis is restricted to the 1975–2014 period because it also relies on data from the Database of Political Institutions (Beck et al. 2001), whose coverage starts in 1975. However, very little substantive data is lost due to this restriction because the vast majority of electoral autocracies covered in the CMP dataset appeared after 1975.

[6] In this sense, the data on Mexico in the CMP dataset provides the broadest coverage of competition in an electoral autocracy. It covers a total of twelve elections in Mexico for 1976–2009, eight of which took place under electoral authoritarian rule (1976–2000).

different structure of various party manifestos. These biases could arise because of peculiarities like different lengths and repetitiveness across party platforms, as well as various linguistic and stylistic differences that can artificially inflate or deflate some indicators of relative issue emphasis.[7] To preempt such problems, I use the following logarithmic scale of issue emphasis in party platforms, proposed by Prosser (2014):

$$\theta_{ike} = \frac{\log(S_{ike} + 1)}{\log(N_{ke} + 1)}$$

where S_{ike} is the number of quasi-statements that the manifesto of party k devotes to policy category i in election e, and N_{ke} is the total number of quasi-statements in the party manifesto for that election.

This scale has several desirable properties. First, it ranges between 0 and 1 for each policy issue, with 0 denoting no mentions and higher values indicating greater emphasis in a given manifesto. This makes the measure easily interpretable and comparable. Second, because of the logarithmic structure of the scale, each additional mention of a policy has a *diminishing impact* on its salience. The underlying rationale here is that the first mention of a certain position reflects its intended salience much more than the hundredth mention or the thousandth mention, for instance – a well-established finding in psychometrics (Stevens 1957; Jakobovits and Lambert 1963; Jakobovits and Hogenraad 1967). This scale property also diminishes the impact of variations in rhetorical exposition across manifestos (e.g. the greater repetitiveness of some party programs). Third, because of its mathematical properties, elaborated in detail by Prosser (2014), the scale is invariant to the different lengths of party manifestos and the addition of irrelevant issues to them. These characteristics ensure that the measures of policy emphasis derived with this scale are consistent, reliable, and valid, and that they can be compared not just across parties and countries, but also across democratic and electoral authoritarian regimes.

Apart from the CMP data, I use the indicator for the largest governing party from the Database of Political Institutions (Beck et al. 2001) to identify the incumbent party for each election. Finally, this analysis relies on the Authoritarian Regimes Dataset (ver. 6) (Wahman, Teorell, and

---

[7] For a more extensive discussion of these issues, see Prosser (2014).

Hadenius 2013), described in detail in the previous two chapters, to distinguish between electoral autocracies and democracies.

Aggregate Patterns in Campaign Emphasis

This book's theoretical framework suggests that contrary to widespread perceptions, electoral autocracies share a common, well-articulated doctrine of strong-armed, but representative (in a plebiscitarian sense) rule, which they use to attract genuine popular support in times of crisis and upheaval. Such regimes argue they are more, not less democratic than liberal democracies, as they claim they can far more efficiently and competently look after the interests of common people in hard times. At the same time, the type of leadership they provide is tutelary and requires societies to give up core freedoms and unite behind the regime's guardianship. As result, in their popular appeals, electoral autocracies will particularly stress the importance of collective values, identities, national unity, and the need to censor certain types of opposition and behavior. Furthermore, electoral authoritarian parties and leaders go to great lengths to showcase their unique competence to restore order, stability, and prosperity, as well as to portray their opponents as too incompetent, corrupt, and dangerous to lead the country.

Analyzing the relative emphasis that parties in the CMP dataset place on these issues provides an opportunity to perform the most general and comprehensive test of this theory. In the broadest sense, if the above hypotheses are true, the greatest difference between the campaign appeals of democracies and electoral autocracies should be on the emphasis they place on democracy, national unity, and governing competence. As a first test of this proposition, I perform a simple, fully inductive analysis: I *rank the mean differences in the emphasis* incumbent parties in electoral autocracies and democracies place on each of the fifty-six policy areas in the CMP from largest to smallest.

The results are displayed in Figure 4.1 below. This chart shows the differences in mean emphasis in the policy areas that are statistically significant at the 5 percent level and greater than 0.04 in absolute value. The differences range between 0 and 1 (the metric of the original log scale of policy emphasis) and are shown in descending order. Positive differences denote issues that have greater emphasis in the election manifestos of electoral authoritarian incumbents; negative ones indicate which issues receive comparatively more attention in the appeals of democratic incumbents.

The pattern that we observe in Figure 4.1 closely matches this book's theoretical expectations. The top five differences between the appeals of democratic and electoral authoritarian incumbents (the darker bars in the graph) include all the key hypothesized traits of the electoral authoritarian doctrine: favorable mentions of democracy, freedom, and human rights, on one hand, and support for strong political authority, emphasis on preserving the constitutional order, and positive appeals to the "national way of life" category, on the other.

The greatest difference overall reflects the much greater frequency of positive mentions of "national way of life" by electoral authoritarian incumbents – an issue category that includes appeals to patriotism, nationalism, and limitation of some freedoms to protect the state against subversion,[8] and closely corresponds to the *Rally-Around-the-Strongman* frame summarized in hypothesis 2. The second largest difference in emphasis between the platforms of electoral authoritarian and democratic incumbents is for the "Political Authority" category in the CMP dataset, which, in turn, matches the *Negative Legitimacy* frame of hypothesis 3. Specifically, the "Political Authority" category includes: (1) references to the manifesto party's or its candidates' competence to govern and/or other parties' or candidates' lack of such competence; (2) "Favorable mentions of the desirability of a strong and/or stable government in general." This is followed by greater emphasis on democracy[9] and individual freedoms and human rights[10] in the platform of electoral

[8] Specifically, appeals classified as positive statements about the "National Way of Life" in the CMP codebook include: (1) "Favorable mentions of the manifesto country's nation, history"; (2) "Support for established national ideas"; (3) "General appeals to pride of citizenship"; (4) "Appeals to patriotism"; (5) "Appeals to nationalism"; (6) "Suspension of some freedoms in order to protect the state against subversion."

[9] According to the Manifesto dataset codebook, the "Democracy" category enumerates "[f]avorable mentions of democracy as the 'only game in town'" and "[g]eneral support for the manifesto country's democracy." It may also include mentions of: (1) "Democracy as method or goal in national, international or other organizations (e.g. labor unions, political parties etc.)"; (2) "The need for the involvement of all citizens in political decision-making"; (3) "Support for parts of democratic regimes (rule of law, division of powers, independence of courts etc.)."

[10] The individual freedoms and human rights category is defined by favorable mentions of the: (1) "importance of personal freedom in the manifesto and other countries"; (2) "importance of human and civil rights in the manifesto and the right to freedom of speech, press, assembly etc."

authoritarian incumbents – categories that reflect the *Democratic Legitimacy* frame of hypothesis 1. Finally, electoral autocracies put much greater stress on appeals to constitutionalism. This issue category tallies statements in support of maintaining the constitutional status quo and the use of constitutionalism to justify policies. Substantively, it can be related to the *Democratic Legitimacy* frame, as it reflects a tendency of electoral authoritarian incumbents to rationalize their actions as measures to protect their countries' democratic constitutions and rule of law.

What is remarkable here is that the analysis in Figure 4.1 has easily distinguished all the hypothesized traits of the electoral authoritarian legitimizing doctrine using a fully inductive approach: by a simple ranking of the differences in mean issue emphasis across all fifty-six substantive policy areas in the CMP dataset. That the contours of the electoral authoritarian legitimizing script stand out so clearly in this

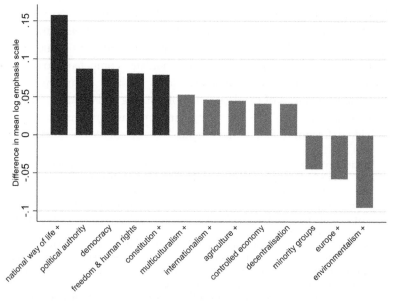

Figure 4.1 Differences in mean policy emphasis of the ruling parties in electoral autocracies and democracies

Note: The graph includes policy components for which the mean difference is statistically significant at p<0.05 and greater than 0.04 in absolute value. The "+" sign after the title of an issue category denotes positive references to it.

completely non-parametric, all-inclusive, and cross-national examination of comparative issue emphasis is a strong indication that these regimes adhere to the same set of legitimizing arguments, intended to justify their rule as a popularly mandated effort to address crises and protect their countries from threats.

The appeal to their societies' authoritarian instinct when survival seems to be at stake is also highlighted by the topics electoral autocracies pay relatively *less* attention to in their campaigns when compared to democratic incumbents. In particular, the results in Figure 4.1 indicate that electoral authoritarian incumbents put far less emphasis than their democratic counterparts on the protection of the environment, underprivileged minority groups (including people with disabilities, immigrants, LGBT, indigenous groups), and the desirability of integration into the European Union (among the countries in this region). The first two issues fall squarely under what Inglehart (2018) has categorized as "post-materialist" values – outlooks that place a premium on self-expression, political participation, freedom, tolerance, and diversity, and that are adopted by societies where the basic material prerequisites for survival are secure. Processes of integration into the European Union, in turn, have been one of the key vehicles for the diffusion of democratic norms, and a major threat to the stability of electoral authoritarianism (Levitsky and Way 2010a).

Campaign Emphasis by Topic and Region

But could these findings reflect the peculiarities of Eastern European electoral autocracies, which tend to be overrepresented in the CMP dataset, rather than more general patterns of electoral authoritarian legitimation? To test the robustness of these results, I examine differences in the mean policy stances of democratic and electoral authoritarian incumbents for each of the key appeals identified in Figure 4.1 in a more disaggregated fashion. Specifically, I calculate mean policy emphasis scores for Mexico under the PRI regime separately from all the other electoral authoritarian regimes in the CMP dataset.[11] This

---

[11] I do not estimate a separate policy emphasis score for Turkey – the other country in the CMP dataset that can serve for potential regional biases – because unlike Mexico, Turkey has had just three election cycles at a time when it was designated as electoral authoritarian, preventing me from estimating standard errors around its mean emphasis score.

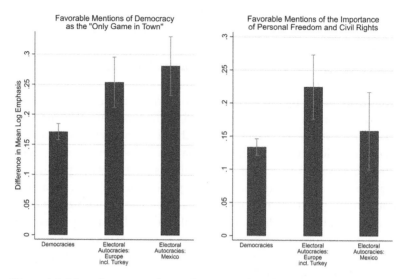

Figure 4.2 Mean frequency of incumbent appeals to democracy and civil rights and personal freedoms
Note: bars presented with 95 percent confidence intervals

allows me to check for potential regional biases: the degree to which the patterns of legitimation in the Mexican case match those of the other, predominantly East European cases, provides some sense of the broader generalizability of the findings of this analysis.

Taking this approach, Figure 4.2 displays the frequency of favorable mentions of democracy as the "only game in town" (the left panel), as well as of the importance of personal freedom and civil rights (the right panel) by incumbent parties in democracies and electoral autocracies. The patterns we observe match the findings from the previous analysis. The panel on the left clearly shows that electoral authoritarian incumbents devote considerably more space to appeals to "democracy" in their manifestos than do their counterparts in liberal democracies. This is especially pronounced in the Mexican electoral autocracy, providing assurance that the pattern is not unique to electoral autocracies in Europe. In the right panel of Figure 4.2, we can see that there is a somewhat smaller gap in the different parties' emphasis on personal freedoms and civil rights, particularly in the Mexican case. But on the whole, electoral autocracies do seem to exhibit a greater rhetorical commitment to these principles, which, as I illustrate in Chapter 5, is justified by claims that individuals will be able to attain greater personal freedoms under the regime's reign because of the stability it will bring.

At the same time, as anticipated by this book's theoretical framework, the emphasis electoral authoritarian incumbents place on democracy is offset by their calls for national unity and for the surrender of freedoms to protect the state from subversion, as well as for stronger, more effective government. We see this in Figure 4.3 below, which plots the different weights democratic and electoral authoritarian governments put on these issues in their electoral programs.

The left panel shows the area where appeals of electoral autocracies differ the most from democracies: the emphasis on patriotism, nationalism, unity and calls for suspension of liberties in the interest of national security – positions coded under the broad rubric of support for the "national way of life" in the CMP dataset. As these results confirm, such themes have been far more prevalent in the appeals of electoral autocracies, confirming the expectation that electoral autocracies will primarily pose as protectors of national unity, integrity, and state security. And on this issue, the rhetorical commitment of both the

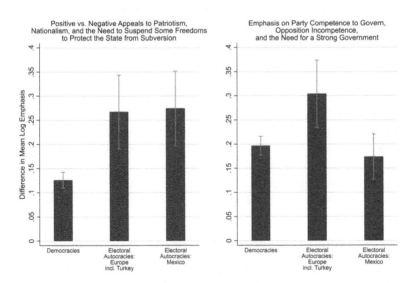

Figure 4.3 Mean frequency of incumbent appeals to nationalism, suspension of freedoms to protect the state, competence, and the need for strong government
Note: bars presented with 95 percent confidence intervals

Mexican and East European electoral autocracies was equally great, providing assurance that this result is more broadly generalizable.

The right panel in Figure 4.3, in turn, suggests that Eastern European electoral autocracies have placed significantly more emphasis than the liberal democracies in the CMP dataset on claims of their competence, the opposition's incompetence, and the need for a strong government. This, again, is in line with this book's theoretical predictions: to portray themselves as their nations' "saviors" in times of danger and crisis, electoral autocracies must claim they have superior ability to provide the effective, strong-armed rule that is fit for the times. The data suggests that this theme was not as pronounced in Mexico's electoral autocracy. However, this "modesty" may be a peculiarity of the electoral manifestos of the ruling PRI party, as previous in-depth studies have shown that claims of superior competence vis-à-vis their opponents were the centerpiece of the regime's campaigns (Magaloni 2006; Greene 2007; Langston and Morgenstern 2009).

Finally, Figure 4.4 depicts the different emphasis that incumbents in electoral autocracies and liberal democracies place on constitutionalist and legalistic appeals. Because of their legitimation as the essential purveyors of stability in times of crisis, I have argued that electoral authoritarian incumbents are especially prone to cast themselves as the protectors of the democratic constitutions and legal order. By the same token, these regimes should regularly refer to constitutional and legal provisions to justify the actions committed in the name of their crusades to restore order and stability. The results displayed in Figure 4.4 support these theses. Electoral authoritarian incumbents have devoted significantly more space in their electoral programs to defending the current constitutional order and to justifying their policies with appeals to legalism and constitutionalism. This was especially true in the Mexican case, where the ruling PRI regime routinely resorted to constitutionalism in its appeals, even as it changed Mexico's constitution more than 400 times to bias legal rules in its favor (Magaloni 2006, 15).

Campaign Appeal Emphasis Over Time

Apart from regional biases, one might also ask whether the legitimation patterns we have observed thus far may be driven by some confounding factor or idiosyncratic differences in how incumbents in some countries justify their rule, rather than substantive differences between electoral

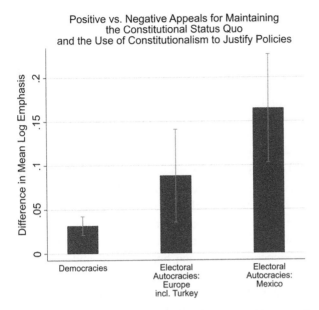

Figure 4.4 Mean frequency of incumbent appeals to constitutionalism
Note: bars presented with 95 percent confidence intervals

autocracies and democracies. One way to address this issue is to examine the over-time trends in incumbent campaign appeals in countries that have experienced *both* democratic and electoral authoritarian rule. This book's theory that electoral authoritarian regimes have a distinct appeal would be invalidated if incumbents in countries that experienced this type of rule *always* adopted the same legitimizing script. In other words, the legitimation pattern I described above cannot be designated as electoral authoritarian if *both* democratic and electoral authoritarian incumbents *in the same country* resort to it. If, on the other hand, the differences in platform emphasis we observed in the cross-national analyses also hold across periods of democratic and electoral authoritarian rule within countries that have had both regime types, we would have additional assurance of the validity of this chapter's claims.

To perform this additional robustness check, I compare the mean differences in emphasis across the platforms of electoral authoritarian and democratic incumbents in countries that have experienced electoral authoritarian rule. This analysis is analogous to running a regression analysis with a fixed effect (e.g. by including a dummy variable), denoting whether a country has experienced a spell of electoral authoritarian rule or not. This approach helps ensure that the differences in emphasis electoral authoritarian incumbents place on some issues are not driven by any country-level confounding factors.

I present the results of this analysis in Figure 4.5 below. The bars in this graph represent differences in emphasis in incumbent campaigns across eighty-four elections, held in the ten countries of the CMP dataset that have experienced spells of *both* electoral authoritarian and democratic rule in the 1975–2014 period. The pattern we observe is very similar to that found in the previous analyses. Across four of the five hypothesized components of the strongman appeal, electoral authoritarian regimes have placed significantly more emphasis on these components than the democratic incumbents that have preceded or followed their rule. These include appeals to democracy, protecting human rights and individual freedoms, nationalism, and constitutionalism.

The only issue category that was somewhat more prevalent in the campaign rhetoric of democratic incumbents was that of appeals in the

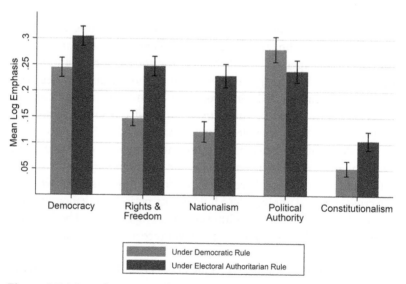

Figure 4.5 Mean frequency of incumbent appeals in the five substantive categories – countries that have experienced electoral authoritarian rule
*Note: bars presented with 95 percent confidence intervals

political authority cluster, which contains statements about one's own competence and the incompetence of one's political opponents. But this may be a relic of the unique circumstances in which these democracies emerged. In eight of the ten countries ruled by both regime types in the CMP dataset, democratic spells are recorded only in the immediate aftermath of the collapse of electoral authoritarianism. As the fledgling democratic incumbents that came to power in these countries had, in many cases, spawned from anti-authoritarian protest movements and were engaged in high-stakes competition against remnants of the former regimes, they may have adopted a particularly combative, negative tone in their campaigns. Thus, taking this peculiarity into account, the differences in campaign-issue emphasis in Figure 4.5 closely match with the electoral authoritarian legitimation script. The stress that electoral authoritarian incumbents placed on appeals to democracy and the need for national unity and strong, competent government, as well as the other associated frames, does not appear to be driven by unaccounted-for characteristics of the countries that experienced this type or rule. On the contrary, it seems to capture the core legitimizing strategy of these regimes.

As an additional test of this proposition, I estimate the mean differences in campaign-issue emphasis separately for 9 of the 10 countries in the CMP dataset that had experienced both democratic and electoral authoritarian rule.[12] The purpose of this exercise is to check whether this chapter's empirical findings are driven by some specific countries that are overrepresented in the CMP dataset, or whether some of these electoral authoritarian incumbents placed particularly high emphasis on the hypothesized components of the electoral authoritarian appeal (i.e. the outliers).[13]

We should also note that this is a particularly stringent test of this chapter's propositions. This is because shifts in campaign appeals in any given country tend to be highly correlated and path dependent: if one party attracts considerably more support by emphasizing some appeals, others tend to follow suit (see e.g. Ansolabehere and Iyengar 1994; Sides 2007); and once there is a broader realignment in issue

---

[12] I omit the ruling regime in Portugal from this analysis, as it was tagged as electoral authoritarian only for the 1975 constituent assembly election. This is because this was a transitional regime, whose purpose was only to ensure the country's democratization after the Carnation Revolution.

[13] Using the regression analogy mentioned earlier, this approach is analogous to re-estimating the original regression analysis with country fixed effects.

emphasis across the party system, it tends to hold across elections, often for long periods of time (see e.g. Carmines and Stimson 1993). For both reasons, differences in incumbents' campaign emphasis in any given country are then minimized across time, making it more difficult to make a distinction between periods of democratic and electoral authoritarian rule.

Nevertheless, the results of the country-by-country analysis, which I present in Figure A.4.2.1 in the Online Appendix to this chapter in the interest of space, indicate that the appeals of democratic and electoral authoritarian incumbents are dissimilar enough to overcome even this hurdle. Indeed, the general pattern of differences in campaign appeals across these countries closely conforms to what we have observed in Figure 4.5. In all the countries that had both regime types, except Ukraine,[14] electoral authoritarian incumbents placed more emphasis on democracy, protecting rights and freedoms, the need for unity and strong government, and constitutionalism than their democratic predecessors or successors. This pattern also holds in Turkey and Mexico – countries that act as controls on potential regional biases due to the overrepresentation of electoral autocracies from Eastern Europe and the former Soviet Union. Turkey is particularly interesting in this regard, because it has experienced two very different spells of electoral authoritarian rule: first under the secular, army-sponsored establishment (the 1995 and 1999 elections) and then under the conservative Islamist AKP of Recep Tayyip Erdoğan (the 2015 election). That these two ideologically divergent electoral autocracies adhered to the same legitimation script is further testament to the role of that script as a defining feature of electoral authoritarianism.

---

[14] Ukraine seems to be the only exception to this pattern: there, democratic incumbents had placed similar, and in some cases, even higher emphasis on these topics. However, this result is based on only one election (the 2002 Parliament election) when Ukraine was tagged as electoral authoritarian by the Authoritarian Regimes Dataset regime indicator. Furthermore, Ukraine's democratic transition in the 2000s was abortive: even though Ukraine was designated as democratic for the 2007 election, the incumbent (and election winner) was the Party of Regions – the former ruling party under the electoral authoritarian regime, dismantled in the pro-democracy Orange Revolution of 2004. As Ukraine was redesignated as electoral authoritarian under the rule of the Party of Regions a few years later, in 2011, the rhetoric it adopted during the supposedly democratic regime in 2007 could have presaged this authoritarian turn. For these reasons, the Ukrainian exception to the pattern in Figure A.4.2.1 in the Online Appendix does not seem to contradict the conclusions of this analysis.

Do the Campaign Appeals of Electoral Authoritarian Incumbents "Stick Together?"

Qualitative Analysis of the Mexican and Russian Cases

Taken together, the empirical results of this chapter thus far demonstrate a clear and consistent pattern of differences between the campaign appeals of incumbents in democracies and electoral autocracies. These differences highlight the individual components of the electoral authoritarian appeal, as articulated by this chapter: calls to unite society behind their strong and competent leadership, coupled with appeals to democracy, protection of individual rights and freedoms, and the rule of law. But do these seemingly contradictory appeals represent the same legitimizing script? Do they, in other words, "stick together" well enough to form a coherent narrative, justifying electoral authoritarian rule?

We can address this question in two steps. First, to unpack the content of these appeals and how well they match together, we can perform a *qualitative analysis* of representative appeals in the CMP categories we have focused on so far. This will not only provide a better sense of the actual language used in each issue category but could also serve as a test of how well they match the hypothesized electoral authoritarian legitimation strategy. With this goal in mind, I extract representative statements in the three defining categories of the electoral authoritarian appeal (the *Democracy, Rally-Around-the-Strongman,* and the *Negative Legitimacy* frames) from two paradigmatic cases: post-communist Russia under the reign of Vladimir Putin and Mexico during the Institutional Revolutionary Party (PRI) regime.[15]

---

[15] I have drawn these statements from the Manifesto Project Primary documents archive, available on https://manifesto-project.wzb.eu/information/documents/corpus (accessed on 5/3/2021). They are representative in the sense that they reflect the clearest, most explicit, or most strongly highlighted statements by United Russia or the PRI in these categories. In the case of United Russia's relatively short electoral program for the 2011 parliament elections (containing only 179 statements), the statements in Table 4.1 also represent a relatively high proportion of the total number of statements in the respective categories. In particular, this party manifesto contained nine statements in the "national way of life" and ten in the democracy category, and four of each of these are provided in Table 4.1 (or about 45 and 40 percent of the total number of statements in these categories, respectively).

Comparing these cases offers particular leverage for analyzing the content of the legitimizing appeals of electoral authoritarian regimes. Russia and Mexico not only have very different geographic, political, economic, and cultural backgrounds, but their electoral autocracies emerged in very different periods and had very different institutional characteristics. But despite these dissimilar backgrounds, they both developed robust electoral authoritarian regimes that were extensively copied across the world. Therefore, a paired comparison of the electoral authoritarian appeals in Mexico and Russia can be thought of as a most different systems analysis: an approach allowing us to isolate the most essential commonalities in the campaign appeals of electoral autocracies more broadly.

With this goal in mind, Table 4.1 provides several representative statements that Russia's and Mexico's ruling parties made across the three core appeal categories in the Russian 2011 parliamentary election and the 1994 general election in Mexico, respectively. I have deliberately chosen these elections as they took place in post-crisis periods, when these electoral autocracies faced unprecedented challenges to their legitimacy.[16] From the perspective of this book's theory of the crisis origins of electoral authoritarianism, "challenging" election campaigns like these should prompt electoral authoritarian incumbents to turn up the volume on their strongman appeal, making its basic contours more apparent. As these regimes' legitimacy as national "saviors" is contested by crises that happened under their watch, they should even more assertively promote the innate democraticness of their rule and their unique ability to unify the nation and prevent further turmoil, as well as highlight the flaws of their opponents.

The statements in Table 4.1 match these expectations. Faced with a challenge to their core legitimizing narratives, the United Russia and PRI parties aggressively promoted themselves as the guardians of national interests, order, and stability, and as legitimate representatives

---

[16] The 1994 election campaign in Mexico was waged against a backdrop of extraordinary turmoil, marked by economic instability, divisions in the ruling party, the murder of the PRI's main presidential candidate, and an armed insurgency in the Chiapas region (Oppenheimer 1998). Russia's 2011 parliamentary election, in turn, took place in the aftermath of the 2009 global financial crisis, which hit Russia particularly hard, and the controversial decision of Vladimir Putin to return to the presidency, which triggered the largest countrywide wave of protest since the beginning of his rule (Judah 2013).

Table 4.1 *Representative statements in the three key categories of electoral authoritarian appeals – Russia and Mexico*[*]

	Positive references to "national way of life"	Positive references to democracy	References to political authority
United Russia (2011 Russian Parliament elections)	"We will not give up our Russia." "Together we have preserved and restored our beloved Homeland – Our Russia" "We are millions of citizens of our country, a Great Nation of a Great State!" *"We will not surrender to those who want to destroy it, we will not surrender to those who deceive people by giving empty and unrealistic promises."*	"Our party will continue to consistently improve the conditions for political competition and the development of intra-party democracy." "Our position is to have effective control of civil society over the bureaucracy, and the nomination of enterprising and honest people that will revitalize our government." "These are extremely important stages in creating the basic conditions for political stability in Russia." *"We have formed our program on the basis of popular initiatives. Based on the proposals of our voters."*	"The global financial crisis [of 2009] has become a serious test for us. *We did not allow a repeat of the devastating shocks of the past, did not allow everyday poverty to return to our lives,* did not allow the crisis to cross out everything that was done in health care, education, social sphere." "United Russia has already proved that it is able to act as a national political leader, not just to lead, but also to rise above narrow group interests. To hear not only their supporters, but also opponents. To follow strategic goals, not short-term benefits, to work in

Table 4.1 (*cont.*)

	Positive references to "national way of life"	Positive references to democracy	References to political authority
			the interests of all regions, all social groups, all citizens of our country. To be in the full sense of the national and all-Russian party."*
Institutional Revolutionary Party – PRI (1994 Mexico general election)	*"The Mexican Revolution is the founding event of contemporary Mexico and constitutes the civic and moral heritage of all Mexicans. Our party has emerged to give continuity and validity to the principles and objectives of the Mexican Revolution ... As a National Revolutionary Party, it unified the political forces and institutionally channeled the great social movement initiated in*	"The PRI is a democratic party. It assumes that the government of the country is representative and that its fundamental legitimacy rests on free elections and on the effectiveness of the suffrage. It competes responsibly and peacefully with other policy options within the framework of the constitutional state	"We know that today society is demanding certainty and security. It wants to face the future with clarity and without fear; it wants security in its employment and income; security for its savings and investments; it wants security in its daily life and it wants certainty in the institutional order, in political

1910; as Party of the Mexican Revolution it represented and organized the aspirations of the popular and nationalist sectors; as an Institutional Revolutionary Party, it has contributed to the development of the country with justice and freedom."

"Our party has a clear offer, which recognizes the value of our history, which assumes the demands of society and foresees the needs that in the future the country will have to guarantee its progress."

and the unrestricted respect for the law."

"For the PRI-istas, the vote is the source of legitimacy for the government."

"For our party, human freedoms must be recognized, defended and promoted by the state and, also, by society."

life, in the exercise of rights."

"The government must guarantee the security, order and stability that democracy requires."

* NB: Italics in the texts above are mine. Translations by the author.

Sources: Platforms of the United Russia party, 2011 Russian legislative election, and of the Institutional Revolutionary Party, 1994 Mexican general election. Manifesto Project [https://manifesto-project.wzb.eu/information/documents/corpus]

of the democratic will of their societies. Both parties showcased their pivotal role in rescuing their countries from the worst tribulations in their histories (the turmoil before the Mexican revolution and the Russian post-communist collapse), as well as their patriotic credentials as the custodians of the most sacred national legacies (the spirit of Mexico's revolution and Russia's great nation/power status). And they both framed the current challenges their countries faced in terms of grave threats and uncertainty that they were uniquely able to address. Even though the tone of United Russia's appeals in 2011 was somewhat more aggressive than that of the PRI in 1994, both parties followed essentially the same script: justifying their strong-armed rule as democratically mandated and indispensable to preserving the stability and prosperity of their fragile societies.

Factor Analysis of the CMP Data

The second, quantitative method of verifying whether the hypothesized components of the electoral authoritarian appeal combine into a coherent narrative is to perform a factor analysis. This statistical technique explores the common patterns of variation between a set of indicators to determine if they are related to a broader, overarching substantive construct, which is not directly observed. For the present purposes, a factor analytic approach would ask: do the appeals in the five categories we have focused on exhibit a sufficient degree of *co-variation* to be combined into a single latent scale, corresponding to the hypothesized legitimizing narrative of electoral authoritarian regimes? And if yes, can this latent scale predict not just rhetoric, but actual electoral authoritarian behavior?

To examine the first question, I use an iterative procedure for scale-component selection and validation, described by Prosser (2014). This procedure is better suited for analyzing the CMP data than traditional factor analysis methods, as these are relatively insensitive to exclusion or miscoding of individual components. They also have serious problems when dealing with count data with many zeros, which emerges when many components are not mentioned in party manifestos.[17] To address these issues, Prosser's method starts with an initial, "naïve" additive scale of a given construct and explores its correlations with

---

[17] For a more detailed discussion of these issues, see Prosser (2014, 92–98).

each component in the CMP dataset that is not part of the scale. If any additional component is correlated with the original scale above an empirically derived threshold, it is included (or conversely, excluded), and the iteration continues until no new components are added.[18]

I initiate this scale-component selection validation test using an additive scale that contains the five hypothesized components of the electoral authoritarian appeal: positive mentions of democracy; freedom and human rights; preserving the national way of life; the need for a strong, competent political authority; and appeals to constitutionalism. For each iteration, I estimate the correlations between this scale and each CMP dataset item *not* included in the scale using party manifestos of incumbents from *both* democracies and electoral autocracies. This ensures that the results are not biased by selecting on what is, in effect, the dependent variable (by narrowing the sample to electoral autocracies, for instance), and provides a relatively stringent test of the consistency and broad validity of the hypothesized scale. I provide a full description of the steps in this analysis in Part 3 of the Online Appendix to this chapter.

The procedure achieves convergence in three iterations, with two changes. First, the positive-appeals-to-constitutionalism item falls just below the 0.43 threshold in the last iteration, so it is excluded from the scale. This correlation is close enough to the exclusion criterion to be of substantive significance and may be driven by measurement errors in constructing the appeals-to-constitutionalism component. Still, to stay true to the inductive nature of this analysis, I exclude this item from the final scale.

Second, and more importantly, an additional item is added because its correlation with the latent scale is higher than the estimated thresholds. This is the "civic-mindedness" category, which according to the CMP codebook, includes: (1) "Favorable mention of the civil society and volunteering"; (2) "Decrying anti-social attitudes in times of crisis"; (3) "Appeal for public spiritedness"; and (4) "Support for the public interest."[19] Adding these appeals makes intuitive sense, as they

---

[18] This threshold is selected by exploring breaks in the distribution of the correlations of the individual components with the scale; such breaks typically separate clusters of highly correlated components from those that have little substantive relation to the underlying construct. For more details, see Part 3 of the Online Appendix to this chapter.

[19] For the CMP codebook, see https://manifesto-project.wzb.eu/datasets (accessed 25/05/2021).

are substantively related to the other key components in the scale, particularly the "national way of life" category. They also closely correspond to this book's conception of the electoral authoritarian doctrine as an appeal to unity and the subordination to collective interests in times of crisis. From this standpoint, this scale-component selection and validation not only converged on the CMP issue categories that most closely correspond to the electoral authoritarian appeal, as defined by this book's theoretical framework, but also identified an additional item that validates its substantive interpretation.

Does the Strongman Appeal Predict Electoral Authoritarianism?

How well does the latent scale of the strongman appeal, developed in the previous subsection, distinguish between the rhetoric of democratic and electoral authoritarian incumbents? One way to examine this is to compare its performance to other theoretically derived scales of the authoritarianism of party appeals that exist in the literature. Perhaps the most conceptually proximate and widely used scale based on the CMP dataset that can be used for this purpose is the "Authoritarian Emphasis" index described in Bakker and Hobolt (2013). Like the electoral authoritarian scale developed in this chapter, this scale also includes appeals to the political authority, national way of life, and civic-mindedness categories. However, it diverges on three other items that it contains: positive references to traditional morality and law and order, and negative references to multiculturalism.[20]

To measure the relative performance of the two scales in distinguishing the appeals of democratic and electoral authoritarian incumbents, I compare the differences in their mean scores across the two regime categories. The results, displayed in Figure A.4.3.2 of the book's Online Appendix to this chapter, show that the Electoral Authoritarianism Scale does a much better job in capturing these distinctions than the

---

[20] According to the CMP codebook, the *traditional-morality category* contains calls for the: (1) "Prohibition, censorship and suppression of immorality and unseemly behavior"; (2) "Maintenance and stability of the traditional family as a value"; and (3) "Support for the role of religious institutions in state and society." The *law-and-order category* contains appeals for: (1) "increasing support and resources for the police"; (2) "Tougher attitudes in courts"; and (3) "Importance of internal security." The *negative-references-to-multiculturalism category* classifies appeals for: (1) "The enforcement or encouragement of cultural integration"; and (2) "for cultural homogeneity in society."

alternative scale. In particular, the difference between the authoritarian and democratic appeals in the Electoral Authoritarianism Scale is almost twice as large as those registered by the Authoritarian Emphasis Scale (0.44 compared to 0.24, respectively). Consequently, the Electoral Authoritarianism Scale derived in this chapter is clearly to be preferred when it comes to distinguishing the appeals of these regimes.[21]

But does this chapter's electoral authoritarian appeal scale actually predict electoral authoritarianism? Can we, in other words, tell whether a regime is electoral authoritarian or not based on how high its ruling parties of leaders score on this scale? To explore this, I perform a second, more general test of the external validity of the strongman electoral authoritarian appeal scale: I compare its performance in predicting electoral authoritarianism to a range of other macro-level factors, representing the leading theories of electoral authoritarianism that I have examined in Chapter 3. Specifically, I estimate logit models of electoral authoritarianism[22] using the indicators of GDP per capita, oil and gas wealth, and military personnel per capita – variables representing the alternative theories that these regimes tend to rise in poorer, resource-rich countries, where people are more easily controlled with patronage, and in states with greater repressive capacity. I also use indicators for the period since 1989, years since independence, high- and low-intensity conflict, and the percentage of autocracies in a country's neighborhood, to respectively capture claims that electoral autocracies have tended to emerge after the Cold War, in newly independent and more conflict-prone states (Sambanis 2004; Regan and Bell 2010), and in countries less exposed to external pressures to democratize (K. S. Gleditsch and Ward 2006; Levitsky and

---

[21] There are two potential reasons why the alternative Authoritarian Emphasis Scale underperforms when identifying electoral authoritarian appeals. First, the three extra appeal categories it includes are primarily associated with right-wing, conservative electoral authoritarian regimes. This makes the more ideologically neutral or left-oriented electoral autocracies get lower scores on this scale, deflating the overall average for this regime category. Second, the authoritarian scale of Bakker and Hobolt does not consider the strong emphasis that authoritarian incumbents place on democracy and the democratic nature of their rule in their appeals. This omits a defining characteristic of these regimes' legitimizing narratives, again reducing the score they receive on the scale.

[22] As before, I measure electoral autocracies with a dummy variable constructed with data from the Authoritarian Regimes Dataset (ver. 5.0).

Way 2010a). Finally, to account for the thesis that presidential systems might have a greater propensity to decay into electoral authoritarianism (O'Donnell 1994), I use an indicator for the type of political system, denoting presidential, parliamentary, and assembly-elected president systems.[23] I provide the summary statistics of these variables in Part 4 of the Online Appendix to this chapter.

The results from this analysis, presented as odds ratios in Table 4.2,[24] suggest that the extent to which incumbents subscribe to the doctrine of strong-armed, plebiscitarian rule closely predicts whether a country is as an electoral autocracy or not. Specifically, adding the scale of electoral authoritarian appeal significantly improves the fit of the models (as captured by the lower Akaike and Bayesian Information Criteria scores),[25] even after the other prominent predictors of electoral authoritarianism are accounted for. Also, the coefficient on the Electoral Authoritarianism Scale is highly statistically significant across all models in Table 4.2 that contain it, and it is associated with sizable increases in the odds that a country is an electoral autocracy. Specifically, based on the estimates of Model (6),

---

[23] To reduce problems with reverse causality, I employ first-order lags of all these variables, except the indicators for the number of years since independence and the Cold War dummy. Also, because of the considerable skewness in their distributions, I use natural logs of the GDP per capita, log value of oil and gas production, and military personnel per capita variables.

[24] Models (1)-(3) contain the 25-battle-deaths conflict indicator, while models (4)-(6) are estimated with the 1,000-battle-deaths conflict measure, both extracted from the UCDP/PRIO Armed Conflict Dataset (N. P. Gleditsch et al. 2002). Models (1) and (4) exclude both the electoral authoritarian appeals scale and the variables with a greater number of missing values (the political system indicators and the proxies for repressive capacity and resource rents). Their purpose is to serve as "baseline" models against which to measure the improvements in fit when the electoral authoritarianism scale is added, as well as to guard against potential biases due to data missingness. Models (2) and (5) expand the baseline models with the electoral authoritarian appeals scale, while Models (3) and (6) are the "full" models, which include the political system indicators and the repression and resource rents proxies.

[25] Specifically, according to the rule of thumb proposed by Burnham and Anderson (2002), a model with an Akaike Information Criterion (AIC) score greater than ten units from a competing model with the lower AIC has considerably weaker support and should be excluded from further consideration. Based on this criterion, Models (2) and (5), which include the electoral authoritarian appeals scale achieve much lower AIC scores than the baseline Models (1) and (4) that do not contain this variable and should be considered to have a superior fit with the data.

Table 4.2 *Comparing the predictors of electoral authoritarianism (logit estimates)*

	(1)	(2)	(3)	(4)	(5)	(6)
Electoral authoritarianism scale		4.44 (1.10)**	4.61 (1.29)**		4.42 (1.12)**	4.50 (1.34)**
Conflict with >25 battle deaths in the past 3 years	1.65 (0.54)	1.66 (0.52)	1.42 (0.53)			
Conflict with >1,000 battle deaths in the past 3 years				5.74 (3.13)**	4.86 (2.25)**	3.44 (1.23)**
Log per capita income	0.57 (0.19)+	0.49 (0.13)**	0.47 (0.19)+	0.60 (0.18)+	0.51 (0.12)**	0.47 (0.19)+
Log military size			1.52 (1.13)			1.74 (1.17)
Log value of oil & gas production			1.05 (0.059)			1.04 (0.057)
Assembly-elected president			0.29 (0.28)			0.26 (0.27)
Parliamentary system			0.24 (0.22)			0.22 (0.22)

Table 4.2 (*cont.*)

	(1)	(2)	(3)	(4)	(5)	(6)
Post–Cold War period	24.8	19.1	10.1	18.3	14.3	8.74
	(76.2)	(41.6)	(21.0)	(49.4)	(30.2)	(18.1)
Years since independence	0.99	1.00	1.00	0.99	1.00	1.00
	(0.0037)	(0.0038)	(0.0038)	(0.0044)[+]	(0.0043)	(0.0042)
Share of Neighbors that	1.01	1.01	1.01	1.02	1.02	1.01
are autocracies	(0.0080)	(0.0084)	(0.010)	(0.0082)*	(0.0087)[+]	(0.010)
Observations	3016	3016	2708	3016	3016	2708
Akaike Information Criterion	1557.96	1419.97	1068.5	1534.01	1400.05	1038.38
Bayesian Information Criterion	1588.02	1456.04	1127.54	1564.07	1436.12	1097.42
Log-likelihood	−773.979	−703.986	−524.251	−762.006	−694.024	−509.19

Note: Estimates represent odds ratios. Robust standard errors clustered by country are given in parentheses. $^{+} p < 0.10$, $^{*} p < 0.05$, $^{**} p < 0.01$

a one standard deviation increase in the scale is associated with doubling of the odds that that country is an electoral autocracy, when all other variables are kept constant.[26]

To use a more intuitive example based on these results, a hypothetical country that has a 50 percent baseline probability of being an electoral autocracy, it will see this risk increase to 67 percent if the score of its incumbent's campaign appeals on the Electoral Authoritarianism Scale increases by one standard deviation. By comparison, one standard deviation increases in the levels of high-intensity conflict in the preceding three-year period, the percentage of neighboring countries that are autocracies, and oil and gas income (ignoring the fact that this last variable is not statistically significant), would raise this country's probability of being electoral authoritarian to 59, 62, and 60 percent, respectively. In turn, a one standard deviation *decline* in GDP per capita will increase this probability from 50 to 62 percent, *ceteris paribus*.[27]

It is hard to understate the significance of these results. They suggest that even this relatively crude scale, capturing the strongman plebiscitarian appeal characteristic of electoral authoritarian leaders and parties, has predictive power greater than the major macro-level structural correlates of electoral authoritarianism. Based on these findings, one can guess whether a regime is electoral authoritarian based on how much its campaign appeals emphasize the hypothesized components of the electoral authoritarian appeal – the need for unity, patriotism, and submission to a strong-armed state, as well as the innate democraticness of this kind of rule in troubled societies. And this conjecture will, on average, be more accurate than attempts to infer the character of such regimes by looking at their levels of poverty, conflict, resource wealth, or repressive capacity, or the influence of neighboring autocracies or democracies.

This again underscores the centrality of the strongman plebiscitarian appeal to electoral authoritarian rule. In this sense, the cumulative

---

[26] The odds ratios are obtained by exponentiating the coefficients in Table 4.2. To calculate the probability changes resulting from shifts in the explanatory variables, I used the following formula: $New\ probabilty = 100 \times \frac{Shift\ in\ odds\ ratio}{1 + Shift\ in\ odds\ ratio}$

[27] I checked the robustness of these estimates with a wide range of different controls and specifications, including models with country-level fixed and random effects to control for idiosyncrasies. All of these analyses (results available on demand) closely match those in Table 4.2.

findings of this and the previous chapter are highly consistent with theoretical expectations: by allowing authoritarian forces to take advantage of crises and turmoil and secure genuine popular support, the strongman plebiscitarian appeal contributes to electoral authoritarianism more than these regimes' capacity to repress, bribe, and brainwash societies into submission.

Conclusion

This chapter examines a central tenet of this book's theoretical framework: that electoral authoritarian regimes have legitimized their rule with a coherent set of appeals and a governing doctrine designed to attract the genuine support of broad social strata in countries affected by profound crises and upheavals. Rising against this background, strongman electoral authoritarian incumbents offer an alternative social order that combines the promise of centralized, decisive, and forceful rule, characteristic of authoritarianism, with plebiscitarian legitimation that imposes a degree of representativeness and restraint.

The chapter tests these propositions with a quantitative cross-national content analysis of party manifestos using data from the CMP dataset, as well as with a qualitative analysis of representative appeals from the electoral programs of the ruling parties in Russia's and Mexico's electoral autocracies. The results of these analyses show that compared to incumbents in liberal democracies, elected autocrats have placed much greater emphasis on appeals to patriotism, nationalism, and the need for strong government, as well as on the need to surrender some freedoms to protect the state in times of crisis. At the same time, electoral authoritarian incumbents have placed greater rhetorical emphasis on democratic principles and individual freedoms. These seemingly contradictory appeals closely match the two core legitimizing arguments of these regimes, outlined by this book's theory of the crisis origins of electoral authoritarianism. The first is that in times of crisis, the most democratic system is the one that represents broad popular demands for restoring stability by any means. The second is that in such circumstances, individual and group freedoms can only be achieved by uniting behind the regime that is most capable of guaranteeing order.

The key contribution of this and the previous chapters' analyses is to highlight the doctrine of strong-armed, plebiscitarian, quasi-emergency rule as the most distinctive campaign appeal of electoral authoritarian regimes, and to associate it with a clear set of background circumstances that make it credible to broad social strata. This bridges the critical gap between the key structural conditions – deep security, economic, and political crises, which according to the findings in Chapter 3 have been most closely associated with the rise of electoral authoritarianism – and the ability of these regimes to win genuine popular support and rule through the ballot box.

The findings of this chapter also fill an important gap in the literature, which thus far has not identified a systematic legitimizing doctrine that allows electoral authoritarian regimes to attract sincere popular support. Accounting for this authentic mass appeal of electoral autocracies is crucial for two reasons. First, it is bound to determine the effectiveness of the more traditional instruments of authoritarian control like repression, clientelism, propaganda, and vote fraud. The reasons are simple: if majorities in troubled societies genuinely support electoral authoritarianism as a system that can restore order and stability, they will also be likely to accept the use of repression, clientelism, and propaganda in the name of these goals. Also, when employed with popular backing, these tactics become more vicious, intimidating, and devastating, and far less prone to backfire.

Recognizing the strongman appeal of electoral autocracies can also help us to better identify these regimes. Existing categorizations of political regimes recognize electoral autocracies based on their observed transgressions against the norms of democratic behavior. However, these infringements are often subtle and hard to discern. As a result, electoral autocracies are often identified late in their trajectory, when they commit gross violations of democratic procedures, human rights, and other liberties. This can be remedied to a large extent if we account for the core legitimizing doctrines and public appeals of incumbents in electoral systems, which as Levitsky and Ziblatt (2018, 21) point out, can serve as a "litmus test" for identifying authoritarian political forces even before they consolidate power. As electoral authoritarian leaders and parties quite vocally and consistently signal their intentions to breach democratic principles, this approach allows us not only to better recognize electoral autocracies, but also to predict which leaders and parties are most likely to establish such regimes should they assume power.

The empirical analysis in this chapter has shown that diverse electoral authoritarian political actors from across the world have indeed followed such a clearly identifiable script in their popular appeals. But a crucial question remains: how do these elected strongman appeals work? What kinds of outlooks make popular majorities willing – and in many cases, eager – to sacrifice their liberties and support strongman parties and leaders that promise to solve their problems with a firm hand? Why are these strongman parties and leaders able to regularly trounce their more moderate – and often better established – oppositions even in relatively free and fair elections? And why do popular majorities continue to support many of these regimes, which claim to bring order and stability even after those regimes have themselves become the sources of conflict, economic stagnation, and crisis in their countries? I explore these questions in the next two empirical chapters, which trace the relationships between crises, electoral authoritarian appeals, and popular opinion.

5 | Crises, Popular Opinion, and the Realignment of Political Competition in Russia

[A]ll the great statesmen of every age and every country, including the most absolute despots, have regarded the popular imagination as the basis of their power, and have never attempted to govern in opposition to it.

Gustave Le Bon (1896)

The two preceding chapters tested this book's crisis-origins theory of electoral authoritarianism from a "high-altitude," macro-level perspective.[1] Chapter 3 showed that security and economic crises are the most robust structural predictors of both the rise of electoral authoritarian regimes and their durability. Chapter 4, in turn, demonstrated that electoral autocracies from across the world have adopted a remarkably similar "strongman" appeal, designed to take advantage of their countries' troubled histories and traumatic crises and to help them seize power through the polling booth. Cumulatively, these findings show that rising in the wake of deep turmoil, electoral authoritarian regimes have sought to attract genuine majority support by promising a strong-armed but popularly endorsed leadership, which is "uniquely capable" of resolving their societies' troubles.

These background circumstances and authoritarian appeals do not directly produce electoral authoritarianism, however. According to this book's analytic framework, they only give rise to such regimes by molding and taking advantage of mass opinion. Structural conditions like economic and security crises foster strongman electoral

---

[1] Different versions of parts of this chapter appeared in the author's original article "It's the Stability, Stupid! How the Quest to Restore Order After the Soviet Collapse Shaped Russian Popular Opinion," in *Comparative Politics* (2018) 50(3): 347–390 (© 2020 The Graduate Center, CUNY), and chapter "The Logic of Vladimir Putin's Popular Appeal," in Valerie Bunce, Karrie Koesel, and Jessica Weiss (eds.), *Citizens and the State in Authoritarian Regimes: Comparing Russia and China* (New York: Oxford University Press, 2020, 217–249 [© Oxford University Press 2020]), and are reprinted with the permission of these publishers.

authoritarianism by reshaping the beliefs of decisive majorities in favor of this kind of rule. And for the authoritarian legitimizing strategies to work, they must closely mirror the attitudes of the affected constituencies. Above all, the latent, unarticulated popular desire for strongman electoral authoritarian rule must exist before this type of regime can be successfully promoted by authoritarian parties and leaders. Demand must, in other words, precede and shape the supply. As Beetham (1991, 11) succinctly put it: "[a] given power relationship is not legitimate because people believe in its legitimacy, but because it can be *justified in terms* of their beliefs." Hence, despite the compelling evidence in favor of the crisis theory of electoral authoritarianism in the preceding chapters, the final link in the causal chain remains to be verified. We need to confirm that crises mold mass opinion so that electoral authoritarianism can be successfully promoted as the best – or least bad – regime alternative.

The idea that electoral autocracies achieve much more through mass persuasion than with coercion (in the form of repression, clientelism, propaganda, vote fraud, and so on) is at the heart of this book's argument. But for this sort of persuasion to work, three basic conditions must be in place. First, there must be a receptive audience. In particular, if the rise of electoral authoritarianism is indeed catalyzed by popular demands for restoring order and stability in troubled societies, these outlooks must already dominate mass attitudes about politics, trumping other preferences, attachments, and considerations. To put it differently, for electoral authoritarianism to emerge in societies gripped by turmoil, mass political opinion must have one defining property: the quest for stability must achieve "complete dominion of the spirit, either to crush every other instinct or to enlist it" for its purposes, to use Walter Lippmann's (1922, 10–11) remark. Above all, primordial anxieties about physical and economic security – what Inglehart (2018) calls "survival values" – should take precedence over ideological and policy preferences, demands for greater freedom and opportunities for self-expression. Collectivist values like demands for unity and nationalism ought to displace tolerance and undermine intergroup and interpersonal trust. Ultimately, fears of political instability and weakness of state authority must eclipse concerns about the abuse of power.

Second, for these opinion shifts to provide the fertile soil needed for strongman electoral authoritarianism to sprout, they must follow in the wake of deep, traumatic crises and upheavals. Simply put, the idea that strong-armed rule is the best available government can only hold sway over public opinion when backed up by traumatic and widely shared memories of turmoil and injustice under alternative orders (on this dynamic, see also Slater 2010). And if this book's theory of electoral authoritarian legitimation is valid, the reverse pattern should also apply: gloomy outlooks and authoritarian predispositions will be less prevalent in periods of relative stability, when painful experiences of turmoil have not yet taken hold, or have faded from living memory. These sentiments must therefore vary even in highly unstable countries, which have had spells of electoral authoritarian rule. Most of all, traumas and fears of instability must be at their peak in periods just before the rise of electoral authoritarianism – they must be even higher than during the reign of these regimes.

Finally, if the rise and persistence of electoral autocracies is mainly a product of their strongman appeal in troubled societies, rather than their coercive power, we should observe a specific mechanism which translates popular anxieties into a persistent electoral advantage for these regimes. The strongman appeal of these regimes must be compelling enough to transform the mass obsession with stability in troubled societies into a *new cleavage*: the choice to support or reject a strong-armed, authoritarian government, which will pursue these objectives by any means necessary.

Promoting themselves as champions of stability in this fashion enables authoritarian parties and leaders to draw away the great mass of crisis-weary citizens away from their competitors, and to divide the opposition. This is a mechanism I labeled as the elected strongman heresthetic in Chapter 2, extending the concept of political issue manipulation developed by William Riker (1986, 1996) to autocracies. Struggling to overcome their ideological and programmatic differences against this backdrop, the diverse constituencies opposing electoral authoritarianism will tend to embrace a multitude of competing alternatives, splitting the antiregime vote. Those who put a premium on stability, on the other hand, are likely to set their other, less salient differences aside and unite in support of a strongman regime. By encouraging the opposition to divide and their adherents to band together, the elected strongman regime cleavage may allow even authoritarian incumbents who lack clear majority support to maintain long-term electoral dominance.

The arguments can be summarized in the following propositions:

H1 The desire to restore and preserve stability becomes the primary driver of mass opinion in societies plagued by severe crises, aligning popular attitudes across different domains with this purpose;

H2 Crises precede the rise of stability-seeking outlooks among the population, which, in turn, precedes the rise of electoral authoritarianism;

H3 Authoritarian political forces take advantage of such realignments in mass opinion to introduce a new major cleavage in the political competition – the choice to accept or reject strong-armed but popularly endorsed rule as a remedy for the present crisis;

H4 This new architecture of choice allows authoritarian parties and candidates to discourage, divide, delegitimize, and ultimately defeat mainstream programmatic oppositions at the ballot box and with minimum coercion.

This chapter will trace the interplay between socioeconomic crises, popular opinion shifts, and the rise of electoral authoritarianism in the paradigmatic case of post-Communist Russia. As I have elaborated in detail in Chapter 1, the Russian case provides an unparalleled opportunity to verify the micro-foundations of elected strongman legitimation proposed by this book's theoretical framework, for two reasons. First, Russia is one of the most studied countries beyond the Western established democracies, offering an unparalleled wealth of high-quality data for this analysis. Second, Russia's electoral authoritarianism, consolidated under Vladimir Putin, has been the most influential role model for similar regimes across the globe. I verify this in Chapter 6, which examines whether the link between crises, opinion patterns, and regime legitimation strategies observed in Russia holds across the globe.

The Logic of the Lesser Evil: Why Have Russians Supported Vladimir Putin?

To reliably win and maintain power through the ballot box, autocrats must be popular among their citizens. Very few, however, have managed to endear themselves to their populations so quickly and for so long as Russia's Vladimir Putin. When first appointed as acting prime minister in August 1999, Putin was virtually unknown among ordinary Russians. His popularity ratings were actually negative: as I show in Figure 5.1 below, the share of Russians disapproving his performance was slightly greater than the percent approving. Nevertheless, in just one month, a string of terrorist attacks across Russia and Putin's brutal military response against the breakaway region of Chechnya turned him into an instant star. By November 1999, his approval ratings shot up to over 80 percent. And they have remained high ever since. Over almost two decades since his rise to power, Putin's approval averaged at about 75 percent. It never dropped below 60 percent until 2020 – even when he faced an unprecedented protest wave against his rule in 2011–2013. And his ratings again soared to over 80 percent after the annexation of Crimea in February 2014 – and hovered around this level for four full years after that.

How could a blatantly authoritarian, and personally bland and uncharismatic leader like Putin sustain such a high degree of popular support for so long? None of the existing explanations in the literature

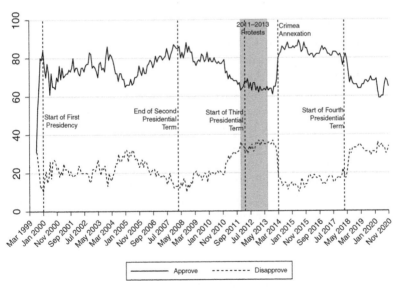

Figure 5.1 Percentage approving and disapproving of Vladimir Putin's performance in office
Source: Levada Center

provide satisfactory answers to this puzzle. One commonsensical explanation of Putin's broad popular acclaim, embraced by many in the West, is that it has been faked: that Russian pollsters and survey responders feign admiration for their leader because they fear reprisals. But this perception is wrong. First, there is consensus that Russia's survey organizations have not tampered with their surveys to paint a rosier picture of Putin's popularity.[2] Second, there is substantial empirical evidence that the overwhelming majority of Russians have not tended to falsely profess admiration for their leaders; indeed, the opposite has been true (Rose 2007). On this topic, a growing number of surveys in recent years have probed Putin's approval ratings with techniques like list and endorsement experiments, which allow researchers to estimate the rate of preference falsification.[3] They have consistently found that only about 6–9 percent of Russian survey respondents profess fake support for Putin when asked a direct question – a proportion that is small, relative to his overall approval, and close to the estimation error of the list experiment technique (Colton and Hale 2014; Frye et al. 2017). These studies, as well as a vast array of diverse and sophisticated opinion research carried out over the years in Russia, suggest that by and large, the popularity of Vladimir Putin has been genuine.

Among those who accepted this fact, the most prominent explanation of Putin's appeal is that it is a product of Russia's robust economic performance under his leadership (see e.g. Treisman 2011a; White and McAllister 2008). But this account has also proven to be inadequate. While economics certainly played a role, it fails to explain the most important shifts in Russian presidential approval. Economic outlooks cannot account for why Russians put up with Putin's predecessor Boris Yeltsin despite the colossal economic disaster he presided over, or why they became so quickly and thoroughly enamored of Putin long before he delivered any tangible improvements. They also cannot tell us why many Russians unexpectedly turned up to protest Putin's rule in 2011–2012, when their economy was doing relatively well (see Treisman 2014) or why they rallied back behind him in unprecedented numbers after the

---

[2] The prime example is the Levada Survey Center, which has been relentlessly persecuted for its independence, professionalism, and objective analysis throughout Putin's time in power (Treisman 2013).

[3] On the design and effectiveness of the list and endorsement experiment techniques, see e.g. Glynn (2013) and Rosenfeld, Imai, and Shapiro (2016).

Crimea annexation, as the economic fallout from the conflict ravaged their living standards (see Hale 2018).

Indeed, there seems to be an even more fundamental disconnect between Putin's perceived performance in office – economic and otherwise – and his popularity. Despite approving Putin's overall conduct, Russian survey respondents have been remarkably critical of his actual achievements in office *throughout his entire reign*. And they have not been afraid to declare this publicly. I illustrate this in Figure 5.2, which chronicles Russian popular evaluations of Vladimir Putin's achievements across eight key substantive areas, ranging from foreign policy to domestic issues such as the standard of living, income inequality, and corruption.[4] The middle panel in this figure shows that on the eve of his second reelection in 2012, a clear majority (of about 60 percent) have registered improvements in *only one* major issue area during Putin's reign: the global influence of Russia. At the same time, less than half of the respondents believed that Russia's political stability and the stability of the North Caucasus – two of Putin's most touted achievements – increased at all during his rule. All other performance assessments were thoroughly negative. Over 70 percent of the respondents found that income inequality increased under Putin, and a majority of 51 percent deemed that corruption worsened in his time in office. Just 33 percent detected improvements in the standard of living – the other oft-brandished accomplishment of Putin's rule – as opposed to 34 percent who thought that living standards had in fact worsened. Yet in the end, despite their remarkably bleak evaluations, a full 66 percent of respondents in the same survey said they had voted for Putin in the 2012 election.

And this pattern is not unique to the 2012 election, when Putin faced historically low ratings and an unprecedented protest wave. Russians had similar, and in some areas, even worse assessments of Putin's performance in 2016, when his ratings were at a record high after the Crimea invasion. In turn, their evaluations were only slightly better in 2008 – the other high-water mark of Putin's popularity. Most Russians, as these results clearly

[4] The data for the left-hand and center graphs in Figure 5.2 are from the 2008 and 2012 Russia Electoral Study surveys carried out by the Demoscope group at the Institute of Sociology of the Russian Academy of Sciences, based on nationally representative samples of 1,130 and 1,682 respondents (see Colton et al. 2014, Colton 2017). The right-hand graph data comes from the 2016 Russia election study that was carried out by the Levada Center based on a nationally representative sample of 2,010 respondents.

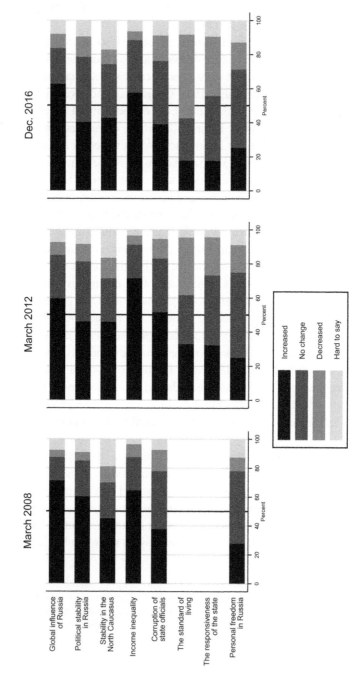

Figure 5.2 In the years since Putin first became president, have the following things increased, decreased, or remained unchanged?
Source: Russia Election Study surveys for 2007–2008, 2012, and 2016

demonstrate, were not drawn to Putin because of his economic and other performance in office. Quite the contrary, they supported him *in spite of* his poor perceived record of achievement in most crucial areas – ranging from the economy to dealing with the North Caucasus.

What explains this inconsistent behavior? I claim that the reasons for the contradictory popular sentiments toward Putin lie in Russia's catastrophic decline in the years before his rise. Deeply traumatized by these experiences, Russians have evaluated Putin's leadership with entirely different criteria from those used by citizens of stable Western democracies. Instead of asking "have things become better under Putin's leadership?" when going to the polls, Russians asked "will things be worse if someone else takes over?" Putin's popularity, in other words, has been primarily rooted in fear. Not the fear of repression for failing to support Russia's "tough" and "unforgiving" leader, but the dread that *without* his strong-armed rule, the country would plunge into chaos and instability, and suffer miseries far worse than life under authoritarian rule. Terrified of the alternatives, most Russians were content to live under Putin's guardianship, thankful for the modicum of protection he provides, and hoping that he will eventually deliver on the promise of improving their living standards and government.

We see direct evidence of this outlook in the responses to a survey question that Russia's premier independent polling center Levada has fielded almost every year during Putin's reign. I display these responses in the left panel of Figure 5.3. Asked why their compatriots trusted Vladimir Putin, only about 15–30 percent of Russians across the entire 2001–2015 period said they did so because he was adequately tackling the country's problems. A combined total of between 65 and 80 percent believed that people had faith in Putin either because they *hoped he would deal with Russia's problems in the future*, or because they *saw no other reliable alternative*. Put differently, most Russians embraced Putin not for what he achieved, but for what they thought he prevented and for what they hoped he might eventually deliver.[5]

---

[5] In responding to this question, Russian survey respondents did not rationalize the behavior of their fellow citizens, with whom they did not necessarily agree. Instead, as I show in Part 1 of the Online Appendix to this chapter, they seemed to project onto them their own reasons for supporting Putin. Furthermore, this logic of delayed and suspended accountability, as I also demonstrate in Part 1 of the Online Appendix, allowed Putin to maintain support even among dissatisfied citizens, who might have voted him out of office in different circumstances.

And Russians did not only tolerate Putin's mediocre governing performance. Throughout his reign, they also wished to live in a considerably more democratic system from the one he maintained. I capture these outlooks in the right panel of Figure 5.3, which records the average assessments Russians gave their *actual* and *desired* political systems on a 1–10 scale, ranging from closed authoritarianism to full democracy.[6] This graph shows that even in the first, "honeymoon" decade of Putin's rule, Russian citizens gave his regime a remarkably accurate grade of slightly above 5 on this scale – the midpoint between democracy and full dictatorship. At the same time, they constantly expressed a desire to live in a system that was about 2 points higher on this scale – a system much closer to a proper democracy. In other words, for the average Russian, Putinism was always far from her or his ideal, more democratic system. Still, they kept on supporting their underperforming and overly authoritarian leader.

Popular majorities, especially those of the size of Russia's, do not willingly put up with a leadership that falls so far short of their expectations unless they believe that it serves another, more immediate and essential purpose. This overriding purpose of the Putin regime, which underpinned its leader's extraordinary popularity, was to restore and maintain Russia's stability. Its attitudinal roots, as I hinted above, lay in the extraordinary trauma that stemmed from Russia's cataclysmic decline since the late 1980s.

Russia's Formative Crises and the Search for a Strongman "Savior"

[T]he collapse of the Soviet Union was a major geopolitical disaster of the century. As for the Russian nation, it became a genuine drama. Tens of millions of our co-citizens and compatriots found themselves outside Russian territory. Moreover, the epidemic of disintegration infected Russia itself.

Vladimir Putin, 2005 Annual Address to the Federal Assembly[7]

---

[6] The data in the left panel of Figure 5.3 is drawn from the New Russia Barometer surveys (Rose 2010), carried out by the Levada Center on behalf of the Center of Study of Public Policy at the University of Strathclyde, UK. For more details, see www.cspp.strath.ac.uk/catalog1_0.html (accessed 05/25/2021).

[7] Official website of the Kremlin (2005, April 25). http://en.kremlin.ru/events/president/transcripts/22931 (accessed on 5/7/2021).

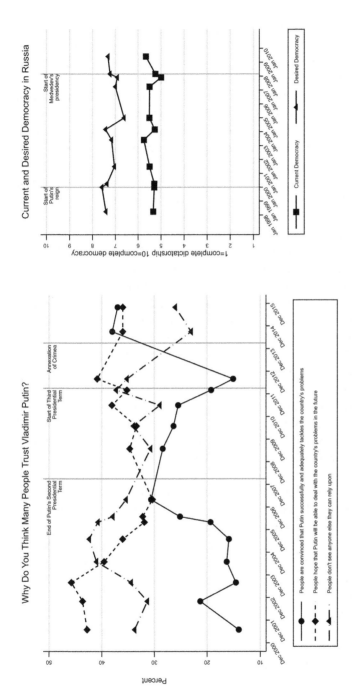

Figure 5.3 Reasons for trusting Putin and democracy assessments and preferences
Source: Levada Center

The popular mood that has underpinned Putin's rule was forged not by one, but three successive catastrophic crises, which struck Russia in the last two decades of the twentieth century. The Russian case, in this sense, is extreme not only in terms of economic decline and conflict – the minimal prerequisites for an electoral autocracy-enabling crisis, according to this book's analytic framework. At every stage of Russia's process of decay, ordinary Russians also suffered a massive existential shock, which gradually realigned popular opinion in favor of elected strongman rule.

The first of Russia's triple crises was the collapse of Communism; it was set off in the late 1980s, when Mikhail Gorbachev's attempt to resuscitate Soviet socialism through political and economic liberalization backfired spectacularly. Despite all the flaws of the Communist belief system, its sudden collapse had a devastating effect on Russia's collective psyche. When faith in Communism crumbled, there was no compelling guiding philosophy or belief system left in its wake to provide direction and hope as Russia plunged into an existential crisis. This produced a rootless and cynical population (Inglehart 2018, 159) that rejected elaborate ideologies and partisan attachments in favor of charismatic leaders who promised results and strong leadership, or who could at the very least supply the emotional gratification of populism (Hanson 2010, ch. 6). Hopelessly disillusioned with parties and ideologies, many Russians became inclined to seek messiahs.

The second crisis that decisively shaped contemporary Russia and Putinism was a political and security breakdown. It was triggered by the actual disintegration of the Soviet Union, which began when Gorbachev's reforms mobilized a cascade of ethno-nationalist protest movements across the republics of the USSR. These were quickly hijacked by local officials, seeking to carve out more power and to secure their political future (Beissinger 2002). However, the centrifugal tendencies generated by the nationalist mobilizations, coupled with the failure of the hardliner coup aimed to contain them, pushed the Soviet Union beyond the point of no return, leading to its dissolution in December 1991.

Most Russians vehemently opposed the dissolution of the USSR – a sentiment that persists to this day. They wanted the Communist system to be reformed or abolished, but to preserve the Soviet Union, as they strongly identified with its achievements and superpower status. For them, the dismemberment of the USSR instilled a permanent sense of diminished national self-worth, betrayal, and resentment (see Kasamara and Sorokina 2012; Guillory 2014). The crumbling of the Soviet Empire did not just hurt Russian national pride; it also had a direct personal effect on the lives of many Russians. Virtually over-night, 70 million (or 1 in 5) inhabitants of the Soviet Union – the vast majority of them ethnic Russians – found themselves living outside of their national "homeland," in hostile newly independent states, all of which were seeking to break free from the Russian orbit (Kotkin 2002, 27). This trauma of imperial collapse led most Russians to seek leader-ship that would stop the seemingly endless disintegration of their country, restore the dominance it had enjoyed in the former USSR, and reclaim its place among the world's major powers.

The third and arguably most consequential crisis that presaged Putin's rise escalated as Russia attempted to complete its political and economic liberalization under the leadership of Boris Yeltsin. Always the consummate populist, Yeltsin embarked on the task of rapidly transforming the most dysfunctional state structure and largest rust belt in history with radical "shock therapy" market reforms. This turned into a catastrophe. The weakened and bankrupt central state could not enforce the necessary fiscal discipline and property rights, so Russia's transition quickly deteriorated into a process more akin to highway robbery than the rise of an orderly capitalist society (Goldman 2003). The result was the largest peacetime decline in history – an economic cataclysm more than twice as intense as the Great Depression of the 1930s (Balzer 2002, ch. 5; Kotkin 2008). To put things in perspective, during the Great Depression of the 1930s, the particularly hard-hit German economy contracted by about 20 percent at its peak decline between 1928 and 1933, and recovered to pre-Depression levels in about seven years, by 1935. In contrast, the Russian economy experienced a monstrous 42 percent decline between 1990 and 1998, and it took sixteen years to recover to pre-collapse levels in 2006.[8]

The sheer scale of human suffering caused by this calamity can only be compared to the effects of full-scale warfare. By a conservative estimate, Russia's population declined by about 5 percent, or 7 million people, in the decade and a half after the Soviet collapse in

---

[8] Trends calculated using the Maddison Project economic data (Bolt and van Zanden 2019).

1991.[9] This is three times higher than the casualty rate Russia suffered in World War I, which was, in turn, the highest of any nation participating in the first global conflict. It is also greater than the death tolls of both the Bolshevik revolution and the Stalinist collectivization and purges. Outside of major global conflicts, only China's "Great Leap Forward" and resulting famine produced a larger population loss (Eberstadt 2010). The psychological toll of this collapse was equally unprecedented. As life expectancy and living standards declined to below third-world levels, the Russian population developed feelings of hopelessness unseen even under the worst wartime circumstances (Gessen 2014).

The political fallout from Russia's disastrous transition made things even worse. Right from the outset, Yeltsin's authority was challenged by a coalition of opportunists and hardliners, who controlled the newly empowered Parliament and sought to take advantage of the turmoil. The standoff escalated into the first major armed conflict on the streets of Moscow since the Bolshevik revolution, with a casualty toll of over 1,000 as Russian army tanks pummeled Yeltsin's opponents, barricaded in the Parliament building, into submission. Another armed conflict erupted on Russia's periphery a year later, in 1994, when Moscow intervened to crush the tiny rebellious province of Chechnya. By 1996, the invasion had turned into a nightmare. With 14,000 Russian military casualties and 100,000 civilian deaths, this conflict prompted a humiliating retreat, which once again underscored how far Russia had fallen from its superpower status (S. Smith 2006, ch. 8; Treisman 2011b).

These conflicts fortified the sense of impending doom among ordinary Russians. Coupled with apocalyptic socioeconomic decline and the bewildering surge of lawlessness and violence on Russia's streets (Glenny 2009, ch. 3; Volkov 2016), they instilled a palpable fear that the country would soon disintegrate in a bloody civil war, much like Yugoslavia (Colton 2008). One of the most common metaphors ordinary Russians used to describe the situation was that they felt as if they

---

[9] Even this figure is substantially lower than the actual depopulation rate in Russia, as it does not account for the large migration inflows Russia experienced in this period (mostly from the former Soviet Central Asian republics). Removing the effect of migration almost doubles the Russian population decline, bringing it to about 13 million (Eberstadt 2010, 6).

were living on a volcano, which could erupt at any moment (Shevchenko 2008).

The Russian case offers an unparalleled wealth of empirical data showing how such popular anxieties translate into support for strongman rule. But the most straightforward summary of this process comes from one survey question, asked repeatedly since 1989 by the Levada Center. It was formulated as follows: "are there, in your opinion, sometimes situations in our nation when the people need a strong and imperious leader, a 'strong hand?'" Respondents could choose from three substantive responses: (1) "our people always need a strong hand"; (2) "there are situations (such as now), when you have to concentrate all power in the same hands"; and (3) "concentrating all power in one person's hands should never be allowed."

I display the aggregate distribution of these attitudes over time in Figure 5.4 (for reference, I include vertical lines denoting key events). The pattern we observe is striking. In November 1989, at a time of the fall of the Berlin Wall, a strong plurality of 45 percent of the Russian population believed that executive power should *never* be put in the hands of one person. This is an impressive level of support for liberal principles for a society that had spent seventy-two years under the yoke of one of history's most brutal dictatorships and had never experienced democracy before. At this time, only a quarter of the Russian population insisted that their country always needed a heavy-handed ruler, and another 15 percent thought that the current situation warranted one. This clearly contradicts theories that Russians have been somehow culturally predisposed to embrace authoritarianism (see e.g. Pipes 2004). In 1989, as these results indicate, most of them were willing to embrace a far more liberal order than Russia had ever experienced.

But then disaster struck. Traumatized by the Soviet collapse and the political and economic cataclysm of the transition, Russians sharply reversed their views on the kind of leadership Russia needed. By 1996, a solid majority of almost 70 percent supported either a temporary or permanent strong-armed rule. Only about 20 percent held on to liberal outlooks and rejected any calls for concentration of executive power. This was the most crucial shift in Russian popular opinion. A decisive majority of Russians demanded a strong-armed leader – someone in Vladimir Putin's mold – many years *before* he entered politics on the national stage. And these sentiments have remained virtually frozen

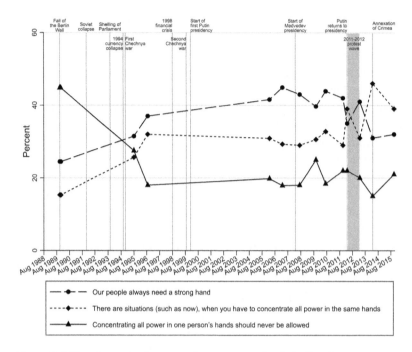

Figure 5.4 Popular attitudes toward strong-armed rule in Russia
Source: Levada Center

since 1996, changing very little throughout the reign of Putin since 2000.

This pattern of support for strongman rule in Russia closely matches one of this book's key predictions, summarized by hypothesis 2 in this chapter: that popular majorities embrace a strongman regime only in the wake of a deep, traumatic crisis which has threatened their existential security. And this popular demand for strongman rule emerged *before* a viable leader, who could consolidate such a regime, stepped into the limelight – and long before he fully seized the reins of power. Clearly, Russians did not develop a penchant for strongman rule because of some cultural fondness for authoritarianism (see also Hale 2011), or under the influence of Putinist propaganda or coercion. On the contrary, Putin rode to power on a rising wave of authoritarian mass sentiment, which had formed in response to Russia's cataclysms many years before Russia's future leader held any sway over public opinion, or the levers of power.

But could it be that the authoritarian shift in Russian mass attitudes was somehow manufactured by Putin's predecessor and mentor Boris Yeltsin? It is indeed true, as I elaborate further in the next section, that Russia's electoral autocracy was, in fact, established by president Yeltsin, who, despite being perceived as Russia's great liberalizer, regularly resorted to authoritarian tactics to survive politically and gain some control over the chaotic post-Soviet transition. Nevertheless, Russia's beleaguered first president could not muster the capacity to produce monumental opinion shifts like those in Figure 5.4 by any stretch of the imagination. For one thing, the Yeltsin-era Kremlin did not have enough control of the Russia's media to control the public discourse (Burrett 2011). Instead, causality flowed in the opposite direction: Yeltsin's authoritarian behavior – the subduing of Parliament, the Chechnya invasion, and ultimately, appointing Putin as his successor – was, for the most part, an effort to appease the growing popular demand for strong-armed leadership that would restore order in Russia (see Colton 2008, chap. 11 and Jack 2005). Similarly, the propaganda machines of the Yeltsin, and later the Putin presidencies, did not manufacture the growing authoritarianism of the Russian public. They rode on its coattails.

Yeltsin's, and later Putin's brands of authoritarianism were shaped by these opinion currents in another crucial way. The Russians who endorsed an authoritarian shift in the wake of their country's cataclysms did not want just any kind of strongman rule. They desired a strong-armed, but electoral regime. Support for multiparty elections among all Russian respondents never dropped below 60 percent even in some of the worst periods of the post-transitional crisis in the 1990s. After Putin's rise, it actually increased to above 80 percent.[10] Thus, even as they demanded a strongman, most Russians wanted him to rule through the voting booth. To Russian citizens, reeling from decades of mismanagement under a completely unchecked Communist dictatorship and an abortive process of democratization, electoral authoritarianism under Boris Yeltsin and later, Vladimir Putin, seemed like the most attractive, middle-ground solution for their problems.

This cautious outlook also made Russians remarkably tolerant of their regime's poor performance. Because of their overriding emphasis on stability, which the electoral authoritarian system seemed best able

---

[10] This data on support of multiparty elections and closed dictatorship is drawn from the New Russia Barometer (NRB) surveys (Rose 2010).

to provide, Russian citizens had put up with an astounding degree of government incompetence, corruption, and blatant unresponsiveness. And they were willing to suppress their underlying aspiration to live in a more democratic system as unsuitable for Russia's dire circumstances, at least until better times arrived.

This sentiment is perfectly captured by an oft-used Russian adage: "[w]hen there is a fire, you don't ask who the fireman is" (cited in Garrels 2016, 35). Assuming the role of this proverbial fireman in Russia's most catastrophic and combustible crisis allowed Yeltsin and especially Putin – along with the electoral authoritarian regimes they led – to literally get away with mass murder (see e.g. Dunlop 2014; Politkovskaya 2007), as well as with a tremendous degree of incompetence, mismanagement, and corruption.

But the popular attitudes that gave such tremendous leeway to Russia's leaders did not materialize on their own. Before they could be wielded as tools for maintaining electoral dominance, people's demands for stability had to be appropriated by Putin, and to no small degree, his predecessor Boris Yeltsin. They had to be pushed to center stage and framed so that most Russians would see their electoral authoritarian regime as the only viable alternative for maintaining order and addressing the crisis. In other words, the demand for strongman rule had to be met by supply. This was primarily achieved through persuasion – not coercion, clientelism, or "brainwashing," but by making a compelling case for electoral authoritarian rule as the only sensible solution for Russia's woes.

The Strongman Heresthetic in Post-Soviet Russia

To put it bluntly, somebody had to be the boss in the country; that's all there was to it.

> Boris Yeltsin, on why he pushed through the
> country's "superpresidential" constitution (cited
> in Gel'man 2015, 55)

The strongman heresthetic that I described in Chapter 2 is an powerful campaign strategy based on a simple ploy: an authoritarian candidate seeks to associate himself (so far, they have always been male) with a compelling solution to the most essential problem of society – restoring order in the wake of crisis – for which the other political alternatives have no good answers. When successful, this maneuver allows the authoritarian contender to reconfigure political competition in his favor. It does so by putting his opponents on the losing side on the most important issue of governing, and displacing their other ideological or programmatic appeals as irrelevant. The other crucial facet of the strongman heresthetic is that it gains extra credibility because it is applied by *elected* autocrats. For one thing, it allows them to paint themselves as pragmatic moderates, who can avoid the excesses of both liberal democracy and closed dictatorship in troubled societies. But more importantly, it enables them to claim that their rule is democratic, as it is popularly endorsed at regular elections and because it represents the most fundamental interest of society: national preservation.

In all these regards, the legitimation strategies of Russia's leaders since the Soviet collapse are archetypal examples of the strongman heresthetic. While Vladimir Putin perfected this appeal, the trailblazer, as I have noted earlier, was Russia's first president and presumed democratizer Boris Yeltsin. He discovered the strongman heresthetic as he tried to survive politically and hold the country together in the chaos after the Soviet collapse. Following his populist instincts, Yeltsin framed his 1993 confrontation with Parliament as a crusade against Communist and nationalist hardliners set to throw the country into the throes of another totalitarian dictatorship. This worked well enough with the Russian public, freshly disillusioned by Communist rule, to justify Yeltsin's use of force against his opponents. It also brought him victory in two crucial referendums, inaugurating the "superpresidential" constitution that gave Yeltsin practically unchecked executive powers. This was the "original sin" of Russia's electoral authoritarianism (Fish 2005). In the true spirit of the strongman heresthetic, Yeltsin was able to able to convince enough moderates and democrats to support this curtailment of Russia's democracy as a measure that was meant to save it. In Yeltsin's own words:

I will not deny that the powers of the president in the draft [of the "super-presidential" constitution] really are significant. But what else would you want to see? [This is] a country habituated to tsars and chieftains; a country where clear-cut group interests have not developed, where the bearers of them have not been defined, and where normal parties are only beginning to be born; a country where discipline is not great and legal nihilism runs riot. In such a country, do you want to depend only or mostly on parliament? If you did, within a half-year, if not sooner, people would demand a dictator.

I assure you that such a dictator would be found, and possibly from within that very same parliament. (cited in Colton 2008)

By casting himself in this oversized role of Russia's protector against the evils of another totalitarian dictatorship, Yeltsin took advantage of the realignment of Russian popular opinion after experiencing the catastrophic Soviet decline. He and the system he had built became the country's primary cleavage. Every opinion poll and election turned into a referendum on Yeltsin's electoral authoritarianism as the "least bad" system to guarantee Russia's stability and the country's transition to a stable democracy. This allowed Yeltsin to divide and rule: to exploit the bad reputation and divisions among his opponents and to get away with terrible failure.

But it also forced him to live up to the strongman savior role he had cast himself in. In particular, Yeltsin had to deliver the other end of the electoral authoritarian bargain: to protect Russia not just from the danger of sliding into another tyranny, but also from the excesses of unfettered democracy. He attempted to do this by staging the invasion of the restive republic of Chechnya in 1994. When that and the efforts to stabilize Russia's economy failed, Yeltsin had to appease Russia's increasingly illiberal mass sentiment by choosing three KGB veterans as his prime ministers and potential successors. When he ultimately settled on Vladimir Putin, Yeltsin declared that here was the "smart, energetic and strong" leader Russia needed (see Colton 2008, ch. 16, Jack 2005 and Bohlen 2000).

Putin established his extraordinary popular appeal by playing the role of the effective strongman that Yeltsin never managed to assume after all his failures. His first act as anointed successor was to demonstrate his suitability for that role, rather than simply pledge that he would fulfill this task. In the eyes of the weary Russian public, Putin's brutal campaign to subdue Chechnya in 1999 – a task previously deemed impossible – made him look like the strongman "messiah" who could reverse the country's seemingly unstoppable post-Soviet decline. It also made him stand out head and shoulders above any conceivable alternatives. To ordinary Russians, numbed by at least three decades of sclerotic and failed leadership, Putin's heroic style provided the hope that everyone was desperate for.

Having established his *bona fides* as an effective strongman, Putin quickly moved to institutionalize this image and the advantages it gave him. Unlike his mentor Boris Yeltsin, who used the strongman appeal instinctively, haphazardly, and as many would argue, reluctantly and as a last resort, Putin codified it as his official governing doctrine. And he did so right from the outset, in his very first electoral platform for the presidential campaign of 2000. Published on December 30, 1999, this so-called *Millennium Manifesto* is the definitive political statement of the Putin era. It was simultaneously the most accurate and empathetic acknowledgment of everything Russians feared and hoped for at the end of the 1990s, as well as the most candid – and one might say prophetic – disclosure of the core guiding principles of Vladimir Putin's entire reign (Hill and Gaddy 2015).

The *Millennium Manifesto* is no ordinary electoral platform for another key reason. It is perhaps the most articulate official statement of the strongman electoral authoritarian legitimation formula described in this book. Right from its opening statements, this document frames Putin's presidency as a response to Russia's disastrous decline. It starts off dramatically, predicting that the country faces an imminent catastrophe of historic proportions if it does not pool its resources and unite behind a campaign of national renewal:

Russia is in the midst of one of the most difficult periods in its history. For the first time in the past 200–300 years, it is facing a real threat of sliding to the second, and possibly even third, echelon of world states. We are running out of time for removing this threat.[11]

Next, the *Manifesto* asserts that if it is to avoid this fate, Russia has no alternative but to embrace a strong, tutelary "state power," exercised from within a democratic framework – a thinly veiled reference to Putin's brand of strongman electoral authoritarian rule. Crucially, Putin showcases this hybrid governing system as both more stable and accountable than naked dictatorship:

Russia needs a strong state power and must have it [my emphasis]. I am not calling for totalitarianism. History proves all dictatorships, all authoritarian forms of government are transient. Only democratic systems are intransient. Whatever the shortcomings, mankind has not devised anything superior.

---

[11] Putin et al. (2000), 209–229. Available at (Robert) Alan Kimball's webpage at University of Oregon (https://pages.uoregon.edu/kimball/Putin.htm) (accessed 05/11/2021). The manifesto was originally published in Russian as a magazine article: Vladimir Putin, "Russia at the Turn of the Millennium" ["Rossiia na rubezhe tysiacheletii"], *Nezavisimaya gazeta* 30 (1999).

A strong state power in Russia is a democratic, law-based, workable feder-
ative state [my emphasis].

The *Manifesto* then completes the case for this hybrid regime as the
ideal, middle-of-the-road governing system by implying that it is the
superior solution to Russia's problems when compared to liberal democracy – all without ceasing to be inherently democratic. To do so, the
document underlines that this "strong state" system is established in
response to overwhelming popular demand to address the catastrophic
weakness caused by Russia's liberalization:

For Russians a strong state is not an anomaly which should be got rid of.
Quite the contrary, they see it as a source and guarantor of order and the
initiator and main driving force of any change [my emphasis]. Modern
Russian society does not identify a strong and effective state with
a totalitarian state. We have come to value the benefits of democracy, a law-
based state, and personal and political freedom. At the same time, people are
alarmed by the obvious weakening of state power. *The public looks forward*
to the restoration of the guiding and regulating role of the state to a degree
which is necessary, proceeding from the traditions and present state of the
country [my emphasis].

Having cast stability provided by a strong executive as the most broadly
endorsed public goal, Putin then leverages it against political alternatives
to this kind of rule. Here, the Manifesto explicitly makes the crucial and
blunt point that change led by any of the three major oppositional
alternatives to Russia's electoral authoritarian regime – the Communists,
nationalists, or liberals – will lead to the collapse of Russia:

Russia has used up its limit for political and socioeconomic upheavals,
cataclysms and radical reforms. *Only fanatics or political forces which are*
absolutely apathetic and indifferent to Russia and its people can make calls to
a new revolution. Be it under communist, national-patriotic or radical liberal
slogans, our country, our people will not withstand a new radical breakup
[my emphasis]. The nation's tolerance and ability both to survive and to
continue creative endeavor has reached the limit: society will simply collapse
economically, politically, psychologically and morally.

These ideas, in a nutshell, capture the essence of the strongman
appeal described in this book. But this legitimation strategy only
works in a very specific, symbiotic relationship with popular opinion.
To enter the political mainstream, the strongman alternative requires

a particular structure of popular opinion – a popular mood defined by traumas, grievances, and fears of unmanageable turmoil. Then, as it catches on, the strongman appeal begins to monopolize these sentiments and dominate popular opinion. By the time strongman electoral authoritarianism is widely considered as the only viable guarantor of order, every belief, fear, prejudice, desire, and evaluation is aligned for or against it. People's concerns and priorities become implicit judgments of this regime. Their policy stances and political allegiances are either abandoned or rallied against it. This is the effect of demand for tough, efficient authoritarian rule in a troubled society meeting its supply. The choice to support or reject strongman electoral authoritarianism, promising to achieve these fundamental goals, becomes the primary cleavage and driver of mass attitudes about politics.

The aggregate opinion patterns I presented in this chapter thus far capture only the broad contours of this process in the Russian case. To unpack and verify these further, we must turn to a more nuanced, in-depth analysis of the structure and dynamics of Russian popular opinion since the early 1990s.

How Russia's Crises Realigned Mass Opinion

Every time I get arrested I am grabbed and thrown in by the same kind of policemen ... and every time I talk to them: "Why are you arresting me? Do you not know that Putin is a thief?" And every time I get the same kind of answers – they all hate United Russia [the regime party], they don't really like Putin – but they throw me into the cell and shout the same thing back at me. "It'll never get any better, mate ... It'll never get any better."

Alexei Navalny, Russian opposition leader
(quoted in Judah 2013, 249)

This book's core prediction is that electoral autocracies thrive in societies traumatized by turmoil, where basic survival instincts trump higher-order political preferences like ideological views or aspirations for equality, pluralism, and free choice. According to this theory, popular opinion in electoral autocracies should have three key characteristics. First, it should be unusually homogeneous, as attitudes from different domains are driven by a single overarching desire for stability. The great diversity of opinion characteristic of modern societies is bound to narrow down dramatically as people's thoughts, judgments, and aspirations are subordinated to the impulse to restore order by any means necessary.

Second, if politically relevant opinions do indeed "march in tune" with this latent purpose, they ought to follow a distinct pattern of variation over time. A greater sense of security will be strongly associated with reduced concerns about basic stability and better economic outlooks. It will also correlate positively with trust in executive power, and lower willingness to protest against it. In turn, higher-order values and issue stances should have no bearing on this narrowed, stability-centric vision. In the pursuit of personal and national survival, mass publics would pragmatically ignore their own preferences for greater justice, tolerance, and respect for human rights.

Finally, existential anxieties of this scale allow elected strongmen to take center stage in the political discourse and in popular opinion. For many, supporting strongman rule becomes synonymous with satisfying their desire for order. When such regimes are in power, their popularity should therefore be a near-perfect reflection of societies' underlying fears of instability. The *less* people are concerned about disorder, and the *more* these concerns matter in their political outlooks, the higher the support for the electoral authoritarian system that promotes itself as the essential guard against these perils.

To verify these expectations in the Russian case, I analyze a uniquely detailed set of monthly and bimonthly surveys produced in the 1993–2011 period by the Levada Center, Russia's premier independent opinion research center.[12] For this purpose, I employ a comprehensive set of 144 questions, asked repeatedly in the same format across 418 representative in-person nationwide polls in Russia since 1993. Drawing on over 818,000 survey interviews that cover an exhaustive range of topics, this analysis provides an unparalleled insight into the structure of Russian mass opinion during the reigns of the three presidents – Yeltsin (1993–1999), Putin (1999–2008), and Medvedev (2008–2011) – who have shaped Russia's electoral authoritarianism. I provide a detailed description of the methodology of the Levada surveys and the full wording of the questions used in this analysis in Part 2 of the Online Appendix to this chapter.

---

[12] These surveys were accessed through the Russian Joint Sociological Data Archive (sophist.hse.ru).

Capturing the contingent logic of opinion formation in turbulent times – the fact that people's attitudes from across different domains are all shaped by an overarching desire for greater stability – requires a method that can analyze the interdependence between many attitudes over time. For this purpose, I utilize Stimson's dyad ratios algorithm, which distills the common underlying dimensions of aggregate opinions, based on their common movements over time.[13] At its core, this technique is based on a very simple intuition: attitudes that shift together over time tend to be driven by some common denominator. Studying the shared patterns of variation of such attitudes should therefore allow us to identify the unseen determinants of mass opinion – the overarching sentiment, "mood," or *Zeitgeist* which shapes the outlooks and behavior of the population across many different domains. The dyad ratios algorithm provides a simple and flexible procedure, akin to principal components analysis, to carry out this sort of analysis.[14]

To perform the dyad ratios analysis of Russian popular opinion, I use *all* available survey questions from the Levada polls that have been asked in identical form in at least fifteen monthly surveys. This approach avoids imposing any selection biases, as no attitudes are purposefully included or excluded from the analysis; it also ensures there are a sufficient number of observations per survey item to obtain reliable estimates (see Stimson 1999). The number of survey questions used for the dyad ratios estimates after applying this criterion is very large,[15] and provides exhaustive substantive coverage. Specifically, I carry out the analysis of the structure of Russian popular opinion with 144 survey items from 5 opinion clusters: principal concerns (21 items), assessments of economic, political, and social conditions and

---

[13] For the technical details of the dyad ratios algorithm, see Stimson (1999), Appendix 1. To perform this analysis, I used the WCALC 5 software (downloaded from https://stimson.web.unc.edu/software/ (accessed on 5/9/2021)).

[14] Beside its ability to capture the interrelationship between many attitudes over time, a key advantage of this method is that it can handle missing values without imposing any substantive assumptions – an essential capability for studies using monthly survey data with many variables and partially overlapping observations.

[15] Because of the large number of cross-sectional surveys available, very few questions were dropped from the analysis due to the minimal inclusion threshold of fifteen survey items.

future expectations in these areas (47 items), trust in key institutions (13 items), policy attitudes (54 items in total), and attitudes toward protest and political participation (9 items).[16]

As the dyad ratios algorithm employs aggregate percentages of survey participants that selected a particular response on a given item, I code all responses in their *positive* direction. Thus, listed by opinion cluster, the items used in the analysis represent the percentage of Russians who: (1) are concerned about the problems listed in the surveys; (2) have positive evaluations and expectations of conditions in Russia; (3) trust the institutions mentioned; (4) support the specified policies; and (5) who are willing to protest, or to participate in politics. This approach greatly simplifies the interpretation of the results from the analysis. Attitudes that have strong positive correlations with the latent dimension of Russian public opinion obtained with the dyad ratios procedure agree with the worldview it represents; those with negative correlations are at odds with it.

Before turning to the results of this analysis, it is useful to recapitulate what they should look like if this book's propositions are correct. If Russians have indeed subordinated their political preferences and outlooks to one central obsession with restoring order, then the latent dimension extracted with the dyad ratios algorithm should explain a large portion of the variation in these attitudes over time. That is to say, attitudes from across these different domains will appear to "march in tune," as if they were driven by the same underlying rationale.

The dyad ratios estimates strongly support this expectation. In particular, the main dimension of Russian popular opinion extracted with this algorithm explains about half (49 percent) of the variance across the extremely diverse set of attitudes used to obtain it. This suggests that Russian popular opinion exhibited a very impressive degree of attitudinal consistency, and confirms that it has closely aligned with one common underlying outlook or "mood." Comparing this result with similar analyses of mass opinion in stable Western democracies might help put it in context. For example, dyad ratios estimates of popular "mood" in the United States and France, which are based on policy attitudes alone, explain 40–50 percent of the variance in this much narrower set of attitudes (Erikson,

---

[16] I provide a full description of the variable selection and coding rules in Part 2 of the Online Appendix to this chapter.

MacKuen, and Stimson 2002, 203; Stimson, Thiébaut, and Tiberj 2012). The main dimension of Russian popular opinion, extracted with this procedure, explains the same degree of variation across *all* the main groups of politically relevant attitudes. That Russian aggregate opinions in areas as diverse as concerns, evaluations, trust, policy stances, and political participation have all shifted in unison is remarkable and suggests that they were all driven by the same underlying outlook and purpose.

But was this latent mood of Russian popular opinion centered on demands for stability and a strong-armed government that would restore it by any means necessary? We can verify the substantive meaning of a latent dimension of opinion extracted with the dyad ratios procedure by observing which survey items are most closely associated with it. Figure 5.5 below shows the correlations for 49 out of the 144 series on the main dimension of Russia's post-Soviet popular opinion extracted with the dyad ratios algorithm. These items are selected using two criteria: (1) their factor loadings or correlations with the latent dimension are greater than 0.6 in absolute value, and they therefore represent the attitudes most closely related to this underlying construct; and (2) they are the most general variant among a set of similar questions. As we also learn about the contents of a common dimension by observing which attitudes are *not* closely related with it, I also include several substantively important items with correlations lower than 0.6 in absolute value.

Starting with the first attitude cluster, the primary concerns of the Russian population most highly and negatively correlated with the primary dimension of mass opinion include concerns about the weakness of state authority, conflicts between government branches, and anxieties related to crime and terrorism. What these sentiments have in common is fear of the disintegration of state authority. Concerns about wage arrears, poverty, and the crisis in the economy, on the other hand, are somewhat less strongly correlated with this dimension. This discrepancy is revealing. It suggests that the main dimension of Russian popular opinion was more closely aligned with concerns about the strength of the state – the primary guarantor of stability – than with the people's own welfare. This fits squarely in line with this book's theoretical predictions.

Also as expected, concerns about restrictions on civil rights are completely unrelated to this main current of Russian popular opinion, achieving a correlation of practically zero. Hence, as Putin himself recognized in his first campaign program quoted in the previous section, since the 1990s, Russians have been primarily concerned about their government's ability to hold the country together. This worry overshadowed even anxieties about poverty and economics. It completely sidelined concerns about civil rights (which achieve a miniscule correlation of only 0.09 with the primary dimension of Russian opinion, according to the results in Figure 5.5) – a higher-order value that does not seem to serve the imperative of restoring order.

The factor loadings of the attitudes in the current assessments and institutional trust clusters reflect a similar emphasis on stability, as well as an underlying desire for strong executive leadership. In the first of these attitude clusters, positive evaluations of the broad national political and economic situation predominate, with correlations of above 0.9. Perceptions that Chechnya is being pacified achieve a comparable loading of 0.85. In turn, assessments that the president plays a significant role in the country, as well as trust in the president, respectively achieve the highest loadings of 0.9 and 0.96 in their clusters. This finding is particularly revealing. Of all the trust items, greater faith in Russia's effectively authoritarian "superpresidential" chief executive had the strongest association with the main common denominator of Russian popular opinion. The other institutions with high loadings in terms of public trust include state security services – the traditional pillar of Russian authoritarian state power – as well as the State Duma (Parliament), which has been substantially co-opted by the presidency during Putin's tenure. On the other hand, trust in the courts, parties, and the media – institutions that typically serve as checks on government power – achieve much lower loadings. On the whole, these findings reveal a clear link between the main dimension of Russian mass opinion and preferences for an essentially unconstrained executive power.

The loadings of the items in the political participation cluster are also in line with this interpretation. Here, expectations of politically motivated protests – particularly against the president – and willingness to participate in them achieve the highest *negative* correlations with the primary dimension of Russian popular opinion. Again, given the centrality of the presidency in Russia's political system, these results are consistent with the idea that the latent dimension captures the extent to which Russians endorsed the country's unchecked executive.

The policy cluster, in turn, has the lowest number of attitudes that are highly correlated with the primary dimension. This is exactly what we might expect in contexts where concerns about stability predominate, and traditional ideological and policy attachments and value judgments take the back seat. Only 17 out of 54 items in the policy attitudes cluster have factor loadings above 0.6, and only 5 of these achieve loadings of over 0.8 in absolute value. This is in stark contrast with the current assessments cluster, where almost half of the 47 items have loadings above 0.8. Gripped by existential fears, Russians were clearly far more interested in positive outcomes than the policies used to achieve them.

But crucially, two policy stances have some of the highest loadings of all 144 attitudes used in this analysis. They confirm this chapter's hypothesis 3, that the main dimension of Russian opinion is an implicit judgment of the country's electoral authoritarian regime: the degree to which people support it for its capacity to maintain order and stability. Specifically, beliefs that the current political system is the best for Russia have the highest loading of 0.95 among policy stances, thus directly confirming that the primary dimension captures not just people's existential anxieties, but also the ability of the strongman executive to address them. The view that Western liberal democracy is the best system for Russia, on the other hand, has the highest negative loading of -0.91 on the common factor – much more negative than even the conviction that the Soviet system is the best regime alternative (which has a loading of -0.57). Taken together, this pattern of loadings is a key indication that the primary dimension of Russian mass opinion is aligned with a cleavage that heavily favors electoral authoritarian rule: the choice of supporting a hybrid regime, which promises to maintain stability and address grievances better than a democratic or a closed authoritarian system.

Here, a skeptic might ask: was the substantive meaning of the primary dimension of Russia's post-Communist opinion the same in the Yeltsin and the Putin/Medvedev eras? In particular, could the findings of the dyad ratios analyses in the later period be driven by the much more robust pro-Kremlin propaganda, which showcased the stabilization of Russia as the purpose of Putin's authoritarian rule? To examine this, I calculated separate dyad ratios dimensional estimates of the Yeltsin and Putin/Medvedev eras, and performed a number of additional analyses to check the potential influence of propaganda on

Primary Concerns

Concerned about: Weakness of state authority
Concerned about: Delays in payment of wages
Concerned about: Crime
Concerned about: Conflicts btw. branches of government
Concerned about: Terrorism
Concerned about: Rise of nationalism
Concerned about: Poverty
Concerned about: Crisis in the economy
Concerned about: Restrictions on civil rights

Institutional Trust

Trusts the President of Russia
Trusts State Duma (Parliament)
Trusts State Security Services
Trusts Unions
Trusts Russian Government
Trusts Republican Authorities
Trusts Russian Courts
Trusts Parties
Trusts Media

Current Assessments

General direction of Russia good
Life satisfaction: fully or largely satisfied
Economy in the next year: good
Current Political Situation: favorable and tranquil
Confident in the future: fully and partially confident
Economy in the next 5 years: good
Russian politics in the coming months: expect to improve
Role of President significant
Russian economy in the coming months: expect to improve
Current Economic Situation: good and very good
Believe most difficult times for Russia are behind it
Current financial condition of respondents' families: good and very good
Current Situation in Chechnya: peace is becoming established
Believe most difficult times for Russia are ahead
Role of Unions significant
Role of Political Parties significant

Policy Attitudes

Best political system for Russia: The Current System
Best political system for Russia: Democracy according to the Western model
Family adapted to changes
Most important policies: Liquidate wage and pension arrears
Market reforms should be continued
Doesn't agree that life before Perestroika was better
Best economic system for Russia: one where state predominates
Favors negotiations with Chechen insurgents to end conflict
Best political system for Russia: The Soviet System
Reforms should be carried out more cautiously

Political Participation

Will support protests calling for the resignation of the President
Will support protests calling for the resignation of the Government
Protests with pol. demands in respondents' area considered likely
Will support protests calling for the dissolution of the State Duma
Will vote in Presidential elections
Protests with econ. demands in respondents' area considered likely
Will participate in protests in local area
Will support protests calling for the resignation of the local administration

Figure 5.5 Correlations of key attitudes with the primary dimension of Russian opinion
Source: Levada Center

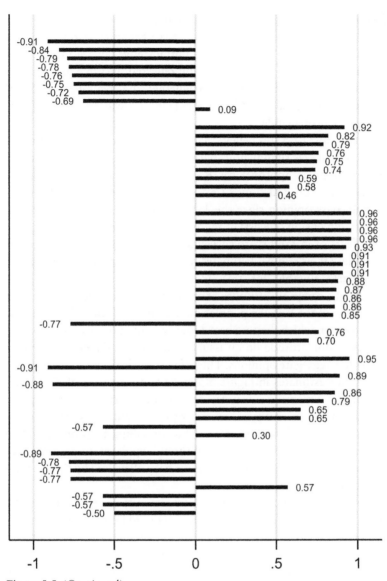

Figure 5.5 (Continued)

Russian popular opinion. The results of these analyses, which I present in full in Part 3 of the Online Appendix to this chapter, strongly suggest that during both the Yeltsin and the Putin/Medvedev presidencies, the primary dimension of Russian opinion reflected the same demands for stability and disagreements as to whether the incumbent electoral authoritarian regime could best provide it, and was not meaningfully affected by propaganda.

But did most Russians believe that supporting their electoral authoritarian system was synonymous with addressing the country's crisis? If yes, the popular approval for Russia's regime should have closely matched the ebb and flow of existential anxieties that had defined Russian mass opinion since the 1990s. To verify this, I compare the primary dimension of Russian aggregate opinion, which captures these latent fears of instability, to survey questions directly asking Russians to evaluate their regime. Estimates from the dyad ratios procedure are particularly suitable for this analysis, as they not only capture a sweeping range of attitudes that contributed to the apprehensive worldview of the Russian population, but are also scaled in the metric of the data on which they are based (the percentage of respondents who have the same attitude on an issue), allowing for direct comparisons with other aggregate opinions. Thus, if we recode the items used for the dyad ratios estimates in Figure 5.5 to have positive correlations with the primary dimension – as percentages *not* concerned about the problems listed in the surveys, having positive evaluations, trusting the institutions named, willing to vote but unwilling to protest, and so on – we will obtain factor scores that should represent the percentage of Russians whose fears of instability have been alleviated by the electoral authoritarian system.

If Russians did indeed embrace electoral autocracy as a pragmatic solution for their country's decline, there should be a close correspondence between this sentiment and the levels of support for the country's post-Communist regime. People's confidence in Russia's stability would, in other words, closely match their approval of the system that was brought in to impose order. I test this claim in Figure 5.6 by comparing the over-time variation of the primary dimension of Russian mass opinion derived with the dyad ratios (displayed as a full line in the left and right panels of the figure) to a set of direct survey questions from New Russia Barometer (NRB) surveys (Rose 2010), asking Russians to evaluate their current political and economic systems on a scale of -100 to 100 (the right panel). The short- and long-dash series in the right panel of Figure 5.6 represent the aggregate responses to these direct survey questions, coded as the percentage of respondents who gave positive ratings to Russia's political and economic systems, respectively.

While the right-hand graph is a coarser representation than the one in the left panel of Figure 5.6, given that only eighteen observations are available for the NRB items for this time interval, the close resemblance between the three series is remarkable. The correspondence between the latent dimension extracted with the dyad ratios algorithm and the political and NRB economic systems ratings is almost perfect – with correlations of 0.93 and 0.95, respectively. The series are also very proximate in levels: the average differences between the latent dimension, capturing people's degree of confidence in Russia's stability, and the NRB economic and political system ratings are 3.8 percent and about 1.3 percent, respectively, which is within the bounds of the sampling error in these surveys.

This near-perfect match between the direct survey ratings of Russia's political and economic system and the dyad ratios estimates of the primary dimension of Russian mass opinion suggests that they represent the same underlying sentiment.[17] The fact that regime approval and mass confidence in Russia's stability moved in lockstep strongly supports the idea, summarized by this chapter's hypothesis 3, that Russian elected autocrats successfully hijacked the existential concerns of the population to justify their rule. Electoral authoritarianism, as these results suggest, earned the backing of Russia's crisis-weary population as they served as a comforting device: posing as the only guarantee against further collapse, which Russians felt compelled to accept in spite of its patchy, unwholesome nature. As Krastev and Holmes (2012) illustrated, "[f]or ordinary Russians haunted by the memories of the Soviet house that humiliatingly fell

---

[17] Also, the close correspondence between the three series is not a relic of the dyad ratios technique, or of the fact that it relies on aggregate opinion data for its estimates. I demonstrate this by extracting the primary dimension of Russian political opinion from individual survey responses with standard cross-sectional principal components analysis, following a procedure developed by Stimson, Thiébaut, and Tiberj (2012). The estimates, which I present in detail in Part 4 of this chapter's Online Appendix, closely match those obtained with the dyad ratios algorithm, despite the fact that they were calculated with a different method and from individual-level survey data.

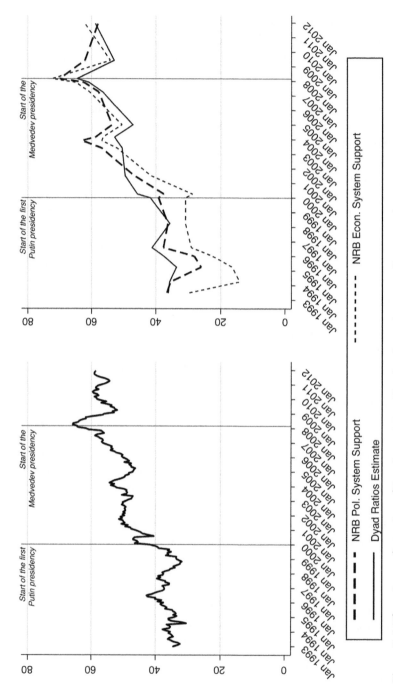

Figure 5.6 The primary dimension of Russian opinion: Dyad ratios estimate vs. direct questions

Source: Levada Center and The New Russia Barometer

apart, rigged elections in which Chechnya votes 95 percent for Putin and United Russia provide psychological reassurance that the country [at least] retains its territorial integrity, however fraught and frayed."

On the whole, the analyses in this section point to one overarching conclusion: that existential anxieties – the primary driver of mass outlooks in Russia since the trauma of the 1990s – perfectly aligned with the appeal of electoral authoritarianism as the only practical remedy for the country's decline. It is striking, given this interpretation, that the confidence in stability and the regime support series in Figure 5.6 reached 50 percent only toward the end of 2001. The series averaged at 35–40 percent during Yeltsin's tenure throughout the 1990s, rising to mean levels of about 50–60 percent during the Putin and Medvedev presidencies until 2011. These underwhelming levels of confidence and systemic support indicate that despite placing their hopes for stability in their post-Soviet system, Russians were actually quite unimpressed by it, and its propaganda. They suggest that Russia's electoral autocracy survived not because of its high performance or overwhelming mass enthusiasm for it, but due to other factors, like the inability of dissatisfied constituencies to unite behind a single oppositional alternative.

This leads us to this book's central argument. The main reason for the failure of the Kremlin's opponents was not their poor organization and leadership, limited resources, or the regime's coercion and manipulations. It was the logic of political competition in a society gripped by turmoil and existential fears. As the obsession with restoring order realigned Russian popular opinion along the one core cleavage I described above – the choice to support or reject strong-armed, electoral authoritarian rule – the opponents of Russia's regime found themselves on the losing side of the debate. The pro-/anti-strongman rule cleavage not only favored a heavy-handed, order-imposing leadership in the Kremlin, but it also put its diverse challengers on the spot by forcing them to offer better solutions for the country's problems. Appealing to constituencies with radically different visions of a more stable future, Russia's Communist, nationalist, and liberal oppositions competed with each other as much as with the regime, as I will show in more detail in the next section. This allowed Vladimir Putin – and even his beleaguered predecessor Yeltsin – to secure and maintain power through the ballot box and with relatively little coercion.

These results also confirm that the mass appeal of an electoral authoritarian system is a more reliable indicator of these regimes' stability than the personal charisma and popularity of their leaders. I illustrate this in Figure 5.7 below, which juxtaposes Boris Yeltsin's and Vladimir Putin's approval ratings with the aggregate regime support extracted with the dyad ratios algorithm. It is clear that popular support for the country's fledgling electoral autocracy carried the day throughout the 1990s, when it outperformed the approval of its leader Boris Yeltsin by an average 15 percentage points, and often by 20–30 percent. This enabled his faltering administration to survive at least two near-fatal crises. One was in the hotly contested 1996 presidential race, when mass support for Russia's system was 12 percent higher than Yeltsin's own approval. This allowed Yeltsin to avoid defeat by turning the election into a referendum on the regime, which Russians still preferred to the Communist alternative (see McFaul 1997). Second, in Yeltsin's final year, when his personal ratings plunged to single digits in the wake of the 1998 financial crisis, the still-relatively-stable 35–40 percent support for the electoral authoritarian system enabled it to survive a highly precarious leadership succession. These patterns show that there was no widely admired, charismatic leader to account for the remarkable resilience of Russia's electoral autocracy in the 1990s. Instead, it was this regime's own attractiveness as the least bad choice for a deeply troubled country that propped up Russia's fumbling and increasingly unpopular leader.

The appeal of electoral authoritarianism remained the cornerstone of Russia's regime in the Putin era, even after Vladimir Putin assumed the mantle of a charismatic strongman. While the trends in Figure 5.7 show that Putin's towering popularity in this role upstaged Russians' faith in the system he led, this gap narrowed significantly over time, dropping from 20 to 25 percent on average to just 4 percent in late 2011. This convergence happened gradually at first, as popular support for Russia's electoral autocracy inched up to 60 percent, and then suddenly, when Putin's ratings plummeted after his return for a third presidential term in 2012 and the unprecedented protest wave it triggered.[18] Thus, despite Putin's imposing popularity, his fortunes remained fundamentally tied to the underlying appeal of Russia's electoral autocracy. High hopes in Putin's leadership certainly helped buoy the ratings of Russia's electoral autocracy, but eventually, the

---

[18] Putin's personal approval reclaimed the lead over mass support for the system he had presided over for four years after his "conquest" of Crimea, but the difference narrowed again as the wartime fervor wore off and his popularity plunged again after 2018 (Kolesnikov 2020).

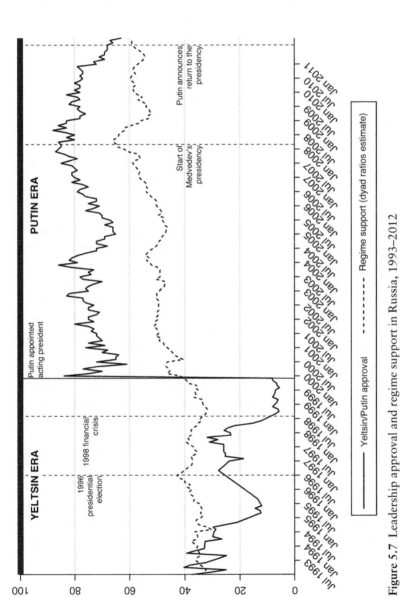

Figure 5.7 Leadership approval and regime support in Russia, 1993–2012
Source: Levada Center

regime's failure to live up to expectations caught up with its leader, undermining his reputation.[19]

All things considered, the preceding passages strongly suggest that the backbone of Russia's electoral authoritarianism has been its own attractiveness as the most pragmatic and benign remedy for Russia's decline. In the next section, I trace how this appeal enabled Russia's electoral autocrats to displace other cleavages and to delegitimize and divide their opponents.

The Regime Cleavage and Political Competition in Russia

The transformation of the strongman appeal into the primary cleavage of popular opinion in troubled societies confers a double electoral advantage to authoritarian forces, which I elaborated in detail in Chapter 2. First, it allows them to displace other cleavages and plat- forms as irrelevant, ineffective, needlessly divisive, and downright dan- gerous. Promising to deliver their societies from turmoil, strongmen draw away two types of voters from their competitors: (1) moderates who have ambivalent, centrist stances on the issues represented by conventional programmatic parties and candidates, and are not com- mitted enough ideologically to resist the cross-pressure of the authori- tarian appeal; and (2) more ideologically committed constituencies that have come to believe their goals cannot be achieved by democratic means, or by a closed dictatorship. Second, the migration of ideologic- ally indifferent voters and disenchanted partisans toward the authori- tarian alternative creates a more polarized and divided oppositional electorate, enabling electoral authoritarian strongmen to win in clean elections even without majority popular support. As the nonideological and ideological pragmatists shift in favor of electoral authoritarianism, the opposition is left with the most entrenched partisans, who are further apart ideologically, and therefore less likely to join forces and form the broad antiregime coalitions needed for victory.

The simplest test of this theory is to examine the party/candidate positioning in the issue space and its electoral consequences. To do this in the Russian case, I plot the mean stances of voters supporting the candidates in the country's presidential polls in 1996, 2000, 2004, and

---

[19]   On these issues, see Rose, Mishler, and Munro (2004), Belanovsky and Dmitriev (2011, 2013), and Rogov (2019).

2008 – elections that marked the consolidation of Russia's electoral autocracy. In the 1996 race, Boris Yeltsin fought Russia's closest presidential race against Communist challenger Gennady Zyuganov. The 2000 election was marked by the rapid ascendance of Vladimir Putin in the wake of the second invasion of Chechnya, while in the 2004 race he entrenched his power, reining in the country's oligarchs and regional elites. In the 2008 election, Putin feigned liberalization and circumvented the constitutional term limit by installing the loyalist and presumed liberalizer Dmitry Medvedev for a stint in office, while he took the back seat as prime minister.

Figure 5.8 displays the mean positions of the voters for each presidential candidate on the NRB regime support scale, discussed in the previous section (the Y-axes), plotted against the most salient economic and political cleavages (the X-axes). The economic issues include the key points of disagreement about Russia's transition to a market economy that are available in the NRB surveys: whether incomes should be equalized or based on individual achievement (the 1996 election), whether state or private ownership of enterprises is better (2000 and 2004), and whether to continue or stop market reforms (2008). The key political cleavage throughout all these elections, in turn, is represented by the main dilemma of Russia's political transition: whether a "tough," closed dictatorship is the best system for the country's current situation.[20]

In all these charts, I plot the mean positions of voters who supported the incumbents Yeltsin and Putin as well as the representatives of Russia's main opposition parties: the Communists (Zyuganov in 1996, 2000, and

---

[20] The full text of the NRB survey question about "tough" dictatorship was as follows: "There are different opinions about the nature of the state. To what extent would you agree with the following statements: a tough dictatorship is best in our current situation?" The response options range from "strongly disagree" to "strongly agree." Unfortunately, the same set of questions on the economic cleavages are not available across all the NRB surveys, as these attempted to tap into specific issues that dominated each campaign. However, their results are comparable as they all apply to attitudes toward Russia's post-Communist market reforms. In 1996, the full question capturing the key economic issues was phrased as follows: "Here are some opinions that different people hold. For each pair, please say which is definitely or somewhat closer to your opinion: Incomes should be made more equal or individual achievement should determine how much people are paid." In 2000 and 2004, the NRB survey item asked "Which of these statements are you more inclined to agree with: State ownership is the best way to run an enterprise or an enterprise is best run by private entrepreneurs" and in 2008, it asked "Do you think that market reforms should be continued or that they should cease?"

2008, and Kharitonov in 2004), liberals (Yavlinsky in 1996 and 2000, and Khakamada in 2004), and nationalists (Zhirinovski in 1996, 2000, and 2008, and Malyshkin in 2004), as well as several independent and Kremlin-co-opted candidates (Lebed and Fyodorov in 1996, Tuleev in 2000, Glazyev and Mironov in 2004, Bogdanov in 2008). The size of diamonds around the names of these candidates are proportional to the share of the total vote they won among the survey respondents, while the dashed lines represent the mean voter positions on the issues.

The patterns we observe in Figure 5.8 closely match the expected effects of the strongman heresthetic in post-crisis societies. As in the two-dimensional electoral competition simulations in Chapter 2, Russia's incumbents clearly "owned" the issue of supporting the electoral authoritarian system of government. Being the most credible representatives of this alternative, they dominated the pro-regime side of the spectrum in the two upper quadrants of the issue space. The choice of whether to support or reject Russia's electoral authoritarian system, in turn, acted as a wedge issue, drawing away voters from the opposition and exacerbating the divisions among those that remained loyal to it.

We can see this from the placement of different opposition constituencies in the graphs in Figure 5.8. In all four elections from 1996 to 2008, Russia's opposition forces failed to converge around a common position on the most basic issue: how much to oppose Russia's electoral authoritarian regime, represented on the y-axis in the graphs. While the Communist candidates Zyuganov and Kharitonov consistently attracted voters with radical anti-systemic stances in the lower corners of the regime support spectrum, nationalists like Zhirinovsky, Malyshkin, and some of the independent candidates like Lebed, adopted far more moderate positions on the regime dimension. In contrast, the less numerous liberals, represented by candidates like Yavlinsky and Khakamada, strategically adopted pro-regime stances, fearing that a move away from electoral authoritarianism would herald a Communist or nationalist-led reversal to a closed dictatorship and a planned economy (on this see also Gel'man 2005).

Voters in Russia therefore faced a fundamental asymmetry of choice, imposed by the regime's strongman appeal. On the regime side of the main political divide, the increasingly consolidated pro-Kremlin bloc offered the clear option of preserving the status quo: the electoral authoritarian system as a pragmatic, centrist (in the sense of representing a system midway between democracy and authoritarianism)

Economic Issues

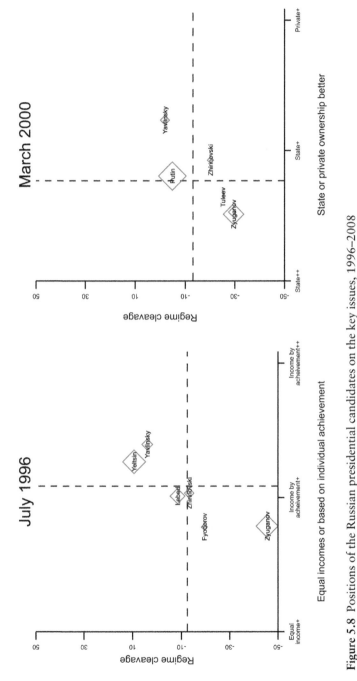

Figure 5.8 Positions of the Russian presidential candidates on the key issues, 1996–2008

Note: the dashed lines represent the mean voters' positions on the issues. Candidate names are placed at the mean positions of those who voted for them; the size of the diamonds is proportional to the candidates' vote share.

Source: The New Russia Barometer.

Economic Issues

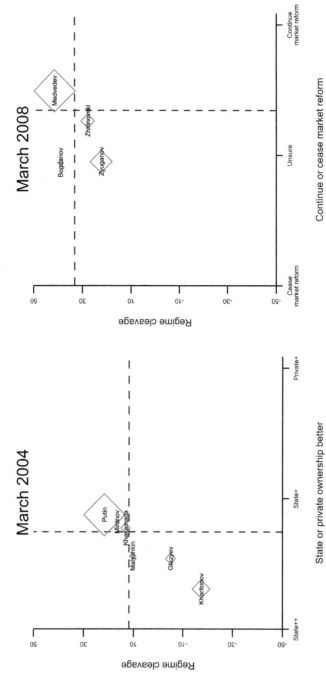

Figure 5.8 (Continued)

Democracy vs. Authoritarianism

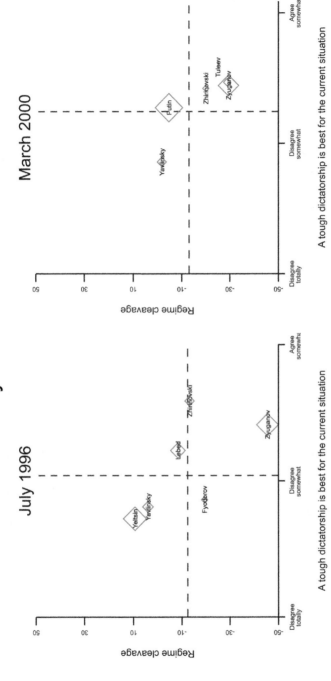

Figure 5.8 (Continued)

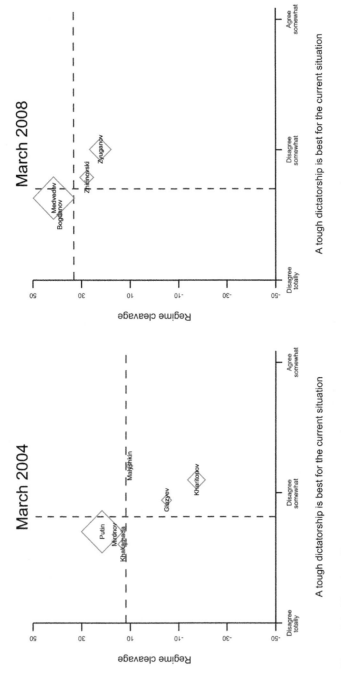

Figure 5.8 (Continued)

solution to the problem of maintaining stability. For many voters, including liberals, this was far from a satisfying choice, but it was certainly the least bad alternative. On the other side of the spectrum, staunch regime opponents with diverse interests and outlooks endorsed conflicting alternatives to the current order. Rooted in programmatic appeals rejected by most other opposition voters (like Communism), none of these alternatives stood out as an obvious substitute to Russia's current electoral authoritarian regime.

These ideological divisions among the opposition are readily apparent in the candidates' stances along Russia's economic and political cleavages. On economic issues, Communist (Zyuganov and Kharitonov) and liberal (Yavlinsky and Khakamada) contenders appealed to constituencies on opposite ends of the median voter position, while nationalists (Lebed, Zhirinovski, and Malyshkin) took more centrist views. On the main political cleavage, Communists and nationalists veered more in favor of closed dictatorship, while liberals vehemently opposed it. These rifts in the opposition allowed Yeltsin, Putin, and Medvedev to portray themselves as the voices of reason and moderation. Taking centrist stances on most of these issues, the incumbent candidates – Putin in particular – provided a refuge for moderates who were turned off by the relative extremism of the opposition forces.

But did the regime cleavage play a decisive role at the ballot box, trumping their other preferences and outlooks? The electoral impact of a cleavage depends on two factors. The most obvious one is its relative salience: the degree to which it matters to voters, compared to other issues. But highly salient issues are not necessarily decisive, as their influence also hinges on how different the alternatives offered by the contestants are (Ansolabehere and Puy 2018). At one extreme, cleavages that are very important to voters may not affect their ballot choices, simply because the contenders take very similar positions on that issue. Conversely, issues that voters do not care as much about could have a disproportionate influence on their ballot choices because of the vast differences in the contenders' positions. The most electorally significant issues, in other words, are usually the ones that both matter the most to voters, and are those on which voters face the most different choices.

Did the regime cleavage have a decisive influence on electoral choices in Russia if we take both of these factors into account? To examine this, I estimate a multinomial logit (ML) model of vote choice in the four Russian presidential elections. ML models are particularly well suited for this analysis as their coefficients capture the combined impact of issue salience and candidate distinctiveness on an issue on the odds of selecting one choice over another (Ansolabehere and Puy 2018).[21] Compared to alternative models of vote choice, ML also provides the added benefit of a disaggregated analysis of vote choice. It does so by estimating how opinion shifts in the issue space affect voter choices for *each pair* of candidates. Thus, based on the ML estimates, we can examine how voter stances on the regime and other cleavages affected the likelihood of choosing between the incumbent and each of the opposition challengers, as well as among the opposition candidates.

To assess the role of the regime cleavage in Russia's electoral competition, I estimate the effects of respondent stances on the issues depicted in Figure 5.8 plus four additional election-specific issues that played prominent roles in the Russian presidential races in 1996, 2000, 2004, and 2008. I provide the ML estimates of the impact of key issue stances on the vote choice for the top-ranking candidates (winning more than 5 percent of the vote) in these elections in Table 5.1 below.[22] The point estimates in Table 5.1 represent multinomial logit coefficients, capturing how preferences for first candidate in the pair over the second candidate change as the respondents' level of agreement with the attitude in question increases by one standard deviation. A positive coefficient indicates that higher respondent values on that attitude boosted the chances of voting for the first candidate of the pair; a negative coefficient suggests the opposite. For ease of comparison, the gray-shaded cells in Table 5.1 highlight the largest coefficient (in absolute value) for each row (i.e. each candidate pair).

The results from these estimates closely conform to the predictions of the strongman heresthetic model, summarized by this chapter's hypothesis 4. When it came down to choosing between the incumbent and the *top* opposition challenger (the first-choice pair for each election), support for Russia's electoral authoritarian system and the issue of adopting a "tough" dictatorship (the issue stances in the first columns) had a greater or equal effect than the other economic and

---

[21] Ansolabehere and Puy (2018) show that the multinomial logit coefficients on voter issue stances are given by $k_x = 2a(x_A - x_B)$, where a is the salience voters attach to the issue x, and s_A and s_B are the stances of candidates, respectively.

[22] To account for the potential vote-stealing and turnout effects in multicandidate races (see e.g. Lacy and Burden 1999), all models also include self-reported abstention from voting as one of the choices. I provide the full estimates of these ML models in Part 5 of the Online Appendix to this chapter.

political cleavages. We can quantify this difference in impact by dividing the issue coefficients for these candidate pairs. For ML models like the ones in Table 5.1, these ratios capture how much stronger or weaker the electoral effect of one issue is relative to another. Based on this metric, a standard deviation shift in voter stances along the regime cleavage in the closely contested 1996 race had 1.4 times greater impact than the issue of price controls on the choice between Yeltsin and Zyuganov, and more than 2.7 and 1.8 times greater effect than improvements in the Russian economy and the respondents' family finances, respectively. This is a remarkable result. Even as Russians were living through the worst peacetime economic decline in history, their economic issue preferences and evaluations had a much smaller influence on how they chose their leaders than their support for Russia's electoral authoritarian political system.

These trends solidified with the rise of Putinism. In Putin's first presidential election in 2000, the effect of a standard deviation shift in attitudes toward Russia's regime on the choice between Putin and Zyuganov was more than double that of an analogous opinion change on the issue of private ownership of businesses, and 1.4 times greater than a standard deviation increase in family finances. In the 2004 and 2008 elections, the pattern seems to have reversed. As the popularity of Putinism solidified, economic issues appeared to take precedence over the regime cleavage when voters decided whether to support Russia's incumbents or its fading opposition. According to the estimates in Table 5.1, in the 2004 and 2008 elections, attitudes toward private ownership and market reforms had a 1.3 and 1.5 times greater impact than stances on the regime cleavage, respectively, when it came down to choosing between the regime candidate and the top-placed Communist challengers Kharitonov and Zyuganov. Similarly, in 2008, standard deviation shifts in attitudes toward market reforms and support for Russia's regime had virtually the same effect on the choice between Medvedev and the nationalist Zhirinovski.

The strongman appeal of Putinism was not losing its influence, however. Quite the contrary, these trends mark its ultimate success: complete dominance over Russian popular opinion and electoral competition. By 2004, Putin's image as a tough-mannered "national savior" became so popular that leading opposition candidates were forced to dampen their opposition to his rule in order to maintain a modicum of support. We can see this behavior in Figure 5.8. As the mean voter position (marked by the dashed lines) swung sharply in the pro-regime direction from 1996 and 2000, to 2004 and 2008, Russia's main opposition candidates dutifully followed suit to avoid alienating their voters. The "adaptation" of Russia's Communists (represented by Zyuganov and Kharitonov in Figure 5.8) was particularly dramatic in this regard: their stance shifted from a fervently antiregime position at about –50 on the political system support scale (ranging from –100 to 100) in 1996 to a cautiously pro-regime score of 20 in 2008.

Thus, the apparent decline in the influence of the regime cleavage came after it had effectively neutralized the main opposition to Putinism. As the share of Russians with antiregime views declined dramatically, from 46 percent in 1996 and 2000 to 22 percent in 2004, and ultimately, just 8 percent in 2008, electoral competition between Russia's fading opposition alternatives and the incumbent became centered on the issues that mattered most to their most hardcore, ideologically motivated supporters. By that point, the Kremlin's mainstream challengers were not looking to contest power, but to survive politically. Seeking to compensate for their disadvantage on the main regime cleavage, they embraced more radical stances on the other, programmatic cleavages.

But in doing so, they further narrowed their appeal and reinforced the splits in the opposition camp. The clearest example is that of the widening programmatic differences between the voters for the Communist Zyuganov and the nationalist Zhirinovsky in Table 5.1. While the choice between these two opposition candidates was unaffected by economic issues in 1996 (as evidenced by the nonsignificant effects of the equal incomes and price control issues), it had become so by 2008, when attitudes toward market reforms and Russia's relation to the West was the most significant differences between voters who supported these alternatives. This is the opposition-splitting effect of the strongman appeal, predicted by this book's theoretical framework. By forcing the regime's opponents to survive by reaching out to fringe constituencies, it pushed them further apart from each other, and from a unified opposition front that could mount a more serious challenge.[23]

---

[23] This same pattern is observed by Greene (2007) in Mexico's electoral autocracy: unable to compete with the PRI regime on the primary issues of interest to the voters, Mexico's opposition parties attempted to survive by appealing to fringe constituencies with radical ideological outlooks.

Table 5.1 *Multinomial logit estimates of the effect of issue stances in Russia's presidential elections*

1996 presidential election (first round)

	Regime cleavage	Support "tough" dictatorship	Favors achievement-based incomes	Favors free prices	Russian economy better	Family financial situation better
Zyuganov vs. Yeltsin	-0.76 (0.13)**	0.41 (0.10)**	-0.18 (0.10)+	-0.53 (0.11)**	-0.28 (0.13)*	-0.43 (0.12)**
Lebed vs. Yeltsin	-0.18 (0.14)	0.44 (0.13)**	-0.13 (0.11)	-0.35 (0.13)**	-0.00 (0.13)	-0.46 (0.13)**
Yavlinsky vs. Yeltsin	-0.06 (0.16)	0.14 (0.16)	0.18 (0.15)	0.03 (0.15)	-0.01 (0.15)	-0.52 (0.16)**
Zhirinovsky vs. Yeltsin	-0.14 (0.17)	0.71 (0.15)**	-0.03 (0.15)	-0.62 (0.16)**	0.00 (0.19)	-0.52 (0.19)**
Nonvoters vs. Yeltsin	-0.29 (0.12)*	0.15 (0.10)	-0.03 (0.10)	-0.21 (0.11)+	-0.09 (0.10)	-0.38 (0.11)**
Lebed vs. Zyuganov	0.58 (0.14)**	0.03 (0.13)	0.05 (0.11)	0.18 (0.13)	0.28 (0.15)+	-0.03 (0.13)
Yavlinsky vs. Zyuganov	0.70 (0.17)**	-0.27 (0.17)	0.36 (0.15)*	0.56 (0.15)**	0.27 (0.17)	-0.09 (0.18)
Zhirinovsky vs. Zyuganov	0.62 (0.17)**	0.30 (0.15)*	0.15 (0.14)	-0.09 (0.15)	0.28 (0.20)	-0.09 (0.19)
Yavlinsky vs. Lebed	0.13 (0.18)	-0.30 (0.18)+	0.31 (0.16)+	0.38 (0.16)*	-0.01 (0.17)	-0.01 (0.17)
Zhirinovsky vs. Lebed	0.04 (0.18)	0.27 (0.17)	0.11 (0.16)	-0.27 (0.17)+	0.00 (0.20)	-0.07 (0.20)
Zhirinovsky vs. Yavlinsky	-0.09 (0.20)	0.57 (0.20)**	-0.20 (0.19)	-0.66 (0.19)**	0.01 (0.22)	-0.01 (0.23)

Table 5.1 (*cont.*)

2000 presidential election

	Regime cleavage	Support "tough" dictatorship	Private ownership better	Prevent separation of Chechnya	Russian economy better	Family financial situation better
Zyuganov vs. Putin	-0.36 (0.11)**	0.06 (0.10)	-0.16 (0.11)	0.00 (0.09)	-0.15 (0.11)	-0.25 (0.10)**
Yavlinsky vs. Putin	-0.07 (0.19)	-0.32 (0.16)*	0.09 (0.14)	-0.11 (0.15)	-0.08 (0.19)	-0.29 0.17)+
Nonvoters vs. Putin	-0.19 (0.10)+	-0.20 (0.09)*	-0.05 (0.09)	-0.01 (0.10)	0.17 (0.10)+	-0.30 (0.09)**
Yavlinsky vs. Zyuganov	0.29 (0.20)	-0.38 (0.17)*	0.25 (0.16)	-0.11 (0.16)	0.07 (0.20)	-0.05 (0.19)

2004 presidential election

	Regime cleavage	Support "tough" dictatorship	Private ownership better	Prevent separation of Chechnya	Russian economy better	Family financial situation better
Kharitonov vs. Putin	-0.56 (0.16)**	0.38 (0.12)**	-0.71 (0.19)**	-0.19 (0.14)	-0.20 (0.15)	-0.35 (0.16)*
Nonvoters vs. Putin	-0.14 (0.10)	0.23 (0.09)**	-0.20 (0.09)*	0.06 (0.08)	-0.12 (0.10)	-0.08 (0.09)

2008 presidential election

	Regime cleavage	Support "tough" dictatorship	Continue market reforms	Future of Russia is with the West	Russian economy better	Family financial situation better
Zyuganov vs. Medvedev	-0.41 (0.12)**	0.25 (0.12)*	-0.60 (0.11)**	-0.26 (0.14)+	-0.22(0.12)+	-0.31 (0.14)*
Zhirinovsky vs. Medvedev	-0.31 (0.16)+	0.18 (0.16)	-0.30 (0.17)+	0.04 (0.14)	-0.10 (0.15)	-0.04 (0.20)
Nonvoters vs. Medvedev	-0.43 (0.11)**	-0.07 (0.10)	-0.31 (0.10)**	0.11 (0.10)	-0.15 (0.11)	-0.33 (0.11)**
Zhirinovsky vs. Zyuganov	0.10 (0.18)	-0.07 (0.19)	0.30 (0.18)+	0.31 (0.18)+	0.11 (0.17)	0.27 (0.23)

Note: Estimates represent multinomial logit coefficients representing the effects on vote choice as voter positions on the attitude scales increase by one standard deviation, with robust standard errors provided in parentheses. Shaded areas represent the highest coefficient for each row (i.e. each candidate pair). $^+ p < 0.10$, $^* p < 0.05$, $^{**} p < 0.01$.

The regime cleavage also directly divided the Russian opposition, according to the estimates in Table 5.1. In the crucial 1996 election, constituencies that voted for the liberal Yavlinsky, the nationalist Zhirinovsky, and the independent Lebed did not share the staunch opposition to Russia's electoral authoritarian regime of the supporters of the top-ranked opposition candidate: the Communist Zyuganov. As suggested by the significant and positive coefficients of the regime cleavage for the choices between each of these candidates and Zyuganov, more favorable outlooks toward Russia's electoral authoritarian system considerably increased the odds of voting for Yavlinsky, Zhirinovsky, and Lebed. The choices between these self-styled third-party candidates (i.e. not incumbent and not Communist) and Yeltsin, on the other hand, were not significantly affected by the regime cleavage.

This confirms that on the decisive issue of the 1996 presidential race – attitudes toward Russia's electoral authoritarian system – supporters of the nationalist and liberal oppositions would rather have voted for the incumbent Yeltsin than unify behind the opposition front-runner Zyuganov. The regime cleavage, in other words, served to isolate the strongest antiregime contender from the rest of the opposition, just as the strongman heresthetic model would predict. This is what indeed happened in the second round of the 1996 ballot: third-party opposition voters threw their support behind the regime candidate, delivering a landslide win for Yeltsin despite the widespread dissatisfaction with his rule (McFaul 1997, chs. 5–6).

The ML estimates in Table 5.1 also confirm that differences among the Russian opposition constituencies on the related issue of imposing a "tough" dictatorship made them at least as likely to support the incumbent as each other's candidates. In particular, a one standard deviation increase in opposition to a "tough" dictatorship in the 1996 election is associated with 1.3–1.7 times greater increases in the odds of voting for the incumbent Yeltsin than for the liberal candidate Yavlinsky, when pitted against Zyuganov, Lebed, or Zhirinovsky.[24] In turn, more

---

[24] Specifically, if we exponentiate the coefficients in Table 5.1 to obtain odds ratios (using the formula $odds = 100 \times exp(coefficient - 1)$), we would see that a standard deviation *decrease* in support for "tough" dictatorship in the 1996 election was associated with 50, 55, and 103 percent increases in the odds of voting for Yeltsin instead of Zyuganov, Lebed, and Zhirinovsky, respectively. The same shift would have respectively produced 30, 34, and 76 percent increases in the odds of voting for Yavlinsky over these other oppositional alternatives.

authoritarian stances on this issue in the presidential race in 2000 were about as likely to draw votes from Yavlinsky to Putin as from Yavlinsky to Zyuganov.[25] Paradoxically, as voter opinions shifted between the extremes on the democracy/authoritarianism spectrum, Russia's electoral authoritarian incumbents garnered at least as much support as their oppositional alternatives because they were seen as *moderates* – favoring a hybrid regime that supposedly avoided the chaos of a laissez-faire liberal democracy and the tyranny of a unbridled Communist or nationalist dictatorship.

This centrist, ideologically uncommitted stance of Russia's strongman incumbents also allowed them to exploit opposition divisions across the other key programmatic cleavages. In 1996, for instance, supporters of achievement-based incomes or free prices would have abandoned the Communist Zyuganov and the independent Lebed to vote for the liberal Yavlinsky (captured by the significant and positive coefficients on this variable in the equations comparing these candidates to Yavlinsky) – but not the incumbent Yeltsin (captured by the nonsignificant coefficient on the Yavlinsky–Yeltsin pair for this issue). In 2008, the advocates of Russia's Western identity would have preferred the nationalist Zhirinovsky over the Communist Zyuganov, but would have remained ambivalent when choosing between Zhirinovsky and the incumbent Medvedev. By adopting relatively moderate stances on these and other programmatic cleavages while touting strongarmed, efficient rule, Russia's electoral authoritarian incumbents made themselves appear as the safer, "saner," and more acceptable choices than their more ideologically committed oppositional alternatives.

These divisions allowed Russia's leaders to win crucial votes even among the regime's staunch opponents. The closely fought 1996 election is a case in point. The results from the 1996 NRB survey suggest that the widely unpopular Boris Yeltsin was still able to win an astonishing 21 percent of the vote among the great many Russians (46 percent) that had negative views of the regime he had established. This allowed him to prevail over Zyuganov, who despite the tremendous popular discontent, attracted only about half (49 percent) of the anti-systemic vote. Putin's

---

[25] Here, a standard deviation boost in support for "tough" dictatorship is associated with a 37 percent increase in the odds of voting for Putin over Yavlinsky and 46 percent for Zyuganov over Yavlinsky.

rise as a viable strongman allowed him to press this advantage much further. In his first election in 2000, Putin actually won the anti-systemic vote with 44 percent, while Zyuganov got 38 percent. In 2004, he extended this margin further, winning 52 percent of the vote among voters with antiregime outlooks, compared to the 29 percent of the top-ranked opposition candidate Kharitonov. By 2008, even Putin's proxy Medvedev managed to secure 45 percent of the vote among the regime's opponents, relative to Zyuganov's 44 percent. This is a remarkable achievement. Even as the number of Russians with negative outlooks toward their country's regime drastically declined – from almost half the voting population to below 10 percent in 2008 – Russia's incumbents won a larger share of the anti-systemic vote than any opposition candidate.

Against this backdrop, it was easier to establish and maintain authoritarianism in Russia by facing off the ill-reputed opposition forces in elections than by banning them. When the country's electoral autocracy delivered on its promises of stabilization, there were few reservations for popular mood to swing in the pro-regime direction. But even when Russia's electoral autocracy performed miserably, its leaders still attracted more votes than its challengers in the opposition, who were seen as too extreme and outlandish to provide better leader-ship. In these circumstances, "resigned acceptance" (Rose, Mishler, and Munro 2004) of electoral autocracy as a lesser evil than its alter-natives seemed the only reasonable response for most voters. This is the *Zeitgeist* that the strongman appeal is designed to produce.

Conclusion

This chapter tests the claim that popular majorities support electoral autocracy not just because they are pressured to do so, but primarily because they believe it serves a useful purpose: restoring stability and prosperity, and addressing core grievances in the wake of deep and persistent crises. Exploring the crucial case of Russia with a uniquely detailed set of popular opinion data, I show that the logic of electoral choice that emerges in such contexts makes it difficult for voters to rally behind an oppositional alternative even when they dislike their elect-oral authoritarian leaders. First, as long as electoral authoritarian strongmen can credibly justify their rule as a response to a crisis, popular majorities will be reluctant to replace them out of fear of renewed instability. Second, in the turbulent contexts in which electoral autocracies emerge, standard ideological and issue-based oppositional platforms lose their appeal, or produce mutually exclusive alternatives to the current order, dividing the antiregime vote.

These findings indicate that to a large degree, the roots of electoral authoritarianism lie in its ability to take advantage of such opinion currents with the heresthetic strategy of legitimizing its rule as a response to a national emergency. In the Russian case, this has allowed the country's regime to persist even when substantial majorities perceived its performance as abysmal and harbored negative views against it. Vladimir Putin's ability to restore a modicum of order and prosperity after the disastrous decade of post-Soviet decline, in turn, allowed him to completely displace any conceivable political alternatives in the popular imagination, and entrench a hegemonic electoral authoritarian system. Having survived the greatest peacetime decline in history, ordinary Russians eagerly traded their diverse political and ideological preferences, as well as their desires to live in a more democratic society, for the stability of Putin's strongman rule.

6 | Is Russia Unique? The Strongman Heresthetic in Comparative Perspective

It is [fear of not preserving themselves] that makes people so willing to follow brash, strong-looking demagogues with tight jaws and loud voices: those who focus their measured words and their sharpened eyes in the intensity of hate, and so seem most capable of cleansing the world of the vague, the weak, the uncertain, the evil. Ah, to give oneself over to their direction – what calm, what relief.

Ernest Becker (1971, 161)

Can the findings of the previous chapter be generalized beyond Russia? In particular, is the success of the strongman appeal, perfected by Vladimir Putin, a peculiarity of Russia's distinct circumstances? Or does it represent a global template for establishing robust electoral authoritarianism in post-crisis societies? To address these questions, I examine the patterns of popular opinion and electoral competition in democracies and electoral autocracies over the past thirty years by using cross-national data from the European and World Values Surveys (EVS 2011; WVS 2014).[1] Covering 104 countries in the 1981–2014 period, this dataset provides the most extensive currently available comparative data for exploring the popular opinion currents that lead to the rise and persistence of electoral authoritarianism throughout the globe.

From the standpoint of this study, European and World Values Surveys (WVS/EVS) have two essential advantages. First, because these surveys have repeatedly asked the same questions across countries and over time, analyzing them allows us to track mass attitudes in countries that have experienced electoral authoritarianism – before, during, and after the reign of these regimes – as well as to contrast these attitudes with popular opinions in stable democracies. Second, the WVS/EVS contain questions very similar to those used in the analysis of Russian popular opinion in the previous chapter, allowing to

[1] See EVS 2020, Inglehart et al. 2020.

replicate it on a cross-national level. Finally, the WVS/EVS data contain a composite index of "survival" values: a set of outlooks that reflect emphasis on physical and economic security, as well as low levels of intergroup tolerance and trust.[2] A high prevalence of survival values should be typical for societies that have faced existential threats and crises and should be closely associated with support for strongman rule. Hence, tracking these sentiments across political regimes and over time provides the simplest and most direct way to verify the link between systemic crises, popular opinion, and the rise of electoral autocracy.

Survival Values and Electoral Authoritarianism

Comparing the prevalence of survival values across populations is the most natural starting point for this analysis. In particular, if this book's theory of electoral authoritarianism is valid, survival values should be most prevalent in the immediate periods before the consolidation of electoral autocracies, as systemic crises lead to growing popular demands for restoring order and stability. Furthermore, the spread of survival values across the population should be comparatively higher before the rise of electoral authoritarianism than ahead of transitions to democracy or closed authoritarianism. This is because electoral autoc-racies are uniquely capable of harnessing popular demands for stability through their appeal as a pragmatic, middle-ground solution to acute crises. Promising to avoid both the fecklessness of liberal democracy and the unbridled tyranny of closed dictatorship, electoral authoritar-ianism should be more attractive than either of these alternatives in stability-craving societies.

To test these claims, I compare the means of the survival values indices in the electoral autocracies and democracies covered by the WVS/EVS surveys across three different periods: (1) Five years before the rise of each of these regimes; (2) during their reigns; and (3) all other periods. This analysis includes survey data from forty-two countries from across the globe that have had spells of electoral authoritarianism, seventy-one that have had periods of democratic rule, and nine that

---

[2] For a full list of the survey items and the procedure used to derive "survival" values" indicator in the WVS/EVS surveys, see Inglehart and Welzel (2005).

experienced military dictatorship.[3] To avoid biasing results in favor of my hypotheses, I exclude survey data from Russia.

The results of this comparison, which I display in Figure 6.1, closely align with the crisis theory of electoral authoritarianism. Starting in the left panel of Figure 6.1, we can see that five-year periods *before* the rise of electoral authoritarian regimes had the highest average prevalence of survival values among populations that experienced this regime type. In turn, this emphasis on physical and material security and well-being was somewhat lower *during* the tenure of these regimes, and much lower in periods when these countries were ruled by other systems. This is consistent with the idea that electoral authoritarianism typically emerges in the wake of the most traumatic periods in the histories of the countries governed by such regimes and is legitimized by acute fears about physical and material security.

The link between high existential anxieties and the rise of electoral authoritarianism becomes even more apparent if we compare the prevalence of these sentiments across regimes. Looking across the three panels of Figure 6.1, five-year periods preceding the rise of electoral authoritarianism have the highest average prevalence of survival values of *all periods* in *all regime types*. This is a key result. No other period in the histories of the 104 countries covered in the WVS/EVS dataset for 1981–2014 that had democratic, military, or electoral authoritarian regimes display such a high prevalence of existential anxieties as the five-year intervals preceding the rise of electoral autocracies.

Furthermore, only countries that had experienced electoral authoritarianism had opinion patterns matching the strongman theory of authoritarian legitimation. Neither democracies nor military dictatorships, as these findings suggest, were preceded by peak levels of existential anxieties among the underlying populations. Indeed, in the nine

---

[3] In total, this analysis draws on 202,313 survey responses collected in 127 surveys carried out in 42 countries that experienced electoral authoritarian rule; 386,743 survey responses collected in 276 surveys carried out in 71 countries that had democratic rule; and 33,141 survey responses collected in 23 surveys carried out in 9 countries that had been ruled by military juntas. The data on the five-year periods before the rise of these regimes come from nineteen electoral autocracies, twenty-three democracies, and four military dictatorships. Other closed dictatorships, including monarchies and single-party regimes, are excluded from the analysis due to the lack of surveys in the WVS/EVS dataset covering the periods before their rise and after their demise.

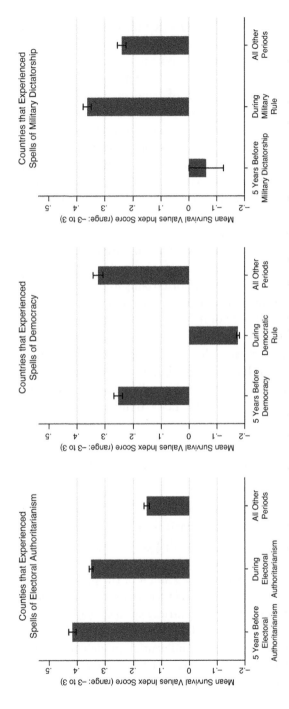

Figure 6.1 Mean "survival" values in countries that have experienced electoral authoritarian, democratic, and military rule

* *Note*: bars presented with 95 percent confidence intervals

countries surveyed in the WVS/EVS dataset that had been ruled by military dictatorships, the five-year periods before their rise registered the *lowest* prevalence of survival values compared to any other time – the exact opposite of what the strongman legitimation theory would predict. And in countries that had spells of democracy, survival values were highest in the periods of *nondemocratic rule*, rather than the immediate five-year periods before democratization. Democracies, in other words, were not preceded by a spike but a relative decline in survivalist outlooks, which then decreased even further during their rule. All these patterns point to the same conclusion: unlike electoral autocracies, transitions to democracies and military dictatorships could not, on average, have been legitimized by unprecedented existential anxieties among their populations.

In the broadest sense, the findings in Figure 6.1 indicate that mass opinion is a key mediating variable between background circumstances and the rise of electoral authoritarianism. While the analyses in Chapter 3 identified acute conflict and economic decline as the closest precursors of electoral authoritarianism, the opinion patterns in Figure 6.1 suggest that heightened existential anxieties, presumably activated by these upheavals, have been the key intervening variable. This is in line with the findings of the Russian case study, where electoral autocracy was not a direct product of crisis but was only made possible by the mass opinion shifts that it engendered.

Existential Anxieties and the Regime Cleavage in Electoral Autocracies

But does this heightened sense of existential insecurity and mobilization of survival instincts allow authoritarianism to be established and sustained through the ballot box? To verify that the strongman heresthetic of the sort we observed in Russia operates across the globe, two conditions – summarized in hypotheses 3 and 4 of the previous chapter – must be satisfied. First, authoritarian forces must focus people's choices on the issue of whether their countries need a strong-armed but electorally accountable regime, which promises to restore stability. Second, this regime cleavage must be influential enough to displace any other salient issues and attachments that allow the opponents of strongman regimes to vie for popular support.

To test the first proposition, I examine whether support for the existing political system in electoral autocracies is associated with existential fears and demands for strong-armed plebiscitarian rule. I do this by measuring the associations of the current political system support scale in the WVS/EVS surveys, which asks respondents to rate their governing system, and a range of issue stances, ideological outlooks, evaluations, and demographic controls. These include respondent survival values scores, attitudes toward democracy and having a strong leader unchecked by parliament or elections, views on the issue of whether the government's main priority should be to guarantee freedoms or to maintain order, positions on the left/right ideological scale, trust in key institutions (government, parliament, political parties, the justice system, the press, and the army), and sense of pride in one's nationality. To account for confounding factors in the cross-national setting, all least-square regressions models I use for this purpose also contain country-year fixed effects, capturing country-and year-specific unmeasured or idiosyncratic factors, as well as individual-level demographic and other controls.

Because these questions were fielded in the WVS/EVS surveys only for 1996–2001 in electoral autocracies and 1994–2002 in democracies, the analysis is limited to this period. However, the narrow focus on the mid-to-late-1990s is, in some ways, an advantage, as it provides a stricter test of the strongman heresthetic mechanism, for two reasons. First, because the analysis takes place before the rise and consolidation of Putinism, similarities with the Russian case should increase our confidence in its broader generalizability. Second, the 1990s came in the wake of the largest democratization wave in history, when democratization pressures were the greatest. To survive, the electoral autocracies from this period would have been compelled to closely adhere to the strongman heresthetic legitimation strategy – ruling with minimal coercion and on the basis of their popular appeal – helping us verify the content of this appeal with the WVS/EVS survey data.

The regressions I estimate for this purpose represent a cross-national analogue of the analysis of the main dimension of Russian popular opinion in the previous chapter. As in Russia, identifying the attitudes that are most strongly associated with support for the current political system allows us to triangulate people's motives for embracing their regimes. The cross-national analysis of political system support also allows us to contrast the sources of regime support in electoral autocracies and democracies. This is another opportunity to verify the strongman heresthetic account of electoral authoritarian legitimation. If this book's theory is valid, existential anxieties, and demands for order and strong-armed rule should be strongly and positively associated with support for the current political system in electoral authoritarian regimes, but not in democracies. To confirm whether this is the case, I estimate the same models separately for electoral autocracies and democracies.

The results of these analyses, provided in Table 6.1, closely conform to the strongman heresthetic model. First, the estimates from models 1–4 indicate that survival value scores and views that governments should prioritize maintaining order over protecting freedoms are strongly and positively associated with support for the current political system *only* in electoral autocracies. In democracies, these sentiments have negligible and statistically insignificant effects on systemic support. Second, just as in the Russian case, regime support in electoral autocracies is most strongly related with trust in the government, the (typically co-opted) legislatures, and the army. In democracies, on the other hand, these correlates of systemic support are also balanced by trust in political parties and judicial system – institutions that are more likely to check executive power.

These legitimation differences across the two regime types closely match with the strongman electoral authoritarian appeal, which calls for unrestrained executive and repressive power, and the weakening of institutionalized pluralism, political competition, and checks and balances. In turn, demands for a strong leader who does not have to bother with parliament and elections have a positive association with regime support in electoral autocracies that is just below 10 percent statistical significance level. This kind of muted association is exactly what this book's theory would predict, given that the attitude in question also implies rejection of electoral authoritarianism in favor of a traditional closed dictatorship.

We observe a similar relationship with the view that democracy is a better system of governance despite its problems. From this book's perspective, there should be a nonlinear, inverted-U relationship between preferences for democracy and regime support in electoral autocracies. As the appeal of electoral authoritarianism lies in its hybrid nature, providing a pragmatic, middle-of-the-road solution to acute crises, support for these regimes peaks among those who prefer

Table 6.1 *The correlates of regime support in electoral autocracies and democracies, 1994–2002*

	(1) Electoral autocracies	(2) Democracies	(3) Electoral autocracies	(4) Democracies	(5) Electoral autocracies	(6) Democracies	(7) Electoral autocracies	(8) Democracies
"Survival" values scale	0.21 (0.06)**	0.00 (0.06)						
Government's main responsibility is to maintain order			0.32 (0.08)**	−0.00 (0.06)				
Good to have a strong leader who does not have to bother with Parliament and elections					0.11 (0.06)	−0.04 (0.05)		
Trust in government							0.40 (0.04)**	0.36 (0.04)**
Trust in Parliament							0.12 (0.05)*	0.19 (0.02)**
Trust in political parties							−0.04 (0.04)	0.06 (0.02)*

Table 6.1 (*cont.*)

	(1) Electoral autocracies	(2) Democracies	(3) Electoral autocracies	(4) Democracies	(5) Electoral autocracies	(6) Democracies	(7) Electoral autocracies	(8) Democracies
Trust in the justice system							0.06 (0.05)	0.06 (0.02)*
Trust in the press							-0.05 (0.04)	0.02 (0.01)
Trust in the army							0.10 (0.03)*	-0.00 (0.03)
Democracy has problems but is better than the alternatives	0.21 (0.07)*	0.49 (0.09)**	0.18 (0.08)+	0.47 (0.09)**	0.19 (0.06)*	0.49 (0.09)**	0.18 (0.08)*	0.40 (0.08)**
Proud of one's nationality	0.44 (0.11)**	0.39 (0.07)**	0.53 (0.07)**	0.37 (0.05)**	0.40 (0.08)**	0.41 (0.06)**	0.39 (0.04)**	0.30 (0.06)**
Left/right scale (left higher)	-0.07 (0.04)+	-0.06 (0.03)+	-0.09 (0.05)+	-0.04 (0.03)	-0.06 (0.04)	-0.05 (0.03)+	-0.05 (0.04)	-0.01 (0.02)
Respondent feeling of happiness	0.30 (0.05)**	0.12 (0.07)	0.24 (0.07)**	0.13 (0.06)*	0.22 (0.04)**	0.14 (0.05)*	0.18 (0.05)**	0.14 (0.05)*

	(1)	(2)	(3)	(4)	(5)	(6)	(7)	(8)
Satisfaction with financial situation of household	0.05	0.06	0.09	0.07	0.07	0.06	0.07	0.05
	$(0.02)^{**}$	$(0.02)^{**}$	$(0.02)^{**}$	$(0.01)^{**}$	$(0.02)^{**}$	$(0.01)^{**}$	$(0.02)^{*}$	$(0.01)^{**}$
Sense of freedom of choice and control over one's life	0.06	0.07	0.03	0.08	0.03	0.07	0.04	0.08
	$(0.02)^{**}$	$(0.01)^{**}$	(0.03)	$(0.01)^{**}$	(0.02)	$(0.01)^{**}$	(0.02)	$(0.01)^{**}$
Female	-0.04	0.01	0.04	-0.02	0.02	0.01	0.08	-0.00
	(0.10)	(0.05)	(0.07)	(0.06)	(0.07)	(0.05)	(0.06)	(0.05)
Age	0.00	-0.00	0.00	-0.00	0.01	-0.00	0.00	-0.00
	(0.00)	(0.00)	$(0.00)^{+}$	(0.00)	$(0.00)^{*}$	(0.00)	(0.00)	(0.00)
Education	-0.02	-0.00	-0.02	0.07	0.01	0.03	0.13	0.14
	(0.11)	(0.10)	(0.10)	(0.11)	(0.08)	(0.09)	(0.07)	(0.10)
Income	0.03	-0.02	0.00	-0.01	0.02	-0.02	0.03	0.01
	(0.03)	(0.02)	(0.03)	(0.02)	(0.03)	(0.03)	(0.03)	(0.02)
Interest in politics	0.13	0.24	0.14	0.26	0.11	0.24	0.13	0.17
	$(0.04)^{**}$	$(0.04)^{**}$	$(0.04)^{*}$	$(0.04)^{**}$	$(0.04)^{**}$	$(0.04)^{**}$	$(0.04)^{*}$	$(0.04)^{**}$
Country-year dummies	YES	YES	YES	YES	YES	YES	YES	YES
Observations	8798	24484	8810	21108	13684	27371	9031	21830
Countries	12	30	9	28	13	30	9	28
Country-years	12	35	9	28	14	35	9	28
R-squared	0.83	0.84	0.83	0.84	0.80	0.84	0.85	0.86

Robust standard errors in parentheses; $^{+}p < 0.10$, $^{*}p < 0.05$, $^{**}p < 0.01$

more limited forms of democracy/authoritarianism, and weakens among strong devotees of democracy and closed authoritarianism.

To verify this thesis, I estimate models 1 and 2 from Table 6.1 with a squared democracy preference term that can capture such nonlinearities. The results from these analyses are displayed in Figure 6.2 below. They confirm that in electoral autocracies, stronger preferences for democracy translate into greater regime support only up to a point. As expected, this effect peaks for respondents around the middle of the scale, those who somewhat agree that the virtues of democracy trump its flaws, and then declines slightly among "purer" democrats, who strongly agree with this premise. In democracies, on the other hand, greater conviction as to democratic virtues always translates into higher regime support (though at a somewhat diminishing rate). Again, these outlooks are consistent with the idea that popular support for an electoral authoritarian system reflects a clear-cut *desire for a hybrid regime*, which is neither democratic nor fully authoritarian. It is likely to find its greatest supporters, as these results show, among those who prefer a system of limited electoral accountability, which can presumably combine the advantages and avoid the pitfalls of both pure regime types.

The results in Table 6.1 also showcase several other sentiments which according to the strongman legitimation theory should be closely aligned with support for electoral authoritarianism. They suggest that increased sense of national pride has a somewhat stronger positive effect on regime support in electoral autocracies than in democracies. This might be seen as a response to the trademark strongman appeal to nationalism, patriotism, and the need for national unity in times of crisis, highlighted in the analyses in Chapter 4. Respondents' feelings of happiness have an even stronger relationship to regime support in electoral autocracies compared to democracies. This does not seem to be a product of performance legitimacy, however. If it were, the respondents' satisfaction with family finances and their sense of freedom and control over their lives would also correlate strongly with political system support in electoral autocracies. Instead, the effect of these variables is equal to or weaker than in democracies. What the relation between happiness and support for electoral authoritarian rule may instead capture is the ability of these regimes to soothe

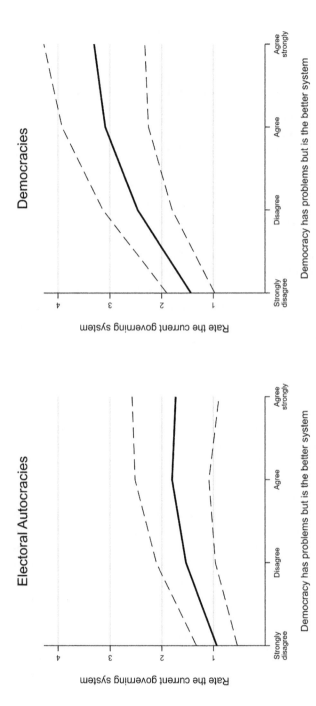

Figure 6.2 Relationship between preferences for democracy and regime support in electoral autocracies and democracies
Note: The dashed lines indicate 95 percent confidence intervals.

people's existential anxieties, and to reinforce the sense of collective identity.[4]

The Elected Strongman Cleavage and Voting Behavior

On the whole, this chapter's analyses thus far leave little doubt that just
as in Russia, the roots of regime support in electoral autocracies from
across the world have been largely driven by existential fears and
demands for strong-armed, yet electorally accountable rule. But is
this electoral authoritarianism cleavage influential enough to enable
strongman incumbents to secure power through the ballot box and
with minimal coercion? The theoretical framework developed in
Chapter 2 suggests strongmen candidates and parties gain the upper
hand if in tumultuous circumstances, the choice to establish an electoral authoritarian regime begins to dominate the voting calculus, displacing other cleavages. Or to state it differently, opposition to
strongman rule crumbles when existential anxieties compel voters to
support authoritarian parties and leaders even when this runs counter
to their other ideological preferences and allegiances.

This theory has two key observable implications. First, demands for
tough, electoral authoritarian rule should affect vote choices *at least as
strongly* as other key issue stances. Second, this skewered pattern of
political competition should only emerge in societies traumatized by
turmoil, which, as Chapter 3 demonstrated, have been increasingly
governed by electoral autocracies since the 1970s. It should have no
sway over popular opinion and vote choice in stable, established
Western democracies.

To test these propositions, I compare the influence of demands for
strong-armed rule on vote choice in electoral autocracies and democracies. For each of these regimes, the analysis asks the same question: are
the odds of voting for the main opposition party instead of the incumbent influenced, above all else, by the respondents' support for a strong-
armed, authoritarian political system? Focusing on races between these
top contenders, as we have seen in the Russian case, allows us to

---

[4] This mechanism was first discussed by Arendt (1966) and Fromm (1941), for
   instance, who argued that discontented and desperate majorities found their
   "escape from freedom" in the classless, atomized totalitarian system, as it
   promised liberation from the rootlessness, uncertainty, insecurity, and general
   lack of cohesion of the deeply troubled societies of the 1920s and 1930s.

capture the most essential features of political competition in a parsimonious fashion.

The key challenge here is to isolate only the portion of regime support that is driven by demands for *electoral* authoritarian rule. For this purpose, I estimate the models of vote choice in two stages. In the first stage, I predict support for the current political system in each country using only the variables that were most closely associated with preferences for electoral authoritarian rule in the analyses in Table 6.1. These include respondent stances on having a strong leader, whether the government's priority should be to maintain order, the level of national pride, trust in the army, and the degree of happiness. I then use the predicted values from the first stage as instruments in models of vote choice for the respective countries. This allows me to indirectly measure the extent to which political system support across different countries and regimes is driven by the same desire for a strong-armed, but *electorally* accountable rule (rather than a closed dictatorship).

Using this approach, I first estimate the effect of preferences for strongman rule in all ten electoral autocracies in the 1995–1998 period for which full data are available in the WVS/EVS surveys. Despite the limited number of cases, this sample is representative of electoral autocracies from across the world. Second, turning to democracies, I analyze the impact of strongman preferences on vote choice in nine established Western democracies for which the key variables are available in the WVS/EVS dataset. This narrowed focus is deliberate. In particular, it allows me to verify that attitudes toward strong-armed rule *do not* meaningfully affect political competition in stable democratic settings. This claim could not be reliably tested in the full sample of democracies, which includes many recent, transitional, and generally unstable democratic regimes.

I display the results of these vote choice analyses in Figures 6.3 and 6.4 below. The results in these graphs represent effects of one standard deviation shifts in two key issue stances: (1) respondents' support for strongman rule; and (2) positions on the left/right spectrum. Figure 6.3 provides the estimated impacts of shifts in support for strongman rule (the left panel) and respondent stances on the left/right scale (the middle and right panels) on their odds of voting for the main opposition parties versus the incumbents in electoral autocracies. I use the left/right cleavage as a benchmark against which to measure the impact of authoritarian preferences for a simple reason: it is the most general ideological "super issue," fusing respondent views on a broad range on policies (see e.g. Bobbio 1996; Gabel and Huber 2000). Hence, if support for strongman rule matches or surpasses the influence of orientations on the left/right spectrum, we can be more confident that it plays the broad diversionary role observed in Russia – drawing people's attention away from issues and platforms that could be used to challenge authoritarian incumbents.

And this is exactly what the results of Figure 6.3 suggest. In a clear majority of electoral autocracies, the strongman regime cleavage had a roughly equal or greater impact on vote choice than orientations on the left/right scale. Specifically, in eight of the ten electoral autocracies examined in Figure 6.3, one standard deviation shifts in demands for a strong-armed regime either had a greater (Croatia, FR. Yugoslavia, Azerbaijan, and Peru) or similar (Belarus, Armenia, Russia, and Mexico) effect on the odds of choosing between incumbents and their main opponents as the left/right scale. Only in two of these cases (Georgia and Albania) did the left/right cleavage have a clearly greater sway in the voter calculus. In line with theoretical predictions and the patterns observed in the Russian case, these results suggest that in most electoral autocracies, the appeal of tough-mannered executive rule trumps other prominent cleavages that could serve as rallying points for the opposition.

I have partially obscured this greater explanatory power of the regime cleavage in electoral autocracies in the middle panel of Figure 6.3 by aligning the direction of the alternative, left/right cleavage so that higher values favor the incumbent.[5] This coding facilitates comparisons with higher support for strongman rule in the left panel, which, in line with this book's predictions, are always aligned in favor of electoral authoritarian incumbents. However, if we use a consistent, unidirectional coding for the left/right orientations, higher (i.e. more left-leaning) values do not always increase the incumbent's odds of victory. In fact, in most of the cases in Figure 6.3 where the effects of this variable are significant, the opposite is true. I show this in the right panel of Figure 6.3. The results there indicate that leftward shifts significantly increased the odds of

---

[5] In other words, I use a scale on which higher values denote more leftist stances when this increases the odds of voting for the current office-holders. When the odds of voting for the incumbent are boosted by more right-leaning orientations, I reverse the scale to reflect rightist stances.

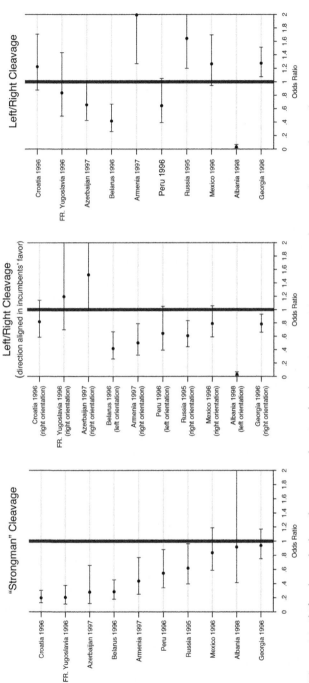

Figure 6.3 Shifts along the key cleavages and voting for the main opposition party vs. the incumbent in *electoral autocracies*

* *Note*: Estimates display the effects of one standard deviation shifts in the issue stances, represented as odds ratios from multinomial logit models, with 95 percent confidence intervals obtained from bootstrapped standard errors.

casting a vote for the main opposition challengers in Armenia, Russia, and Georgia. In Albania and Belarus, on the other hand, shifts to the left meaningfully favored the incumbent.

The left/right cleavage, in other words, does not play favorites – shifts along this spectrum may advantage either incumbents or oppositions. Heightened popular demands for strongman rule, in contrast, *always* favor authoritarian incumbents. This again highlights their crucial role in the rise and persistence of electoral autocracies. By displacing programmatic cleavages that can serve as platforms to challenge them, these sentiments create the conditions for stable authoritarian dominance at the ballot box.

Political competition in stable democracies follows the exact opposite pattern to that of electoral autocracies, according to the results in Figure 6.4. First, the estimates in the leftmost panel of this figure show that support for strongman rule had practically no bearing on voters' choices between incumbents and their main opposition challengers in Western democracies. The effect of authoritarian preferences does not approach statistical significance at the conventional levels in any of the countries examined here. Even if we ignore statistical significance, in nearly half of the democracies examined (the United States, Australia, Switzerland, and New Zealand), increased support for strongman rule behaves in a manner that is contrary to what we observed in electoral autocracies: it is associated, on average, with higher odds of voting for the main *opposition party* instead of the incumbent (as seen by positive mean odds ratios estimates for these countries). Authoritarian preferences, to put it differently, do not systematically favor current office-holders in democracies.

Furthermore, shifts along the left/right cleavage play a much more robust role in established democracies than they do in electoral autocracies. As the results in the middle panel of Figure 6.4 show, the effects of this variable were not only statistically significant in all the Western democracies analyzed here, but they were also substantively much larger than in electoral autocracies. Specifically, these estimates indicate that a one standard deviation shift in the incumbent's direction on the left/right spectrum would reduce the odds of voting for the main opposition party by between 40 and nearly 100 percent. Again, these empirical findings closely match the predictions of the strongman heresthetic model. In sharp contrast to the electoral autocracies in Figure 6.3, where left/right orientations took the back seat to

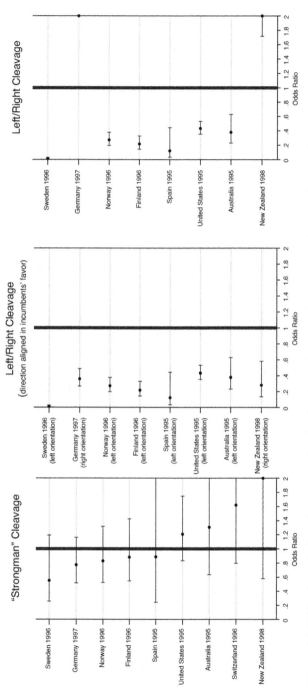

Figure 6.4 Shifts along the key cleavages and voting for the main opposition party vs. the incumbent in *democracies*

* *Note*: Estimates display the effects of one standard deviation shifts in the issue stances, represented as odds ratios from multinomial logit models with 95 percent confidence intervals obtained from bootstrapped standard errors.

preferences for strongman rule, the left/right programmatic cleavage has played a decisive role in determining the electoral winner in Western democracies. Unaffected by authoritarian impulses, electorates in these stable democracies have chosen their leaders by relying, for the most part, on issue stances that do not systematically favor incumbents.

Conclusion

The cross-national analyses in the preceding passages show that the patterns of electoral authoritarian legitimation that we observed in Russia in the previous chapter are broadly generalizable to similar regimes from across the world. Examining popular opinion trends in a diverse set of regimes surveyed by the WVS/EVS project, I find that just like in post-Communist Russia, periods before the rise of electoral autocracies have been characterized by record levels of existential anxieties among the underlying populations. At the same time, analyses of vote choice in these settings show that long before the rise of the Putinist model in Russia, electoral authoritarian incumbents from across the globe exploited similar kinds of fears to rearrange political competition in their favor. Transforming elections into referenda on strongman rule that guarantees stability and a modicum of representativeness and restraint, they have displaced traditional programmatic cleavages and appeals that can be used to challenge them, dramatically shrinking the scope for oppositional victory – even in perfectly clean elections.

7 | *Conclusions and Implications*

Nothing appears more surprising to those who consider human affairs . . . than the easiness with which the many are governed by the few . . . When we inquire by what means this wonder is achieved, we shall find that . . . the governors have nothing to support them but opinion. It is, therefore, on opinion only that government is founded; and this maxim extends to the most despotic and the most military governments, as well as to the most free and most popular.

David Hume (1742)

Why are some dictatorships genuinely popular and capable of sustaining their rule through regular multiparty elections? This book argues that the main force behind the emergence of electoral autocracies – the most widespread and resilient form of authoritarianism since the end of the Cold War – lies in these regimes' ability to justify their reign as a response to seemingly intractable crises in societies traumatized by turmoil. Such upheavals discredit the existing political forces and create broad popular demands for stability and for grievances to be addressed. This allows political parties and candidates which call for strong-armed rule to seize and hold power through the ballot box and with minimal repression. At the same time, the nominally democratic constitutional framework and plebiscitarian nature of electoral autocracies provide a degree of popular legitimacy, representativeness, and restraint, enabling such regimes to maintain the pretense of a democratic order.

These traits make electoral authoritarianism appear an attractive remedy for both democracies and closed autocracies gripped by instability and dysfunction. In liberal democracies embroiled in conflict or socioeconomic cataclysms, majorities often yearn for the firm hand of an elected leader with unchecked powers, who will overcome institutional paralysis, wipe out corrupt elites and special interests, and bring order and justice, but still stop short of imposing naked tyranny.

In closed autocracies plagued by strife, economic decay, and declining legitimacy, electoral authoritarianism provides a path to a revitalized and more representative system without risking the instability of full pluralism.

In Chapter 1 and throughout this book, I show that the rise and resilience of electoral autocracies cannot be fully attributed to the use of the traditional coercive tactics of nondemocracies – repression, patronage, propaganda, and electoral fraud. These methods have a well-documented tendency to backfire, particularly when used by unpopular regimes in partially open settings. Thus, electoral autocracies can only afford to use mass-scale repression, patronage, propaganda, and vote fraud when they have the stable support of popular majorities or substantial pluralities. Shifting patterns of popular support also determine the loyalty of the elites in autocracies. I also claim that ambitious or disgruntled regime insiders and powerful elites stand little chance against a popular regime, which can mobilize the masses. However, those elites readily turn against an electoral autocracy that has fallen out of favor. For this reason, the only stable electoral autocracies are majority tyrannies: regimes that have genuine mass support in spite of, or indeed, because of their authoritarian nature.

Convincing electoral majorities to willingly submit to authoritarian rule is therefore the most essential prerequisite for the rise and survival of electoral authoritarianism. In Chapter 2, I develop a full theoretical framework linking popular consent to electoral authoritarianism with these regimes' ability to persuade majorities that they are the most pragmatic governing system for societies plagued by turmoil. Contrary to the prevailing view in the literature that electoral autocracies have superficial and inconsistent legitimizing strategies, I argue that the secret of success of these regimes lies in a distinct elected "strongman" doctrine and appeal, which seeks to justify electoral authoritarianism as a form of emergency rule, suited to unstable and dysfunctional societies. This broad appeal of strong-armed regimes rationalized as a sort of a popularly mandated emergency rule in times of trouble has allowed electoral authoritarianism to emerge and be sustained from within nominally democratic constitutional frameworks, in the name of the people, and with their explicit backing in regular elections.

I argue that the content and strategic purpose of this strongman appeal of elected autocrats lies hidden in plain sight, obscured by the seemingly impulsive, vulgar, populist, and cynical language through which it is delivered to mass audiences. But behind these theatrics lies a finely nuanced and carefully orchestrated ploy to take advantage of the most powerful instincts of societies beset by turmoil and despair: fears of instability and the urge for self-preservation. Such sentiments have motivated people to accept, and indeed demand, iron-fisted rule, giving rise to a remarkably stable equilibrium. As long as people dread anarchy and dysfunction more than they resent dictatorial malice, their consent serves as the main pillar of a robust electoral authoritarian Leviathan.

By connecting the top-down supply of electoral authoritarianism with the bottom-up popular demand in some circumstances, this book challenges the dominant elite-centric view of how these regimes rise and persist. Contrary to conventional wisdom, I claim that in societies besieged by crises, ordinary citizens are often more reliable backers of authoritarianism than the political, military, economic, intellectual, and bureaucratic elites. It is far easier to convince average citizens threatened by turmoil to sustain autocracy by simply not resisting it, than to maintain the loyalty and active cooperation of the notoriously fickle elites, who need to temper their ambitions, invest their resources in and tie their fortunes to this regime. Capable of stopping any revolution and elite coup in their tracks, the collective inertia and apathy of the masses is the most powerful guarantee of autocratic stability.

Chapter 3 tests the key macro-level implication of this theory: that electoral autocracies emerge in the wake of severe and sustained crises and cataclysms. Based on a comprehensive cross-national event history analysis of regime transitions for 1960–2014, it confirms that security and economic crises are the structural factors most closely associated with transitions to electoral authoritarianism from democracies, single-party systems, and military dictatorships – the categories accounting for the overwhelming majority of regime changes in this period. I find that while other factors, such as economic development, resource rents, and the diffusion of democracy, had a significant influence on the rise of electoral authoritarianism, they account for far less variation in this outcome over time, and do not predict it across all modes of transition.

Crucially, the effects of these factors are also moderated by the presence of systemic crises. Economic development, for instance, protects democracies from backsliding into electoral authoritarianism only in the absence of conflict. Resource rents, in turn, prevent the collapse of military dictatorships only during economic downturns, while a higher share of neighboring democracies promotes the liberalization of single-party regimes only in the absence of economic and security crises. Major systemic crises, in other words, confound the effects of other key predictors of electoral authoritarianism. In line with this book's theory, they amplify or diminish the effects of coercive power and resources, and external democratization pressures, helping electoral autocracies to emerge even where they seem to be at a structural disadvantage.

The findings in Chapter 3 also reveal that traumatic histories of economic and security crises not only increase the probability of electoral authoritarian rule, but also boost its longevity. They do so by greatly diminishing the odds of these regimes' democratization or collapse into closed dictatorships like military juntas. This result is consistent with the book's thesis that electoral authoritarianism is preferred to both democracy and closed autocracies in societies traumatized by cries, as such backgrounds allow these regimes to compellingly justify their rule as a more balanced, middle-ground option: one that is authoritarian enough to ensure steady and effective rule, and at the same time, sufficiently representative to make sure that it is relatively restrained and broadly accepted.

Chapter 4 shows that the campaign appeals of electoral autocracies have followed a remarkably consistent pattern, seeking to take advantage of their "strongman savior" appeal in countries with tumultuous backgrounds. Through a study of cross-national data from the Comparative Manifestos Project dataset (Volkens et al. 2016) and a qualitative analysis of the appeals of the archetypal Russian and Mexican electoral autocracies, I find that to a much greater degree than liberal democracies, these regimes have stressed the need for national unity, strong government, and the surrendering of some freedoms in order to protect society in difficult times, as well as their unique competence to carry out this task. At the same time, electoral autocracies have, in their campaigns, emphasized their allegedly greater respect for democracy and the interests of the people in comparison to the opposition parties. These seemingly contradictory appeals closely match the main tenets of the strongman legitimizing doctrine, outlined in Chapter 2 – the *Rally-Around-the-Strongman, Negative Legitimacy,* and *Democratic Legitimacy* frames – as well as the overarching claim that in times of crisis, the most democratic system is the one that reflects popular demands to restore stability by any means necessary.

In Chapter 5, I test the thesis that deep systemic crises refashion mass attitudes in ways that provide durable electoral advantages to strongmen parties and leaders. This chapter performs an in-depth study of the case of Russia, which has served as the preeminent global model of robust electoral authoritarianism since the rise of Vladimir Putin. To trace the trajectory of Putinism, I first outline the scope and consequences of Russia's catastrophic post-Communist cataclysm and how it reshaped popular opinion. Based on a longitudinal analysis of a uniquely detailed set of 418 surveys for 1993–2011, produced by Russia's independent Levada polling center, this analysis shows that people's desire for stability and effective government in the wake of crises allowed the country's increasingly authoritarian incumbents to realign political competition along a new cleavage: the choice to support or reject their strongman rule, which promised to restore and maintain order by all means necessary while also remaining electorally accountable. I also confirm that this cleavage structure fostered deep divisions in the opposition camp. This enabled Russia's electoral autocracy to survive despite its poor record of performance and the fact that, at times, it had the approval of less than a third of the country's population.

In Chapter 6, I perform a broad spectrum of cross-national opinion analyses, which show that the patterns observed in Russia are also prevalent in other electoral autocracies. Examining comparative cross-national opinion data from forty-two electoral autocracies in the 1981–2014 period, drawn from the European and World Values Surveys (EVS 2011; WVS 2014), I find that just as in Russia, electoral authoritarian incumbents from across the globe have exploited traumas resulting from unmanageable turmoil to reconfigure mass opinion and political competition in their favor. Turning elections into referenda on strongman rule that promises stability and protection, they have displaced traditional programmatic cleavages and appeals that can be used to challenge them, dramatically shrinking the scope for the rise of a robust, unified opposition. The final segment of Chapter 6 shows that this cleavage structure and logic of vote choice differs substantially from those in stable Western democracies, confirming again that the advantages electoral autocracies enjoy at the polls are largely owing to the extraordinarily subversive power of the strongman appeal in troubled societies.

Taken together, this book's sweeping empirical analyses provide strong support for the strongman appeal theory of electoral authoritarianism, which associates the rise and endurance of these regimes with their distinct attractiveness in the wake of deep systemic crises. The empirical findings of this study are unique in that they combine evidence from three very different perspectives and levels of aggregation: (1) the standpoint of the "high-altitude," macro-level structural factors associated with the rise and persistence of authoritarianism; (2) the level of political discourse, looking at the "supply side" of authoritarian appeals during electoral campaigns; and (3) the micro-level, attitudinal "demand-side" perspective of electoral authoritarianism, exploring popular opinion and voting behavior patterns that might contribute to electoral dictatorship. Not only do these separate analyses independently verify the strongman theory of electoral authoritarianism, but they also pool together a uniquely rich set of data for a wide variety of robustness tests.

The Role of Crises in the Rise of Electoral Authoritarianism

This book's findings highlight an uncomfortable truth: that broad popular strata are often willing, though perhaps unenthusiastic, participants in sustaining electoral authoritarianism. I show that electoral autocracies establish and maintain their rule by exploiting mass anxieties and appealing to broad popular demands for stability and justice in the wake of deep systemic crises. Prompted by self-preservation impulses in the wake of major crises, substantial majorities become tolerant of systematic encroachments on political freedoms and democratic institutions – violations they may otherwise resist. And in many cases, sizable constituencies actively cheer the authoritarian behavior of these regimes: the stacking of institutions with loyalists, the clamping down on free speech and the media, and the persecution of opposition figures and various "troublesome" minorities.

Democracy, from this perspective, is not merely hijacked by elected strongmen but is voluntarily traded away by popular majorities seeking their protection. The crucial enabler of this social contract is the presence of deep, systemic, and unmanageable upheaval and dysfunction. Without widespread traumas from such turmoil, and credible threats that it might return, electoral autocracies would simply lack a compelling rationale to justify their existence. Crises therefore stand at the beginning of a causal chain resulting with the rise and persistence of electoral autocracies. No crises, no stable, robust electoral authoritarianism.

This perspective challenges the long-standing assumption that electoral authoritarian regimes are mainly a product of the democratization pressures that have built up since the end of the Cold War. Instead, this book's findings paint a more nuanced, and in many ways, more troubling picture. They indicate that the proliferation of electoral autocracies after 1989 owed more to the emergence of new, unstable countries and regions than to the pressure for dictatorships to mimic democracy in order to appear more respectable. The rise of electoral authoritarianism, to put it simply, was facilitated by the rise in instability more than it was driven by the spread of democracy. This burgeoning turmoil of the post–Cold War era allowed electoral autocracies to defuse democratization pressures far better than by simply imitating democracy: it enabled elected strongmen to pose as essential providers of order, stability, and justice, securing genuine popular support at the polls.

These findings also shed new light on the roots of the sustained democratic recession that the world has been experiencing since the mid-2000s. They point to the string of global security, economic, and political crises – ranging from the terror attacks on September 11, 2001 and the ensuing global war on terrorism, to the global financial crisis in 2009 and its consequences – as the primary catalysts of democratic backsliding toward electoral authoritarianism. The distinct pattern of this wave of democratic deconsolidation fits squarely with the strongman theory of electoral autocracy. Democracies affected by socioeconomic, political, and security upheavals have been degraded and dismantled through the ballot box and with virtually no coercion – by tough-mannered incumbents elected in largely free and fair elections, promising to restore their nations' stability, prosperity, and pride in the wake of traumatic crises and decline.[1]

This strongman appeal, as this book's findings suggest, has been the critical factor that has enabled authoritarian forces to penetrate in

---

[1] On these processes, see Svolik (2013), Bermeo (2016), and Levitsky and Ziblatt (2018).

societies seen as permanent converts to democracy. Such stunning breakdowns included the cases of the EU and NATO members and previously eager democratizers Hungary and Poland, where authoritarian incumbents dismantled democracy by catering to mass dissatisfaction, resentments, and demands for strong-armed rule, built up as a result of successive crises of governance and representation (Lendvai 2017; Applebaum 2018). More ominously, the success of the strongman appeal has encouraged a proliferation of authoritarian populist parties and leaders throughout the world, seeking to take advantage of it. These political forces have often gained in the polls even in established Western democracies, which are still reeling from the lingering effects of the 2009 financial crisis, and resentments spurred by globalization, demographic shifts, and various local schisms (Inglehart 2018; Norris and Inglehart 2019).

Popular Dictatorships offers a comprehensive analytic framework for understanding some key and underappreciated aspects of these processes. It does so by showing how collective traumas from deep and sustained political, economic, and security crises create opportunities to dismantle democracy. By turning electoral dictatorship into a compelling alternative, the mass opinion currents that emerge in such circumstances make democracies exceptionally susceptible to takeover by authoritarian parties and leaders who take on the strongman mantle. This danger is compounded by the fact that more than any other political order, democracy requires a considerable degree of stability to function properly. Even long-standing democracies, as the historical record shows, will break down if they are kept under significant duress for long enough.[2]

This book highlights another fundamental reason why democracies are exceptionally vulnerable to such threats: they provide the full legal, institutional, and legitimation framework for their transformation into electoral autocracies in times of crisis. Sweeping emergency powers and executive privileges, which can be used to erode and eventually suspend democracy, are a feature of practically every democratic legal order.[3] And where such instruments are not readily available, legislatures can

---

[2] See e.g. Dahl (1971), Linz (1978), Huntington (1991), and Levitsky and Ziblatt (2018).

[3] According to data from the Comparative Constitutions Project (Elkins, Ginsburg, and Melton 2009), for instance, about 67 percent of the constitutions adopted between 1789 and 1990 had state-of-emergency provisions; after 1990,

enact new ones under pressure from anxious and resentful majorities or substantial pluralities. Most importantly, elections can be used to bestow popular legitimacy to a state of suspended democracy even when these arrangements are entirely informal and are carried out by controlling key institutions through loyalists. As long as voting majorities are willing to encourage, or even simply tolerate such transgressions, there is little that can stand in the way of elected dictatorship. To paraphrase Lincoln, just as in democracies, majority sentiment in electoral autocracies is everything: with it, nothing can fail; against it, nothing can succeed.

The distinct popular opinion currents that emerge after acute crises are therefore the key ingredient in turning democratic institutions against democracy itself. This is the most troubling implication of this study. Given their sensitivity to sustained upheavals and exposure to popular opinion swings, virtually all democracies – even the long-established, mature ones – are one sufficiently traumatic crisis away from sliding into electoral authoritarianism.

From this perspective, the growing list of potential crises affecting democracies across the globe indicates that the threat of strongman electoral authoritarianism will likely increase in the future. A particularly worrisome catalyst for the spread of such regimes in the coming decades may be the impact of sweeping transcontinental crises like financial meltdowns and global warming, which, as a growing body of research predicts, will produce unprecedented increases in conflict, resource scarcity, migration, and socioeconomic pressures.[4] As societies pushed to the brink of collapse struggle to cope with these disruptions and upheavals, the strongman "savior" appeal of elected autocrats, outlined in this book, seems poised to become stronger than ever.

The Elected Strongman Appeal

Perhaps the most distinctive contribution of this book lies in its ability to identify the structure and logic of the mass appeal of electoral autocracies. Focusing on this appeal has enabled me to do far more

---

they have appeared in over 90 percent of constitutions. On this, also see Agamben (2005).

[4] See e.g. M. B. Burke et al. (2009), Fritsche et al. (2012), Carleton and Hsiang (2016), Kim (2016), Missirian and Schlenker (2017), and Mach et al. (2019).

than tackle the thorny issue of these regimes' legitimation. It has also allowed to identify what I argue is the most fundamental feature of electoral authoritarianism, which ties together all its attributes, causes, and consequences. The elected strongman appeal itself, as this book demonstrates, is the attribute that connects electoral autocracies to a specific set of structural and historical circumstances – the aftermaths of deep systemic crises – and the mass opinion currents that emerge from them. It also provides a compelling justification for electoral authoritarianism, allowing such regimes to attract sincere popular support, employ coercion with impunity, resist external democratization pressures, and quite often, survive despite their poor economic and general performance.

This account turns current understandings of electoral authoritarianism, which mainly attribute the rise and persistence of these regimes to manipulation and sophisticated coercion, on their heads. It also makes three distinct advances in the study of authoritarian legitimation. First, it shows that far from being "ideologically homeless" (Schedler 2013, 55), electoral autocracies rely on a coherent, well-defined legitimation script to justify their regime as quasi-emergency rule to societies gripped by crisis and dysfunction. This elected strongman doctrine is the kind of ideology with a small "i" – a smaller-scale ideational narrative that takes advantage of specific contexts and mass sentiments to justify dictatorships – that has been the missing link in the understanding of contemporary authoritarian legitimation (see Dukalskis and Gerschewski 2017).

Based on an attraction to popular strong-armed rule in nations in turmoil, this doctrine lacks the grand ambition of the totalitarian and millenarian ideologies of the past (hence the small-"i" designation). But it nevertheless achieves the same purpose – providing a compelling justification and mass support for dictatorship – all while being more versatile and less prone to failure and disenchantment. Thus, by identifying the elected strongman doctrine, I was able to incorporate legitimation as a fully fledged causal variable, and to show that this is not only pivotal in the rise, persistence, and decline of electoral authoritarianism, but that it also conditions the effects of authoritarian tools like repression, clientelism, and propaganda.

The second contribution of *Popular Dictatorships* to the regime legitimation literature is to provide a more nuanced account of the performance and procedural legitimacy of electoral authoritarian regimes. In regard to the former, the book's findings indicate that the core appeal of electoral autocrats as guarantors of order in fragile and dysfunctional societies sets a very peculiar set of performance standards by which these regimes are judged by the masses. Formed against this backdrop, evaluations of economic and other performance of electoral autocracies follow a very different rationale from that which we observe in stable democracies. On the one hand, crisis-weary populations may be reluctant to punish electoral autocracies that perform badly for fear that supporting the opposition – which is often new and untried, or associated with the crises that led to authoritarian rule – will lead to renewed turmoil and hardship (on this, see also Morgenstern and Zechmeister 2001). Performance evaluations in electoral autocracies, from this vantage point, do not proceed under the "what have you done for me or the economy lately?" logic typical for stable democratic settings. Rather, the question "will things become worse if the opposition wins?" is more likely to drive voters' calculus in such contexts.

At the same time, the crisis legitimation theory predicts that, paradoxically, highly performing electoral autocracies will tend to gradually lose popular support. This is a function of their narrow mandate: by delivering on their legitimizing promise of restoring stability and prosperity, these regimes make themselves redundant in the eyes of the population. For why would people tolerate the restrictions and unwholesome nature of authoritarian rule if their countries were stable and there was no need for strongmen to protect them against danger and dysfunction?

Taken together, these findings indicate that the logic of elected strongman appeal imposes *floor and ceiling effects* on the performance legitimacy of electoral autocracies – a dynamic not accounted for in existing analyses. The floor effect is what allows electoral autocracies with abysmal records of performance – regimes like Zimbabwe under Robert Mugabe, Venezuela under Hugo Chávez and Nicolás Maduro, or Serbia under Slobodan Milošević – to maintain dominance for a long time just because they are seen to be only slightly more competent (or rather, less incompetent) than their tarnished oppositional alternatives.[5] The ceiling effect, in turn, explains why societies have

---

[5] This account also provides fresh insight into the so-called "tragic brilliance" of poorly performing yet highly persistent electoral autocracies. While current accounts attribute this phenomenon to the skillful use of clientelism and repression to maintain citizen loyalty (Diaz-Cayeros, Magaloni, and Weingast

turned against elected autocracies when their economic and other performance has been relatively high (see e.g. Treisman 2014). This is because electoral dictatorships that have secured their countries from upheavals and dysfunction have, from the standpoint of their mandate of restoring order, outlived their usefulness. As result, many of their autocracy-weary citizens come to see these regimes as obstacles to further progress.

This study also challenges current understandings of the procedural legitimacy of electoral autocracies: their ability to claim they have the same moral authority as democracies because they follow the same norms and procedures for leadership selection. In particular, I dispute the prevailing assumption in the literature that such regimes reap the benefits of electoral legitimacy only by *faking* electoral accountability – by staging largely coerced and fraudulent plebiscites to assume a veneer of democratic legitimacy (see e.g. Schedler 2002, 37; Morgenbesser 2016, 184–187; and von Soest and Grauvogel 2017). The crisis legitimation framework suggests that the opposite is true: that electoral dictatorships have become widespread and resilient because the support they receive at the polls is, for the most part, genuine, and reflects deep-seated mass anxieties and demand for strong-armed rule. These regimes certainly coerce, bribe, brainwash, and otherwise manipulate to secure their dominance, but these tools serve to inflate rather than create popular support. The main purpose of elections in dictatorships, from this perspective, is not to serve as a façade that hides their authoritarian nature. Instead, their primary function is to sustain a manifestly authoritarian social contract: mass approval for unrestrained executive power in exchange for protection from turmoil, dysfunction, or perceived injustice. Elected strongmen, as a result, do not derive procedural legitimacy from faking democracy, but from adopting elections as a credible commitment mechanism to deliver their end of the bargain.

Due to all these properties, the elected strongman legitimation doctrine also emerges as the most reliable way to identify electoral

2003; Golosov 2016), I argue that societies can consent to electoral authoritarian they consider to be corrupt, immoral, and quite incompetent without any such coercive pressures. All that is needed is for a majority of voters to believe that elected autocracy is marginally more capable of managing society's latent crises and upheavals than any of the available alternatives, or to fear that a regime transition would cause greater turmoil than benefit.

authoritarianism. In Chapter 4, I show that we can more accurately recognize electoral autocracies based on how much incumbents emphasize the core components of the elected strongman appeal in their rhetoric – the calls to unify the nation behind their strong-armed, "uniquely competent" leadership, and the innate democraticness of this kind of rule in troubled societies – than by looking at countries' levels of poverty, resource wealth, repressive capacity, or exposure to external influences.

The diagnostic power of these "rhetorical fingerprints" of electoral authoritarianism confirms a pattern that scholars and observers of these regimes have been intimately familiar with for some time. More than anything else, the elected strongman appeal has been the unmistakable common trait, shared by virtually all electoral autocracies: by leaders and regimes as different as those established by Hugo Chávez in Venezuela, Viktor Orbán in Hungary, Robert Mugabe in Zimbabwe, Recep Tayyip Erdoğan in Turkey, and Vladimir Putin in Russia. These and many other electoral dictatorships have varied greatly in terms of their resource wealth, economic prosperity, coercive power, exposure to Western influences, and virtually every other background characteristic. Each of them has subverted democracy in their own way, relying on a different set of strategies from the "menu" of authoritarian manipulation. But the one thing they always had in common has been tough-talking, opposition-bashing, and democracy-touting rhetoric.

This, I argue, makes the elected strongman appeal an incredibly powerful diagnostic tool and measure of electoral authoritarianism. Its close association with the rise of these regimes not only makes it an ideal alternative indicator, which can be used to supplement existing measures of electoral authoritarianism, but also a crucial prognostic tool. Unlike any other factor, the strongman appeal described in this book may be able to predict whether parties and leaders will seek to establish electoral authoritarianism once they seize power.

This is because the elected strongman legitimation strategy plays such a central role in the ability of authoritarian parties and leaders to seize and sustain power that they effectively become its hostages. If voters in stable democracies punish politicians for "flip-flopping" on non-existential issues, then anxious electorates in unstable and dysfunctional societies are poised to react much more harshly if strongman leaders, who promise to impose order and address grievances, display weakness or seem to become "soft." Hence, few politicians who have staked their fortune on a strongman reputation can back off from it and expect to survive. Instead, they must constantly live up to this image.

For this reason, even outlandish strongman appeals cannot be dismissed as populist "cheap talk." Instead, they tend to be reliable predictors of the future behavior and trajectory of authoritarian politicians. When leaders like Russia's Vladimir Putin, Egypt's Abdel Fattah al-Sisi or Rodrigo Duterte of the Philippines, pledge to "waste" Chechen rebels in the outhouse, "end the Muslim Brotherhood," or "feed drug dealers and criminals to the fish in Manila Bay" (Heydarian 2017), they have strong incentives to deliver on their promises, regardless of the cost. Hence, the analysis of the rhetoric of these and other political leaders and parties has the potential to be used a key prognostic tool – helping us not only to understand the roots of electoral authoritarianism, but to also predict the rise and future actions of these regimes. The findings of this book suggest that this is a very promising area of further research into electoral authoritarianism, especially given the recent advances in data sources and methodology for political discourse and text analysis.[6]

Are Strongman Leaders the Key to Electoral Authoritarianism?

The outsized influence and public image of elected strongmen often makes it seem they are the sole reason why their regimes exist. It is hard to imagine electoral authoritarianism without their televangelist-like sermons, marathon press conferences, grotesque public outbursts, cruel jokes, and general "macho" swagger and bravado. Electoral authoritarian regimes seem unlikely to hold together without the degree of dominance these strongmen exert over their administrations and followers. The fact that most electoral autocracies are established by leaders of this caliber, and dismantled when they fall, instills a strong sense that electoral authoritarianism is all about its charismatic strongmen. Their personality appears so integral to the existence and functioning of electoral authoritarianism that each of these strongmen is assigned his own regime subcategory: Erdoğanism, Orbánism, Chavismo, Putinism, Duterteism, and so on.

---

[6] For a review of these methods, see e.g. Monroe and Schrodt (2008), Grimmer and Stewart (2013), Alvarez (2016), and Wilkerson and Casas (2017). Several notable studies have already made important inroads in using these techniques to study authoritarian appeals (see Windsor, Dowell, and Graesser 2014; Windsor et al. 2018; Maerz 2019; and Maerz and Schneider 2019).

This obsession with leaders is why the opponents of electoral autocracies often instinctively think of them as aberrations: historical accidents that would never have occurred unless a particular demagogue with an authoritarian streak got his lucky moment in the spotlight. The same outlook shapes expectations about the future of electoral authoritarian rule. Much of what is said and written about these regimes is built around the assumption that the removal of charismatic strongmen will spell the end of electoral authoritarianism in the affected countries for the foreseeable future.

Popular Dictatorships acknowledges the integral role individual "strongmen" play in electoral autocracies, but also cautions that their influence is more subtle, indirect, and limited than is commonly thought. The most essential pillar of electoral authoritarianism, as I have shown in the preceding chapters, is the broad and genuine appeal of its governing doctrine and legitimation script: the call to empower a strong-armed, but popularly elected executive as the most expedient remedy for societies plagued by unmanageable crises and dysfunction. The elected "strongman," in this context, is not a particular individual, but a *role* that can be played by different people. Leaders get selected for this role based on their perceived ability to live up to the promise of the electoral authoritarian doctrine in troubled societies. They become credible as strongmen not by writing their own rules, but by following a script. They grow popular not by virtue of their own character, but by molding it to the strongman image that is appealing to the masses.

The success of electoral authoritarianism, to put it differently, owes far more to its compelling legitimation formula, which defines the role of the elected strongman, than to the charm and personality of the leaders who perform it. While a charismatic autocrat can make the strongman role more appealing, even the most capable strongmen will turn the population against them if they overstep the boundaries of the electoral authoritarian legitimizing script and social contract. As the empirical record shows, nothing mobilizes societies against these regimes like overturning electoral results (see e.g. Beissinger 2007, Tucker 2007, and Bunce and Wolchik 2011), or exhausting their mandates to impose order, stability, and justice. At the same time, anxious populations can be very forgiving of those who stick to the electoral authoritarian legitimation script. When survival is at stake, majorities will reluctantly accept even mediocre elected strongmen who stay in character and present themselves as a less dangerous choice than their alternatives.

The rise of Vladimir Putin is a case in point. As Gleb Pavlovsky, one of the top campaign managers for Putin's inaugural election in 2000 admits, the appointment of the successor to the enfeebled Boris Yeltsin was the result of a highly orchestrated plot, set in motion in early 1999 – six months before Putin was *selected for the role.* "I knew the plot; I only needed an actor," Pavlovsky reminisced (Pavlovsky 2017). The scenario was to promote a strongman "savior" replacement for Yeltsin against the backdrop of an antiterror campaign against the runaway province of Chechnya, staged to boost the successor's credentials among the public (see also Jack 2005, 105; Dunlop 2014, 62).

Suitable candidates were selected based on extensive opinion research, and Vladimir Putin got onto the shortlist because he fitted the profile most preferred by the public. After Yeltsin finally settled for him in August 1999, it turned out that Putin still needed extensive training to be able to convincingly play the role. As he had little media experience and was awkward in his press appearances, he required extensive coaching on how to speak and act to project the strongman image the Russian public craved. The PR team carrying out "operation successor" spiced up Putin's demeanor and vocabulary to give him a folksier, down-to-earth appearance. They staged newscasts with Putin practicing Judo, flying fighter jets, and performing other stunts to flaunt his physical prowess and youthful, macho-man vigor.

The result was one of the most remarkable and significant political coups in recent history, and a testament to the power of the electoral authoritarian appeal in troubled societies. That a previously unknown (and initially reluctant),[7] camera-shy apparatchik could be selected, groomed, and successfully promoted as a wildly popular strongman on such short notice underlines the crucial importance of the electoral authoritarian legitimation script, and the circumstances that make it so attractive, over the personal charisma and talent of the "actor" that performs this role.

While this sort of stage-managed "casting" operation is unusual, the historical evidence suggests that most electoral authoritarian rulers

[7] See Jack (2005, ch. 3) and Judah (2013, ch. 1).

rose through a similar process of adjusting their personalities and reputations to fit the elected strongman script.[8] Along the way, personal savvy and charisma certainly boosted their chances of success. But the failure of any of these aspiring strongmen would *not* have prevented the rise of electoral authoritarianism in their countries. As long as there was a strong and persistent popular demand for this kind of leadership, they would have been able to learn their lessons, perfect their act, and try again later. And if that failed, there would likely be someone else to take their place.

These observations indicate that the roots of electoral authoritarianism run deeper than commonly assumed. Electoral authoritarianism is not a simple product of accidental takeovers by charismatic "masterminds" and their henchmen. It is not prevented if a particular strongman and his clique never rises to power, and it does not disappear when they are gone. Instead, such regimes are a symptom of a broader, systemic malaise: an underlying crisis making people desperate, traumatized, and angry enough to trade their freedoms for a modicum of security or perceived justice. As long as these circumstances and outlooks that make elected strongmen attractive persist, electoral authoritarianism will eventually find a way to break through, or to return after it has been deposed. Where there is perpetual upheaval, the elected strongman will constantly be reincarnated.

From a policy perspective, the key takeaway here is that deposing individual dictators, no matter how unique or important they may seem to be, is not enough to root out electoral authoritarianism in their countries. The only sure-fire way to achieve this objective, according to this book's findings, is to carry out the much harder task of bringing about a sufficient degree of stability and fairness to make elected dictatorship redundant in the eyes of popular majorities.

---

[8] Hungary's Viktor Orbán, for instance, had to break into this role for over a decade by learning from his past failures, trying out different nationalist and populist messages, and waiting for sufficient popular demand to materialize (Lendvai 2017, chs. 4–9). Hugo Chávez followed a similar trajectory of gradually perfecting his image and credibility as a popular *caudillo* who cared for Venezuela's impoverished majority (Hawkins 2010, ch. 1).

Are Electoral Autocracies Reliant on Crises and Conflict to Justify Their Rule?

Perhaps the biggest paradox of electoral authoritarianism identified in *Popular Dictatorships* is that the justification of these regimes as a response to crises is simultaneously their main strength and greatest liability. On one hand, the strongman "savior" mission of restoring stability in the wake of severe upheavals has allowed these regimes to attract the genuine support of broad popular majorities, and to rule with minimal coercion and through the polling booth. But on the other hand, by committing to this relatively narrow mandate, electoral autocracies risk becoming *redundant both when they succeed and when they fail* to deliver on their foundational promises of stabilization and overcoming dysfunction and injustice. To sustain support for their rule over the long run, electoral autocracies must therefore maintain, or even manufacture, the crises and conflicts that legitimize their rule, while also appearing to protect against them.

This paradox has profound implications for the domestic and international conduct of these regimes. In particular, it helps explain why electoral autocracies have been so consistently associated with conflict: a question that remains largely open in the existing literature.[9] This book's analytic framework helps address this gap by predicting several key patterns of conflict in these regimes. To begin with, its findings show that the worst episodes of mass violence in countries that have had electoral authoritarian rule tended to precede the rise of the regime, not follow it. The fact that their countries have faced the most horrendous upheavals and hardships *before* the rise of electoral authoritarianism allows strongman incumbents to discredit their alternatives, and to convincingly argue that instability will return without their steady hand at the helm.

Next, this book's analytic framework predicts that during their tenure, electoral autocracies will pursue three divergent patterns of conflict, depending on the degree of popular support they enjoy. First, at the peak of their popular appeal, when their image as indispensable providers of stability and justice is secure, elected autocrats will seek to *minimize conflict* and the risks associated with it. In this phase of their trajectory, electoral dictatorships have strong incentives

---

[9]   See e.g. Fearon and Laitin (2003), Sambanis (2004), Treier and Jackman (2008), Enterline (2010), and Regan and Bell (2010).

to reap the "stabilization dividend": to act as peacemakers and pursue developmental policies that would solidify their reputations as national "saviors" and reformers, and widen the perceived contrast with their predecessors and alternatives. This is electoral authoritarianism on its best behavior – the most benign, "code green" stage in terms of the threat they pose. It is predicated on overwhelming, enthusiastic, and sincere popular support: the kind of environment many elected dictators enjoy in their honeymoon stages.

Second, this book predicts that elected strongmen will abandon this complaisant stance when they lack supermajority appeal, moving to a more aggressive, "code yellow" type of behavior. Threatened by increased opposition and competitiveness, they seek to demonstrate the need for their strong-armed approach and "skill set" by manufacturing *low-grade* crises and disputes, *and controlled* conflicts. The rationale for this belligerent but still cautious diversionary strategy is twofold. On one hand, if electoral autocracies allow upheavals to reach or surpass the levels from before their reign, they could undermine their own legitimacy as providers of order and stability. If, on the other hand, their countries are completely pacified and their societies relatively unconcerned about renewed turmoil and dysfunction, electoral authoritarianism becomes unnecessary. Thus, to sustain mass consent to their rule, electoral dictators that are still relatively popular strive to manufacture *crises that simmer, but do not boil over.*

In the security realm, this implies that electoral autocracies would have a particular penchant for initiating controlled disputes and conflicts that occasionally flare up to serve as reminders that the essential "protective services" they offer are still necessary. It might be argued, from this perspective, that the ideal diversionary crises for legitimizing electoral authoritarianism are domestic ethno-religious purges, and antiterror and anti-crime campaigns, as well as territorial and other disputes with foreign powers. These are not difficult to manufacture and sustain, and could be effectively pursued with limited violence, often carried out by proxy groups, or simply through diplomatic posturing. The world is replete with internal fault lines and contentious international issues that could be exploited for this purpose.

These tactics work for a simple reason. Despite being low-grade, domestic antiterror, anti-crime, and minority-persecution campaigns and all kinds of intra-state disputes have a profound emotional impact on the population – strong enough to maintain the sense of insecurity that justifies the need for emergency rule and authoritarianism, especially in societies traumatized by prior crises.[10] Also, these disputes and conflicts generally lack the collateral damage and escalation potential that can threaten most electoral authoritarian regimes, at least over the short term. Repressing marginalized ethnic and other groups at home is a relatively low-risk diversionary strategy (Tir and Jasinski 2008), and as I highlighted in the preceding chapters, it can significantly boost the popularity of elected strongmen who scapegoat them (see Wintrobe 2018 and The Economist 2020). Antiterrorism campaigns may also be deployed as a low-grade – though potentially riskier[11] – strategy for sustaining the legitimacy of electoral authoritarian rule. If the backlash is contained to minor terrorist incidents, the lingering mass anxiety may sustain popular support for elected strongmen and the security they seem to offer (see Fedotenkov 2020).

But above all else, elected strongmen seeking to bolster their appeal have incentives to pursue international "diversionary spectacles": intra-state disputes with high rallying capacity and low escalation potential. This strategy may have a particularly strong domestic rallying capacity when aimed against more powerful countries.[12] Venezuela's Hugo Chávez, for instance, mastered the diversionary spectacle approach by taking on the United States with flamboyant diatribes and international grandstanding (Corrales and Penfold-Becerra 2015, ch. 5). In recent years, Turkey's Recep Tayyip Erdoğan followed in Chávez's footsteps by staging diplomatic spats and bad-mouthing leading European powers (Gall 2018).

Ultimately, the strongman legitimation theory of electoral authoritarianism suggests that such regimes escalate to their most aggressive, "code-red" diversionary behavior when their popular appeal is low and declining: either before they have established their strongman reputation, or when they become increasingly unpopular and face

[10] See e.g. Merolla and Zechmeister (2009), Grauvogel and Von Soest (2014), S. V. Miller (2015), and Caroline Abadeer, Alexandra Blackman, Lisa Blaydes, and Scott Williamson, "Did Egypt's Post-Uprising Crime Wave Increase Support for Authoritarian Rule?" (unpublished working paper, 2019).

[11] As previous research has shown, autocracies are especially prone to lose their legitimacy in the wake of significant terrorist violence (Park and Bali 2017). From this book's standpoint, such patterns might arise in electoral autocracies because sustained, uncontrollable terrorism undermines these regimes' core legitimation appeal as effective providers of order and security.

[12] On this mechanism, also see Tarar (2006), Oakes (2012), and Haynes (2017).

mass opposition. Critically dependent on majority support, electoral autocracies will, under such circumstances, seek to establish or reclaim their aura as indispensable guardians of national interests, order, and justice by staging much riskier and more dangerous standoffs and conflicts. Faced with mortal danger, electoral autocracies are highly prone, in other words, to "gamble for resurrection":[13] to engage in high-risk confrontations in a desperate attempt to "resurrect" their popular standing by demonstrating relevance and competence.

By highlighting the centrality of these regimes' mass appeal, *Popular Dictatorships* helps account for this seeming inconsistency in the behavior of electoral dictatorships: switching from a benign to a low-risk, limited confrontation posture, and then to high-stakes aggression. It also points to the likely trigger for their most violent, "code-red"-level outbursts: mass contentious mobilization against their rule, which has been the leading cause of regime collapse among electoral autocracies. Wagering their nations' interests and pride in high-stakes conflicts, these regimes strive to defuse protest movements by reactivating their populations' preservation instincts and rally-around-the-flag reflexes. This book's contribution is to underline the attitudinal mechanisms that make this strategy work: the deep-seated traumas of unmanageable turmoil and decline and the resultant demand for strong-armed rule.

The focus on the attitudinal roots of electoral authoritarianism also reveals the key danger of this "gamble for survival" diversionary strategy. Electoral autocracies that start down the path of orchestrating risky conflicts to compensate for their diminishing domestic support may need to constantly raise the stakes to control their increasingly weary publics. Using conflicts as a narcotic, elected strongmen need to supply bigger and bigger "fixes" to successfully sedate their progressively more disillusioned and benumbed populations (on this, see also Mead 2014). The consequence is a vicious circle of devastating conflicts, protest, and decay, which we observe in many electoral autocracies.

The prototypical cautionary tale in this regard is about the reign of Slobodan Milošević in Serbia. A former Communist seeking to retain power in the post–Cold War era, Milošević sought to defuse the growing liberal opposition challenge and mass mobilization against his rule

---

[13] For this mechanism, see Downs and Rocke (1994), Goemans and Fey (2009), Chiozza and Goemans (2011), and Haynes (2017).

by stoking ethnic conflicts and posing as his compatriots' stalwart protector. By thrusting the nation into a string of progressively more devastating conflicts in Croatia, Bosnia, and Kosovo, Serbia's electoral autocracy successfully demobilized major protest waves in 1991 and 1996–7 (Gagnon 2004, ch. 4; Gordy 2010). This allowed the Serbian regime to maintain electoral dominance for over a decade despite its crumbling legitimacy. But to sustain this scheme, it was forced into a deadly spiral of military struggles with catastrophic collateral damage. Milošević's diversionary legitimation strategy led to the bloody disintegration of Yugoslavia, causing Europe's first genocidal wars since 1945. The main casualty, however, was Serbia itself, as its leadership mercilessly sacrificed its country's interests in a series of ill-advised adventures staged to ensure its survival. At the end of Milošević's rule, Serbia had suffered a near-total collapse: economic devastation, international isolation, and a succession of disastrous wars, all resulting in defeat and major loss of territory (Palairet 2001).

Cases like this show is that although electoral autocracies may prefer to sustain their appeal with controlled, low-grade conflicts, they will lash out with risky, wanton acts of violence and aggression when threatened by declining mass approval and protest. This behavior is rooted in these regimes' unique dependence on popular support, and the need to sustain the broad credibility of their mandate to restore security and justice. As such, elected strongmen may have very little latitude to back off when their reputations and legitimacy are at stake. They cannot be reliably contained, appeased, or reasoned, or bargained with. They may, for these reasons, be even more unpredictable and aggressive than closed dictatorships, including the military and single-party regimes that dominated the Cold War era.

This logic of electoral authoritarian legitimation paints a grim picture of the highly destabilizing and malignant global influence of the growing share of electoral autocracies across the globe – an issue I also touch upon in the next section.

Authoritarian Learning and Diffusion

A key recent advance in the authoritarianism literature has been to highlight the processes of authoritarian learning, whereby undemocratic regimes borrow and build upon each other's experiences in curbing oppositional activism and democratization pressures.

Empirical studies of this phenomenon have particularly emphasized the spread of innovative authoritarian tactics for preempting oppositional mobilization and cross-border diffusion of protest movements and activism, curbing information flows and controlling new media.[14]

While confirming the importance of these mechanisms, this book predicts a somewhat different and more sinister emphasis on authoritarian learning. It suggests that electoral autocracies have most to learn from each other about how to create and maintain the crises that can justify their rule as a response to national emergencies. The discussion in the previous section suggests that relatively popular autocracies would greatly benefit from sharing "recipes" for stoking or taking advantage of terrorist threats, ethnic conflicts, crime waves, and various international disputes – the "simmering" types of conflict that are ideal for legitimizing protracted states of emergency. More concerningly, they are also bound to learn and profit from each other's experiences and successes in staging larger conflicts and disturbances – the "gambles for resurrection" designed to defuse mass mobilization and protest against their rule.

There is strong empirical evidence that electoral autocracies have assimilated both kinds of "know-how." In the 1990s, Slobodan Milošević's high-stakes diversionary survival approach inspired neighboring Croatia's electoral autocracy to follow a similar approach (Gagnon 2004, c. 5). In the 2010s, the actions of Russia's regime in Ukraine since 2014 have been widely interpreted as an upgraded version of this strategy. Under the guise of manufactured insurrections claimed to "protect" co-ethnics in neighboring states, Putin's regime – just like Milošević and others before – managed to impose a "nation under siege" mentality at home, diverting attention from its weak governing performance and declining popularity, and demobilizing the domestic opposition.[15]

One can also argue that Putin's successful "resurrection gamble" with the annexation of Crimea had a crucial demonstration effect, inviting other troubled regimes to attempt similar stunts. Turkey's Erdoğan in particular seems to have taken a page from this script after a wave of dissatisfaction and electoral setbacks in 2019.

---

[14] See e.g. Beissinger (2007), Bunce and Wolchik (2011), Robertson (2011), and Koesel and Bunce (2013).

[15] See e.g. Pejić (2014), A. Wood (2014), Bunce and Hozic (2015), Stoner and McFaul (2015), Hale (2018), and Matovski (2020).

To consolidate power at home, he has thrown Turkey into a bewildering array of conflicts, ranging from crackdowns on the Kurdish minority, military interventions in Syria, and proxy wars in Libya and Nagorno-Karabakh, to tense maritime standoffs with Greece (Tol 2019; Keating 2020).

Electoral autocracies have also learned to abuse lower-intensity counterterrorist campaigns to justify their rule and persecute their opponents. Ironically, some of the authoritarian diffusion in this regard since the early 2000s may have been inadvertently catalyzed by the United States–led global war on terror. Taking advantage of demands for counterterrorism assistance, electoral autocracies have forced the United States and its allies to refrain from criticism and democratization promotion and extorted substantial foreign aid in return for their cooperation. But most importantly, they have hijacked the antiterrorism cause as justification for their rule. Electoral authoritarian regimes were, in this sense, the most eager implementers of new counterterror legislation and measures after the 9/11 attacks; they regularly abused these instruments to label their opposition as terrorists, to limit freedom of speech, and to expand the use of repressive tactics (D. M. Jones and Smith 2002; Whitaker 2007, 2010).

Perhaps most insidiously, there are indications that some autocracies may have adapted the tactic of deliberately fueling the growth of terrorist and extremist movements through brutal repression, particularly in the Middle East after the Arab Spring. The resurgent electoral dictatorship in Egypt, for instance, has been particularly brutal in its clampdown on the Muslim Brotherhood, in ways that have pushed the movement's remnants toward terrorism. This seems to be a deliberate tactic used to portray the regime as the "lesser evil," both at home and abroad (see The Economist 2015a).

A key implication here, in line with this book's findings, seems to be that learning how to create the crises that sustain authoritarian rule may be among the most dangerous and widespread form of authoritarian diffusion. From the perspective of what remains of the global "war on terror," electoral dictatorships that learn how to become indispensable in fighting terrorism will strive to remain *permanently* indispensable by sustaining the threats they are supposed to eliminate. To stay in demand, they will strategically employ brutal tactics that may exterminate the current terrorists but also breed new ones that will replace them. Thus, rather than tackling the underlying causes of terrorism, they will nourish novel and potentially more extreme forms over the long run.

This same argument applies more broadly to electoral autocracies that are considered to be key allies and pillars of stability in strategic regions. Seeking to defuse domestic and international pressures for democratization, such regimes have consistently played up their indispensable roles as guarantors of order in troubled regions (this time not just at home, but also internationally). At the same time, they have deliberately sustained and even fueled the crises that provided them with this legitimacy, often exacerbating instability over the long run (see e.g. Bieber 2018, 2020).

Peace, stability, and justice under electoral authoritarianism are therefore bound to remain elusive goals, despite the leadership's self-proclaimed purpose of achieving these objectives. The logic of these regimes' survival, captured by the crisis legitimation theory of electoral authoritarianism, dictates they will tend to perpetuate some of the turmoil that brought them into power. The incentives for such behavior are clear: for elected strongmen to fully resolve their countries' crises is for them to make themselves redundant.

Political Participation, Protest, and the Durability of Electoral Authoritarianism

This book's analytic framework highlights that swings in popular opinion and political participation can make or break electoral autocracies. Ordinary citizens can make these regimes remarkably robust by supporting strongman parties and leaders at the polls. But all they really have to do to sustain electoral authoritarianism is to never rebel against it – at the polls or in the streets. In this sense, electoral autocracies are, to a large degree, legitimized through what Krastev and Holmes (2012) have called the "plebiscite of silence": people's lack of willingness to express their grievances and to mobilize politically as they see no palpable alternatives, or fear further destabilization. As I have argued, these regimes are typically products of crises, which have often left wide swathes of the population disillusioned, apathetic, and estranged from politics. The shocks, upheavals, and repeated disappointments resulting from the crises that typically accompany the rise of electoral authoritarianism have a well-noted propensity to demobilize electorates and push people away from political activism and participation.[16]

This perspective provides additional insights into why electoral authoritarianism is particularly susceptible to the threat of popular protest and rebellion – a topic that has received considerable attention in the literature. For one, strongman regimes stand to lose their core credibility as guarantors of order if they cannot keep large numbers of their citizens from protesting in the streets. Also, elected autocrats cannot sustain their second foundational appeal to democratic legitimacy – the claim that their rule is based on a broad electoral mandate, sustained by overwhelming popular support – if a substantial share of the population becomes willing to challenge them through contentious action. By forcing these regimes to primarily rely on coercive tactics to control their population, a sustained mass protest therefore defeats the purpose of electoral authoritarianism. Instead of stifling discontent and opposition, holding elections in this environment provides the focal point for mobilizing it.

Most importantly, by striking at the core of the strongman appeal, mass contention provides opportunities to overturn the heresthetic that sustains electoral dictatorships – to redefine the issue space in favor of the opposition and to promote fresh, untarnished oppositional alternatives. It does so by injecting new insurgent issues and grievances into public debate that can neutralize the effects of the strongman appeal in societies gripped by turmoil. The processes through which this takes place are beyond the scope of this book, but its analytic framework offers a roadmap for future research on these topics. Specifically, it points to the kinds of shifts in mass attitudes that are most likely to provide opportunities for mobilizing regime-shattering protests of this sort. The core claim of this book is that popular majorities consent to electoral authoritarianism as long as they believe it is uniquely qualified to serve a useful purpose: addressing acute crises and latent instability. The most essential precondition for mobilizing societies against electoral authoritarianism, from this vantage point, is the growing realization that it has outlived its usefulness, either by failing its promise to restore order and stability or by achieving it.

[16] On this dynamic, see also Meirowitz and Tucker (2013).

Bibliography

Acemoglu, Daron, and James Robinson. 2006. *Economic Origins of Dictatorship and Democracy*. Cambridge; New York, NY: Cambridge University Press.

Achen, Christopher H., and Larry M. Bartels. 2017. *Democracy for Realists: Why Elections Do Not Produce Responsive Government*. Princeton, NJ: Princeton University Press.

Adams, James F., Samuel Merrill, and Bernard Grofman. 2005. *A Unified Theory of Party Competition: A Cross-National Analysis Integrating Spatial and Behavioral Factors*. New York, NY: Cambridge University Press.

Agamben, Giorgio. 2005. *State of Exception*. Chicago: University of Chicago Press.

Albertus, Michael, and Victor Menaldo. 2012. "Coercive Capacity and the Prospects for Democratization." *Comparative Politics* 44(2): 151–169.

Allred, Nathaniel, Kirk A. Hawkins, and Saskia P. Ruth. 2015. "The Impact of Populism on Liberal Democracy." Prepared for the 8th Congreso de la Asociación Latinoamericana de Ciencia Política, Lima, Peru, July 22–24, 2015.

Alvarez, R. Michael (ed.). 2016. *Computational Social Science: Discovery and Prediction*. New York, NY: Cambridge University Press.

Ansolabehere, Stephen, and Shanto Iyengar. 1994. "Riding the Wave and Claiming Ownership Over Issues: The Joint Effects of Advertising and News Coverage in Campaigns." *Public Opinion Quarterly* 58(3): 335–357.

Ansolabehere, Stephen, and M. Socorro Puy. 2018. "Measuring Issue-Salience in Voters' Preferences." *Electoral Studies* 51: 103–114.

Applebaum, Anne. 2018, Sep. 13. "A Warning from Europe: The Worst Is Yet to Come." *The Atlantic*, 53–63. www.theatlantic.com/magazine/archive/2018/10/poland-polarization/568324/ (accessed 05/20/2021).

Arditi, Benjamin. 2005. "Populism as an Internal Periphery of Democratic Politics." In *Populism and the Mirror of Democracy*, ed. Francisco Panizza. London; New York, NY: Verso, 72–98.

Arendt, Hannah. 1966. *The Origins of Totalitarianism*. New York, NY: Harcourt, Brace & World.

Bakker, Ryan, and Sara Hobolt. 2013. "Measuring Party Positions." In *Political Choice Matters: Explaining the Strength of Class and Religious Cleavages in Cross- National Perspective*, ed. Geoffrey Evans and Nan Dirk de Graaf. New York, NY: Oxford University Press, 27–45.

Balzer, Harley. 2002. "Human Capital and Russian Security in the Twenty-First Century." In *Russia after the Fall*, ed. Andrew Kuchins. Washington, DC: Carnegie Endowment for International Peace, 163–184.

Bateson, Regina. 2012. "Crime Victimization and Political Participation." *American Political Science Review* 106(3): 570–587.

Baumeister, Roy F., Ellen Bratslavsky, Catrin Finkenauer, and Kathleen D. Vohs. 2001. "Bad Is Stronger Than Good." *Review of General Psychology* 5(4): 323–370.

BBC. 2014, May 6. "Egypt Election: Sisi Vows End to Muslim Brotherhood." *BBC News*. www.bbc.com/news/av/world-middle-east-27289931/egypt-election-sisi-vows-end-to-muslim-brotherhood (accessed 05/20/2021).

Beck, Thorsten, George Clarke, Alberto Groff, Philip Keefer, and Patrick Walsh. 2001. "New Tools in Comparative Political Economy: The Database of Political Institutions." *World Bank Economic Review* 15(1) (Jan. 2001): 165–176.

Becker, Ernest. 1971. *Birth and Death of Meaning: An Interdisciplinary Perspective on the Problem of Man*. New York, NY: The New Press.

Beetham, David. 1991. *The Legitimation of Power*. Atlantic Highlands, NJ: Humanities Press International Inc.

Beissinger, Mark R. 2002. *Nationalist Mobilization and the Collapse of the Soviet State*. Cambridge; New York, NY: Cambridge University Press.

Beissinger, Mark R. 2007. "Structure and Example in Modular Political Phenomena: The Diffusion of Bulldozer/Rose/Orange/Tulip Revolutions." *Perspectives on Politics* 5(2): 259–276.

Belanovsky, Sergey, and Mikhail Dmitriev. 2011. *Politichyeskiy Krizis v Rossii I Vozmozhniye Myehanizmi Yego Razvitiya (The Political Crisis in Russia and How It May Develop)*. Report of the Center for Strategic Research (CSR). Moscow, Russia:CSR.

Belanovsky, Sergey, and Mikhail Dmitriev. 2013. *Novoe Jelektoral'noe Ravnovesie: Srednesrochnyj Trend Ili "Vremennoe Zatish'e"? (The New Electoral Equilibrium: A Mid-Term Trend or "Temporary Lull")*. Report of the Center for Strategic Research (CSR). Moscow, Russia:CSR.

Belkin, Aaron, and Evan Schofer. 2003. "Toward a Structural Understanding of Coup Risk." *Journal of Conflict Resolution* 47(5): 594–620.

Bermeo, Nancy G. 1997. *Getting Mad or Going Mad? Citizens, Scarcity and the Breakdown of Democracy in Interwar Europe*. Irvine, CA: Center for the Study of Democracy, University of California, Irvine.

Bermeo, Nancy G. 2003. *Ordinary People in Extraordinary Times: The Citizenry and the Breakdown of Democracy.* Princeton, NJ: Princeton University Press.

Bermeo, Nancy G. 2016. "On Democratic Backsliding." *Journal of Democracy* 27(1): 5–19.

Bieber, Florian. 2018. "The Rise (and Fall) of Balkan Stabilitocracies." *Horizons: Journal of International Relations and Sustainable Development* (10): 176–185.

Bieber, Florian. 2020. *The Rise of Authoritarianism in the Western Balkans.* London, UK: Springer.

Blaydes, Lisa. 2008. "Authoritarian Elections and Elite Management: Theory and Evidence from Egypt." Paper presented at the Princeton University Conference on Dictatorships, Princeton University, Princeton, NJ, April 25–26.

Blickle, Kristian. 2020. *Pandemics Change Cities: Municipal Spending and Voter Extremism in Germany, 1918–1933.* Federal Reserve Bank of New York Staff Reports (920). New York, NY: Federal Reserve Bank.

Bobbio, Norberto. 1996. *Left and Right: The Significance of a Political Distinction.* Chicago, IL: University of Chicago Press.

Bogaards, Matthijs. 2010. "Measures of Democratization: From Degree to Type to War." *Political Research Quarterly* 63(2): 475–488.

Bohlen, Celestine. 2000. "Yeltsin Resigns, Naming Putin as Acting President to Run in March Election." *The New York Times*, Jan. 1. www.nytimes.com/2 000/01/01/world/yeltsin-resigns-overview-yeltsin-resigns-naming-putin-acting-president-run-march.html (accessed 5/16/2021).

Boix, Carles, Michael K. Miller, and Sebastian Rosato. 2012. "A Complete Data Set of Political Regimes, 1800–2007." *Comparative Political Studies* 46(12): 1523–1554. DOI: https://doi.org/10.1177/0010414012463905

Boix, Carles, and Milan Svolik. 2013. "The Foundations of Limited Authoritarian Government: Institutions and Power-Sharing in Dictatorships." *The Journal of Politics* 75(2): 300–316.

Bollen, K. A., and P. Paxton. 2000. "Subjective Measures of Liberal Democracy." *Comparative Political Studies* 33(1): 58–86.

Bolt, Jutta Robert Inklaar Herman de Jong, and Jan Luiten van Zanden. 2019. *Rebasing "Maddison": New Income Comparisons and the Shape of Long-Run Economic Development.* Maddison Project Database, Version 2018. Maddison Project Working Paper 10.

Booth, John A, and Mitchell A. Seligson. 2009. *The Legitimacy Puzzle in Latin America: Political Support and Democracy in Eight Nations.* New York, NY: Cambridge University Press.

Box-Steffensmeier, Janet M., Suzanna De Boef, and Kyle A. Joyce. 2007. "Event Dependence and Heterogeneity in Duration Models: The Conditional Frailty Model." *Political Analysis* 15(3): 237–256.

Box-Steffensmeier, Janet M., and Bradford S. Jones. 2004. *Event History Modeling: A Guide for Social Scientists*. Cambridge; New York, NY: Cambridge University Press.

Box-Steffensmeier, Janet M., Suzanna Linn, and Corwin D. Smidt. 2014. "Analyzing the Robustness of Semi-Parametric Duration Models for the Study of Repeated Events." *Political Analysis* 22(2): 183–204.

Brancati, Dawn. 2014a. "Democratic Authoritarianism: Origins and Effects." *Annual Review of Political Science* 17: 313–326.

Brancati, Dawn. 2014b. "Pocketbook Protests: Explaining the Emergence of Pro-Democracy Protests Worldwide." *Comparative Political Studies* 47 (11): 1503–1530.

Bratton, Michael. 2008. "Vote Buying and Violence in Nigerian Election Campaigns." *Electoral Studies* 27(4): 621–632.

Bratton, Michael, and Eldred Masunungure. 2008. "Zimbabwe's Long Agony." *Journal of Democracy* 19(4): 41–55.

Brinks, Daniel, and Michael Coppedge. 2006. "Diffusion Is No Illusion: Neighbor Emulation in the Third Wave of Democracy." *Comparative Political Studies* 39(4): 463–489.

Brookings. 2014. "President Erdoğan: Turkey's Election and the Future." In *The Project on Middle East Democracy*. Washington, DC: The Brookings Institution. https://pomed.org/wp-content/uploads/2014/09/Turkey-Brookings-event-notes.pdf?x18047 (accessed 5/16/2021).

Brown, Nathan J., and Mai El-Sadany. 2017, Oct. 30. "How a State of Emergency Became Egypt's New Normal." *The Washington Post*, Oct. 30. www.washingtonpost.com/news/monkey-cage/wp/2017/10/30/how-a-state-of-emergency-became-egypts-new-normal/ (accessed 5/16/2021).

Brownlee, Jason. 2007. *Authoritarianism in an Age of Democratization*. New York, NY: Cambridge University Press.

Budge, Ian, Lawrence Ezrow, and Michael D McDonald. 2010. "Ideology, Party Factionalism and Policy Change: An Integrated Dynamic Theory." *British Journal of Political Science* 40(4): 781–804.

Bunce, Valerie, and Aida Hozic. 2015. "National Security, Job Security and Sneaky Wars: The Russian Invasion of Ukraine." Paper presented at the Shambaugh Workshop: Democratic Backsliding, University of Iowa, Iowa City, April 23–25, 2015.

Bunce, Valerie, and Sharon Wolchik. 2011. *Defeating Authoritarian Leaders in Postcommunist Countries*. Cambridge; New York, NY: Cambridge University Press.

Burke, Marshall B., Edward Miguel, Shanker Satyanath, John A. Dykema, and David B. Lobell. 2009. "Warming Increases the Risk of Civil War in Africa." *Proceedings of the National Academy of Sciences* 106(49): 20670–20674.

Burke, Paul J., and Andrew Leigh. 2010. "Do Output Contractions Trigger Democratic Change?" *American Economic Journal: Macroeconomics* 2 (4): 124–157.

Burnell, Peter. 2006. "Autocratic Opening to Democracy: Why Legitimacy Matters." *Third World Quarterly* 27(4): 545–562.

Burnham, Kenneth, and David Anderson. 2002. *Model Selection and Multimodel Inference: A Practical Information-Theoretic Approach.* New York, NY: Springer.

Burrett, Tina. 2011. *Television and Presidential Power in Putin's Russia.* Abingdon; New York, NY: Routledge.

Cagaptay, Soner. 2017. *The New Sultan: Erdogan and the Crisis of Modern Turkey.* London; New York, NY: IB Tauris.

Calvo, Ernesto, and Maria Victoria Murillo. 2013. "When Parties Meet Voters: Assessing Political Linkages Through Partisan Networks and Distributive Expectations in Argentina and Chile." *Comparative Political Studies* 46(7): 851–882.

Canache, Damarys. 2002. "From Bullets to Ballots: The Emergence of Popular Support for Hugo Chavez." *Latin American Politics and Society* 44(1): 69–90.

Carleton, Tamma A., and Solomon M. Hsiang. 2016. "Social and Economic Impacts of Climate." *Science* 353(6304): aad9837.

Carmines, Edward, and James Stimson. 1993. "On the Evolution of Political Issues." In *Agenda Formation*, ed. William H. Riker. Ann Arbor, MI: The University of Michigan Press.

Carothers, Thomas. 2002. "The End of the Transition Paradigm." *Journal of Democracy* 13(1): 5–21.

Caryl, Christian. 2015, Feb. 13. "New Model Dictator: Why Vladimir Putin Is the Leader Other Autocrats Wish They Could Be." *Foreign Policy.* https://foreignpolicy.com/2015/02/13/new-model-dictator-putin-sisi-erdogan/ (accessed 5/16/2021).

Caryl, Christian. 2018, May 8. "How Vladimir Putin Became the World's Favorite Dictator." *The Washington Post.* www.washingtonpost.com/news/democracy-post/wp/2018/05/08/how-vladimir-putin-became-the-worlds-favorite-dictator/ (accessed 5/16/2021).

Cassani, Andrea. 2017a. "Do All Bad Things Go Together? Electoral Authoritarianism and the Consequences of Political Change Short of Democratisation." *Politikon* 44(3): 351–369.

Cassani, Andrea. 2017b. "Social Services to Claim Legitimacy: Comparing Autocracies' Performance." *Contemporary Politics* 23(3): 348–368.

Castañeda, Jorge G. 2000. *Perpetuating Power: How Mexican Presidents Were Chosen*. New York, NY: The New Press.

Cheibub, José Antonio. 2007. *Presidentialism, Parliamentarism, and Democracy*. Cambridge: Cambridge University Press.

Cheibub, José Antonio, Jennifer Gandhi, and James Raymond Vreeland. 2010. "Democracy and Dictatorship Revisited." *Public Choice* 143(1): 67–101.

Chiozza, Giacomo, and Hein Erich Goemans. 2011. *Leaders and International Conflict*. Cambridge; New York: Cambridge University Press.

Chzhen, Kat, Geoffrey Evans, and Mark Pickup. 2014. "When Do Economic Perceptions Matter for Party Approval?" *Political Behavior* 36(2) 291–313.

Cingranelli, David L., David L. Richards, and K. Chad Clay. 2014. "The CIRI Human Rights Dataset, Version 2014.04.14." www.humanrightsdata.com (accessed 11/24/2018).

Collier, David, and Steven Levitsky. 1997. "Democracy with Adjectives: Conceptual Innovation in Comparative Research." *World Politics* 49 (03): 430–451.

Colton, Timothy. 2000. *Transitional Citizens: Voters and What Influences Them in the New Russia*. Cambridge, MA: Harvard University Press.

Colton, Timothy. 2008. *Yeltsin: A Life*. New York, NY: Basic Books.

Colton, Timothy. 2014. "Russian Post-Presidential Election Survey in 2012." *Harvard Dataverse*. https://doi.org/10.7910/DVN/24202.

Colton, Timothy. 2017. "Russian Election Study, 2007–2008." *Harvard Dataverse*. https://doi.org/10.7910/DVN/PTHUG6.

Colton, Timothy, and Henry E. Hale. 2014. "Putin's Uneasy Return and Hybrid Regime Stability: The 2012 Russian Election Studies Survey." *Problems of Post-Communism* 61(2): 3–22.

Converse, Philip E. 2006. "The Nature of Belief Systems in Mass Publics (1964)." *Critical Review* 18(1–3): 1–74.

Corrales, Javier. 2006. "Hugo Boss." *Foreign Policy* 152(13): 32–40.

Corrales, Javier. 2015. "Autocratic Legalism in Venezuela." *Journal of Democracy* 26(2): 37–51.

Corrales, Javier, and Michael Penfold-Becerra. 2015. *Dragon in the Tropics: Hugo Chavez and the Political Economy of Revolution in Venezuela*. Washington, DC: Brookings Institution Press.

Dahl, Robert A. 1963. *A Preface to Democratic Theory*. Chicago, IL: University of Chicago Press.

Dahl, Robert A. 1971. *Polyarchy: Participation and Opposition*. New Haven, CT: Yale University Press.

Davenport, Christian. 2007. "State Repression and Political Order." *Annual Review Political Science* 10: 1–23.

Davis, Darren W., and Brian D. Silver. 2004. "Civil Liberties vs. Security: Public Opinion in the Context of the Terrorist Attacks on America." *American Journal of Political Science* 48(1): 28–46.

De Bromhead, Alan, Barry Eichengreen, and Kevin H. O'Rourke. 2012. *Right-Wing Political Extremism in the Great Depression* (Working Paper No. 17871). Cambridge, MA: National Bureau of Economic Research. https://www.nber.org/papers/w17871 (accessed 5/16/2021).

De Jouvenel, Bertrand. 1962. *On Power: Its Nature and the History of Its Growth*. Boston, MA: Beacon Press.

De Mesquita, Bueno, Alistair Smith, Randolph Siverson, and James Morrow. 2003. *The Logic of Political Survival*. Cambridge, MA: MIT Press.

Desai, Raj M., Anders Olofsgård, and Tarik M. Yousef. 2009. "The Logic of Authoritarian Bargains." *Economics & Politics* 21(1): 93–125.

Diamond, Larry J. 2002. "Thinking About Hybrid Regimes." *Journal of Democracy* 13(2): 21–35.

Diaz-Cayeros, Alberto, Beatriz Magaloni, and Barry R. Weingast. 2003. "Tragic Brilliance: Equilibrium Party Hegemony and Democratization in Mexico." Hoover Institution, Stanford University. http://dx.doi.org/10.2139/ssrn.1153510

Djankov, Simeon, Jose G. Montalvo, and Marta Reynal-Querol. 2008. "The Curse of Aid." *Journal of Economic Growth* 13(3): 169–194.

Dmitriev, Mikhail. 2015. "Lost in Transition? The Geography of Protests and Attitude Change in Russia." *Europe-Asia Studies* 67(2): 224–243.

Dominguez, Jorge I., and James A. McCann. 1998. *Democratizing Mexico: Public Opinion and Electoral Choices*. Baltimore, MD: The Johns Hopkins University Press.

Downs, George W., and David M. Rocke. 1994. "Conflict, Agency, and Gambling for Resurrection: The Principal-Agent Problem Goes to War." *American Journal of Political Science* 38(2): 362–380.

Duch, R. M., H. D. Palmer, and C. J. Anderson. 2000. "Heterogeneity in Perceptions of National Economic Conditions." *American Journal of Political Science* 44(4): 635–652.

Dukalskis, Alexander, and Johannes Gerschewski. 2017. "What Autocracies Say (and What Citizens Hear): Proposing Four Mechanisms of Autocratic Legitimation." *Contemporary Politics* 23(3): 251–268.

Dunlop, John. 2014. *The Moscow Bombings of September 1999: Examinations of Russian Terrorist Attacks at the Onset of Vladimir Putin's Rule*. Stuttgart: ibidem Press.

Eberstadt, Nicholas. 2010. *Russia's Peacetime Demographic Crisis: Dimensions, Causes, Implications*. Seattle, WA: National Bureau of Asian Research.

The Economist. 2015a. "Repression in Egypt: Worse than Mubarak." *The Economist*, May 2. www.economist.com/middle-east-and-africa/2015/05/02/worse-than-mubarak (accessed 05/20/2021).

The Economist. 2015b. "The Singapore Exception." *The Economist*, July 18. www.economist.com/special-report/2015/07/16/the-singapore-exception (accessed 05/20/2021).

The Economist. 2017a. "How Chávez and Maduro Have Impoverished Venezuela." *The Economist*, April 8. www.economist.com/finance-and-economics/2017/04/06/how-chavez-and-maduro-have-impoverished-venezuela (accessed 05/20/2021).

The Economist. 2017b. "The Man Who Ruined a Country: How Robert Mugabe Held on to Power for So Long." *The Economist*, Nov. 16. www.economist.com/middle-east-and-africa/2017/11/16/how-robert-mugabe-held-on-to-power-for-so-long (accessed 05/20/2021).

The Economist. 2014. "Hungary's Election: To Viktor the Spoils." *The Economist*, April 7. www.economist.com/eastern-approaches/2014/04/07/to-viktor-the-spoils (accessed 05/20/2021).

The Economist. 2018. "Tilting the Playing Field: How Malaysia's Next Election Will Be Rigged." *The Economist*, Mar. 10. www.economist.com/asia/2018/03/08/how-malaysias-next-election-will-be-rigged (accessed 05/20/2021).

The Economist. 2020. "Rodrigo Duterte's Lawless War on Drugs Is Wildly Popular." *The Economist*, Feb. 22. www.economist.com/briefing/2020/02/20/rodrigo-dutertes-lawless-war-on-drugs-is-wildly-popular (accessed 05/25/2021).

Elkins, Zachary, Tom Ginsburg, and James Melton. 2009. *The Endurance of National Constitutions*. New York, NY: Cambridge University Press.

Enelow, James M., and Melvin J. Hinich. 1984. *The Spatial Theory of Voting: An Introduction*. Cambridge; New York, NY: Cambridge University Press.

Enterline, Andrew J. 2010. "Introduction to CMPS Special Issue Diversionary Theory." *Conflict Management and Peace Science* 27(5): 411–416.

Erikson, Robert S., Michael MacKuen, and James Stimson. 2002. *The Macro Polity*. New York, NY: Cambridge University Press.

EU. 2018. "Key Findings of the 2018 Report on Turkey." *European Commission*. http://europa.eu/rapid/press-release_MEMO-18-3407_en.htm (accessed 07/18/ 2018).

Evans, Geoffrey, and Robert Andersen. 2006. "The Political Conditioning of Economic Perceptions." *The Journal of Politics* 68(1): 194–207.

EVS. (2020*). European Values Study Longitudinal Data File 1981-2008 (EVS 1981-2008). GESIS Data Archive, Cologne. ZA4804 Data file Version 3.1.0,* https://doi.org/10.4232/1.13486

Fearon, James D., and David D. Laitin. 2003. "Ethnicity, Insurgency, and Civil War." *American Political Science Review* 97(1): 75–90.

Fedotenkov, Igor. 2020. "Terrorist Attacks and Public Approval of the Russian President: Evidence from Time Series Analysis." *Post-Soviet Affairs* 36(2): 159–170.

Feldman, Stanley, and Karen Stenner. 1997. "Perceived Threat and Authoritarianism." *Political Psychology* 18(4): 741–770.

Fish, Steven. 2005. *Democracy Derailed in Russia: The Failure of Open Politics.* New York: Cambridge University Press.

Fraenkel, Ernst. 2017. *The Dual State: A Contribution to the Theory of Dictatorship.* New York, NY: Oxford University Press.

Frantz, Erica, and Andrea Kendall-Taylor. 2014. "A Dictator's Toolkit: Understanding How Co-Optation Affects Repression in Autocracies." *Journal of Peace Research* 51(3): 332–346.

Freedom House. 2020. "Freedom in the World 2020: A Leaderless Struggle for Democracy." Freedom House. https://freedomhouse.org/report/free dom-world/2020/leaderless-struggle-democracy (accessed 05/20/2021).

Fritsche, Immo, J. Christopher Cohrs, Thomas Kessler, and Judith Bauer. 2012. "Global Warming Is Breeding Social Conflict: The Subtle Impact of Climate Change Threat on Authoritarian Tendencies." *Journal of Environmental Psychology* 32(1): 1–10.

Fromm, Erich. 1941. *Escape from Freedom.* New York, NY: Farrar & Rinehart.

Frye, Timothy, Scott Gehlbach, Kyle L. Marquardt, and Ora John Reuter. 2017. "Is Putin's Popularity Real?" *Post-Soviet Affairs* 33(1), 1–15.

Funke, Manuel, Moritz Schularick, and Christoph Trebesch. 2016. "Going to Extremes: Politics after Financial Crises, 1870–2014." *European Economic Review* 88: 227–260.

Gabel, Matthew J., and John D. Huber. 2000. "Putting Parties in Their Place: Inferring Party Left-Right Ideological Positions from Party Manifestos Data." *American Journal of Political Science* 44: 94–103.

Gagnon, Valère Philip. 2004. *The Myth of Ethnic War: Serbia and Croatia in the 1990s.* Ithaca, NY; London: Cornell University Press.

Gall, Carlotta. 2018. "Sermons and Shouted Insults: How Erdogan Keeps Turkey Spellbound." *The New York Times*, April 2. www.nytimes.com/201 8/04/02/world/middleeast/erdogan-turkey.html (accessed 05/20/2021).

Gandhi, Jennifer, and Adam Przeworski. 2007. "Authoritarian Institutions and the Survival of Autocrats." *Comparative Political Studies* 40(11): 1279–1301.

Garrels, Anne. 2016. *Putin Country: A Journey into the Real Russia.* New York, NY: Macmillan.

Gasiorowski, Mark. 1995. "Economic Crisis and Political Regime Change: An Event History Analysis." *American Political Science Review* 89(4): 882–897.

Gassebner, Martin, Michael J. Lamla, and James Raymond Vreeland. 2013. "Extreme Bounds of Democracy." *Journal of Conflict Resolution* 57(2): 171–197.

Gates, Scott, Håvard Hegre, Mark Jones, and Håvard Strand. 2006. "Institutional Inconsistency and Political Instability: Polity Duration, 1800–2000." *American Journal of Political Science* 50(4): 893–908.

Geddes, Barbara. 1999. "What Do We Know About Democratization After Twenty Years?" *Annual Review of Political Science* 2(1): 115–144.

Geddes, Barbara. 2005. "Why Parties and Elections in Authoritarian Regimes?" Annual Meeting of the American Political Science Association, Washington DC, Sept. 1–4, 2005, 456–471.

Geddes, Barbara, Erica Frantz, and Joseph G. Wright. 2014. "Military Rule." *Annual Review of Political Science* 17: 147–162.

Gehlbach, Scott. 2010. "Reflections on Putin and the Media." *Post-Soviet Affairs* 26(1): 77–87.

Gehlbach, Scott, and Alberto Simpser. 2015. "Electoral Manipulation as Bureaucratic Control." *American Journal of Political Science* 59(1): 212–224.

Gelfand, Michele J., Jana L. Raver, Lisa Nishii, Lisa M. Leslie et al. 2011. "Differences Between Tight and Loose Cultures: A 33-Nation Study." *Science* 332(6033): 1100–1104.

Gel'man, Vladimir. 2005. "Political Opposition in Russia: A Dying Species?" *Post-Soviet Affairs* 21(3): 226–246.

Gel'man, Vladimir. 2015. *Authoritarian Russia: Analyzing Post-Soviet Regime Changes.* Pittsburgh, PA: University of Pittsburgh Press.

Gerschewski, Johannes. 2013. "The Three Pillars of Stability: Legitimation, Repression, and Co-Optation in Autocratic Regimes." *Democratization* 20(1): 13–38.

Gessen, Masha. 2014. "The Dying Russians." *The New York Review of Books*, Sept. 2. www.nybooks.com/daily/2014/09/02/dying-russians/ (accessed 05/20/2021).

Gibney, Mark, Linda Cornett, Reed Wood, Peter Haschke, Daniel Arnon, and Attilio Pisanò. 2017. "The Political Terror Scale 1976–2016." www.politicalterrorscale.org (accessed 11/24/2018).

Gibson, James L. 1997. "The Struggle Between Order and Liberty in Contemporary Russian Political Culture." *Australian Journal of Political Science* 32(2): 271–290.

Gleditsch, Kristian Skrede, and Michael D. Ward. 1997. "Double Take: A Reexamination of Democracy and Autocracy in Modern Polities." *Journal of Conflict Resolution* 41(3): 361–383.

Gleditsch, Kristian Skrede, and Michael D. Ward. 2006. "Diffusion and the International Context of Democratization." *International Organization* 60(4): 911–933.

Gleditsch, Nils Petter, Peter Wallensteen, Mikael Eriksson, Margareta Sollenberg, and Håvard Strand. 2002. "Armed Conflict 1946–2001: A New Dataset." *Journal of Peace Research* 39(5): 615–637.

Glenny, Misha. 2009. *McMafia: A Journey Through the Global Underworld*. New York, NY: First Vintage Books.

Glynn, Adam N. 2013. "What Can We Learn with Statistical Truth Serum? Design and Analysis of the List Experiment." *Public Opinion Quarterly* 77 (S1): 159–172.

Goemans, Hein E., and Mark Fey. 2009. "Risky but Rational: War as an Institutionally Induced Gamble." *The Journal of Politics* 71(1): 35–54.

Goldman, Marshall I. 2003. *The Piratization of Russia: Russian Reform Goes Awry*. New York, NY: Routledge.

Golosov, Grigorii V. 2016. "Voter Volatility in Electoral Authoritarian Regimes: Testing the 'Tragic Brilliance' Thesis." *Comparative Sociology* 15(5): 535–559.

Gordy, Eric D. 2010. *Culture of Power in Serbia: Nationalism and the Destruction of Alternatives*. University Park, PA: Pennsylvania State University Press.

Grauvogel, Julia, and Christian Von Soest. 2014. "Claims to Legitimacy Count: Why Sanctions Fail to Instigate Democratisation in Authoritarian Regimes." *European Journal of Political Research* 53(4): 635–653.

Greene, Kenneth F. 2007. *Why Dominant Parties Lose: Mexico's Democratization in Comparative Perspective*. Cambridge; New York, NY: Cambridge University Press.

Greitens, Sheena Chestnut. 2016. *Dictators and Their Secret Police: Coercive Institutions and State Violence*. Cambridge: Cambridge University Press.

Grimmer, Justin, and Brandon M. Stewart. 2013. "Text as Data: The Promise and Pitfalls of Automatic Content Analysis Methods for Political Texts." *Political Analysis* 21(3): 267–297.

Grofman, Bernard. 1985. "The Neglected Role of the Status Quo in Models of Issue Voting." *The Journal of Politics* 47(01): 229–237.

Gudkov, Lev. 2011. "The Nature of 'Putinism.'" *Russian Social Science Review* 52(6): 21–47.

Guillory, Sean. 2014. "Is Russia Suffering from Post-Traumatic Stress Disorder?" *The New Republic*, April 23. https://newrepublic.com/

article/117493/russia-suffering-post-traumatic-stress-disorder   (accessed 05/20/2021).

Gutiérrez-Romero, Roxana. 2014. "An Inquiry into the Use of Illegal Electoral Practices and Effects of Political Violence and Vote-Buying." *Journal of Conflict Resolution* 58(8): 1500–1527.

Habermas, Jürgen. 1973. *Legitimation Crisis*. Boston, MA: Beacon Press.

Hadenius, Axel. 1992. *Democracy and Development*. Cambridge: Cambridge University Press.

Hadenius, Axel, and Jan Teorell. 2007. "Pathways from Authoritarianism." *Journal of Democracy* 18(1): 143–157.

Haggard, Stephan, and Robert R. Kaufman. 1995. *The Political Economy of Democratic Transitions*. Princeton, NJ: Princeton University Press.

Hale, Henry. 2011. "The Myth of Mass Russian Support for Autocracy: The Public Opinion Foundations of a Hybrid Regime." *Europe-Asia Studies* 63 (8): 1357–1375.

Hale, Henry. 2014. *Patronal Politics: Eurasian Regime Dynamics in Comparative Perspective*. New York, NY: Cambridge University Press.

Hale, Henry. 2018. "How Crimea Pays: Media, Rallying 'Round the Flag, and Authoritarian Support." *Comparative Politics* 50(3): 369–391.

Hanson, Stephen E. 2010. *Post-Imperial Democracies: Ideology and Party Formation in Third Republic France, Weimar Germany, and Post-Soviet Russia*. New York, NY: Cambridge University Press.

Hawkins, Kirk A. 2010. *Venezuela's Chavismo and Populism in Comparative Perspective*. New York, NY: Cambridge University Press.

Haynes, Kyle. 2017. "Diversionary Conflict: Demonizing Enemies or Demonstrating Competence?" *Conflict Management and Peace Science* 34(4): 337–358.

Hellmeier, Sebastian, and Nils B. Weidmann. 2019. "Pulling the Strings? The Strategic Use of Pro-Government Mobilization in Authoritarian Regimes." *Comparative Political Studies* 53(1): 71–108.

Heston, Alan, Robert Summers, and Bettina Aten. 2012. *Penn World Table Version 7.1*. Center for International Comparisons of Production, Income and Prices at the University of Pennsylvania.

Hetherington, Marc J, and Jonathan D. Weiler. 2009. *Authoritarianism and Polarization in American Politics*. New York, NY: Cambridge University Press.

Heydarian, Richard Javad. 2017. *The Rise of Duterte: A Populist Revolt against Elite Democracy*. Singapore: Palgrave Macmillan.

Hill, Fiona, and Clifford G. Gaddy. 2015. *Mr. Putin: Operative in the Kremlin*. Washington, DC: Brookings Institution Press.

Hobbes, Thomas. 1640. *Elements of Law, Natural and Political*. New York, NY: Routledge.

Houle, Christian, and Paul D. Kenny. 2016. "The Political and Economic Consequences of Populist Rule in Latin America." *Government and Opposition* 53(2): 256–287.

Hume, David. 1742. *Essays: Moral, Political and Literary*. Oxford, UK: Oxford University Press.

Huntington, Samuel P. 1968. *Political Order in Changing Societies*. New Haven, CT: Yale University Press.

Huntington, Samuel P. 1991. *The Third Wave: Democratization in the Late Twentieth Century*. Norman, OH; London: University of Oklahoma Press.

Hyde, S. D. 2007. "The Observer Effect in International Politics: Evidence from a Natural Experiment." *World Politics* 60(1): 37–63.

Inglehart, Ronald. 2018. *Cultural Evolution: People's Motivations Are Changing and Reshaping the World*. New York, NY: Cambridge University Press.

Inglehart, Ronald, and Christian Welzel. 2005. *Modernization, Cultural Change, and Democracy: The Human Development Sequence*. New York, NY: Cambridge University Press.

Inglehart, Ronald, and Christian Welzel. 2009. "How Development Leads to Democracy: What We Know About Modernization." *Foreign Affairs* 88 (2): 33–48.

Inglehart, R., Haerpfer, C., Moreno, A., Welzel, C., Kizilova, K., Diez-Medrano, J., Lagos, M., Norris, P., Ponarin, E. and Puranen, B. et al. (eds.). 2020. *World Values Survey: All Rounds – Country-Pooled Datafile. Madrid, Spain & Vienna, Austria: JD Systems Institute & WVSA Secretariat*: www.worldvaluessurvey.org/WVSDocumentationWVL.jsp (accessed 05/20/2021).

Jack, Andrew. 2005. *Inside Putin's Russia: Can There Be Reform Without Democracy?* Oxford, UK; New York, NY: Oxford University Press.

Jakobovits, Leon A., and Robert Hogenraad. 1967. "Some Suggestive Evidence on the Operation of Semantic Generation and Satiation in Group Discussions." *Psychological Reports* 20(3c): 1247–1250.

Jakobovits, Leon A, and W. E. Lambert. 1963. "The Effects of Repetition in Communication on Meanings and Attitudes." In *Television and Human Behavior*, ed. L. Arons and M. A. May. New York, NY: Appleton-Century-Crofts, 167–176.

James, Spencer L., Paul Gubbins, Christopher J. L. Murray, and Emmanuela Gakidou. 2012. "Developing a Comprehensive Time Series of GDP Per Capita for 210 Countries from 1950 to 2015." *Population Health Metrics* 10(1): 10–12.

Johnson, Jaclyn, and Clayton L. Thyne. 2018. "Squeaky Wheels and Troop Loyalty: How Domestic Protests Influence Coups D'état, 1951–2005." *Journal of Conflict Resolution* 62(3): 597–625.

Johnson, Simon, Daniel Kaufmann, Andrei Shleifer, Marshall I. Goldman, and Martin L. Weitzman. 1997. "The Unofficial Economy in Transition." *Brookings Papers on Economic Activity* 1997(2): 159–239.

Jones, Bradford S, and Regina P. Branton. 2005. "Beyond Logit and Probit: Cox Duration Models of Single, Repeating, and Competing Events for State Policy Adoption." *State Politics & Policy Quarterly* 5(4): 420–443.

Jones, David Martin, and Michael Smith. 2002. "The Perils of Hyper-Vigilance: The War on Terrorism and the Surveillance State in South-East Asia." *Intelligence and National Security* 17(4): 31–54.

Judah, Ben. 2013. *Fragile Empire: How Russia Fell In and Out of Love with Vladimir Putin*. New Haven, CT: Yale University Press.

Kailitz, Steffen. 2013. "Classifying Political Regimes Revisited: Legitimation and Durability." *Democratization* 20(1): 39–60.

Kailitz, Steffen, and Daniel Stockemer. 2017. "Regime Legitimation, Elite Cohesion and the Durability of Autocratic Regime Types." *International Political Science Review* 38(3): 332–348.

Kalinin, Kirill. 2016. "The Social Desirability Bias in Autocrat's Electoral Ratings: Evidence from the 2012 Russian Presidential Elections." *Journal of Elections, Public Opinion and Parties* 26(2): 191–211.

Kaltwasser, Cristóbal Rovira. 2012. "The Ambivalence of Populism: Threat and Corrective for Democracy." *Democratization* 19(2): 184–208.

Kapstein, Ethan, and Nathan Converse. 2008. *The Fate of Young Democracies*. Cambridge: Cambridge University Press.

Kasamara, Valeria, and Anna Sorokina. 2012. "Imperial Ambitions of Russians." *Communist and Post-Communist Studies* 45(3): 279–288.

Keating, Joshua. 2020. "Why Is Turkey Suddenly Fighting with Everyone?" *Slate*, Oct. 28. https://slate.com/news-and-politics/2020/10/turkey-foreign -policy-erdogan.html (accessed 05/20/2021).

Kelley, Judith. 2009. "D-Minus Elections: The Politics and Norms of International Election Observation." *International Organization* 63(4): 765–787.

Kelley, Judith. 2012. *Monitoring Democracy: When International Election Observation Works, and Why It Often Fails*. Princeton, NJ: Princeton University Press.

Kendall-Taylor, Andrea, and Erica Frantz. 2014. "Mimicking Democracy to Prolong Autocracies." *The Washington Quarterly* 37(4): 71–84.

Kennedy, David M. 2003. *The American People in the Great Depression: Freedom from Fear*. New York, NY: Oxford University Press.

Kim, Nam Kyu. 2016. "Revisiting Economic Shocks and Coups." *Journal of Conflict Resolution* 60(1): 3–31.

Knight, Brian, and Ana Tribin. 2018. "The Limits of Propaganda: Evidence from Chavez's Venezuela." *Journal of the European Economic Association* 17(2): 567–605.

Knutsen, Carl Henrik, Håvard Mokleiv Nygård, and Tore Wig. 2017. "Autocratic Elections: Stabilizing Tool or Force for Change?" *World Politics* 69(1): 98–143.

Koesel, Karrie J., and Valerie J. Bunce. 2013. "Diffusion-Proofing: Russian and Chinese Responses to Waves of Popular Mobilizations against Authoritarian Rulers." *Perspectives on Politics* 11(03): 753–768.

Kolesnikov, Andrei. 2020. "Are Russians Finally Sick of Putin?" *Carnegie Moscow Center Commentary*. https://carnegie.ru/commentary/81485 (accessed 11/4/2020).

Kotkin, Stephen. 2002. "Trashcanistan: A Tour Through the Wreckage of the Soviet Empire." *New Republic* 226(14): 26–38.

Kotkin, Stephen. 2008. *Armageddon Averted: Soviet Collapse, 1970–2000.* Oxford, UK: Oxford University Press.

Krastev, Ivan. 2006. "Democracy's 'Doubles.'" *Journal of Democracy* 17(2): 52–62.

Krastev, Ivan, and Stephen Holmes. 2012. "An Autopsy of Managed Democracy." *Journal of Democracy* 23(3): 33–45.

Laclau, Ernesto. 2005. *On Populist Reason.* London & New York, NY: Verso.

Lacy, Dean, and Barry C. Burden. 1999. "The Vote-Stealing and Turnout Effects of Ross Perot in the 1992 US Presidential Election." *American Journal of Political Science* 43(1): 233–255.

Langston, Joy. 2006. "Elite Ruptures: When Do Ruling Parties Split?" In Andreas Schedler (ed.), *Electoral Authoritarianism: The Dynamics of Unfree Competition.* Boulder, CO: Lynne Rienner, 57–76.

Langston, Joy, and Scott Morgenstern. 2009. "Campaigning in an Electoral Authoritarian Regime: The Case of Mexico." *Comparative Politics* 41(2): 165–181.

Le Bon, Gustave. 1896. *The Crowd: A Study of the Popular Mind.* Kitchener, ON: Batoche Books.

Lendvai, Paul. 2017. *Orbán: Europe's New Strongman.* New York, NY: Oxford University Press.

Levitsky, Steven, and Maxwell A. Cameron. 2003. "Democracy Without Parties? Political Parties and Regime Change in Fujimorii's Peru." *Latin American Politics and Society* 45(3): 1–33.

Levitsky, Steven, and Lucan Way. 2010a. *Competitive Authoritarianism: Hybrid Regimes After the Cold War.* New York, NY: Cambridge University Press.

Levitsky, Steven, and Lucan Way. 2010b. "Why Democracy Needs a Level Playing Field." *Journal of Democracy* 21(1): 57–68.

Levitsky, Steven, and Lucan Way. 2015. "The Myth of Democratic Recession." *Journal of Democracy* 26(1): 45–58.

Levitsky, Steven, and Daniel Ziblatt. 2018. *How Democracies Die*. New York, NY: Crown.

Linz, Juan. 1978. "The Breakdown of Democratic Regimes: Crisis, Breakdown, and Reequilibration." In *The Breakdown of Democratic Regimes*, ed. Alfred Linz and Alfred Stepan. Baltimore, MD: Johns Hopkins University Press, 3–124.

Linz, Juan. 1990. "The Perils of Presidentialism." *Journal of Democracy* 1 (1): 51–69.

Lippmann, Walther. 1922. *Public Opinion*. Blacksburg, VA: Wilder Publications.

Little, Andrew T. 2017. "Are Non-Competitive Elections Good for Citizens?" *Journal of Theoretical Politics* 29(2): 214–242.

Loveluck, Louisa. 2018. "Turkish President Threatens to 'Drown' U.S.-Backed Force in Syria." *The Washington Post*, Jan. 15. www.washingtonpost.com/world/turkish-president-threatens-todrown-us-backed-force-in-syria/2018/01/15/e7789850-f9e7-11e7-b832-8c26844 b74fb_story.html?utm_term=.bdb80e9e2a1 (accessed 7/17/ 2019).

Loxton, James. 2016. *Authoritarian Successor Parties Worldwide: A Framework for Analysis*. Notre Dame, IN: Helen Kellogg Institute for International Studies.

Lust-Okar, Ellen. 2008. "Competitive Clientelism in Jordanian Elections." In *Political Participation in the Middle East*, ed. Ellen Lust-Okar and Saloua Zerhouni, Boulder, CO: Lynne Rienner, 75–93.

Luttwak, Edward. 2016. *Coup D'Etat*. Cambridge, MA: Harvard University Press.

Lyall, Jason M. K. 2006. "Pocket Protests: Rhetorical Coercion and the Micropolitics of Collective Action in Semiauthoritarian Regimes." *World Politics* 58(3): 378–412.

Mach, Katharine J., Caroline M. Kraan, W. Neil Adger, and Halvard Buhaug. 2019. "Climate as a Risk Factor for Armed Conflict." *Nature* 571(7764): 193–197.

Machiavelli, Niccolò. 1532. *The Prince and Other Writings*. New York, NY: Barnes & Noble.

Madison, James. 1787. "The Federalist No. 10." In *The Federalist Papers*. Library of Congress. https://guides.loc.gov/federalist-papers/full-text (accessed 05/25/2021).

Madison, James. 1788. "The Federalist No. 51." In *The Federalist Papers*. Library of Congress. https://guides.loc.gov/federalist-papers/full-text (accessed 05/25/2021).

Maerz, Seraphine F. 2019. "Simulating Pluralism: The Language of Democracy in Hegemonic Authoritarianism." *Political Research Exchange* 1(1): 1–23.

Maerz, Seraphine F., and Carsten Q. Schneider. 2019. "Comparing Public Communication in Democracies and Autocracies: Automated Text Analyses of Speeches by Heads of Government." *Quality & Quantity* 54 (2): 1–29.

Magaloni, Beatriz. 2006. *Voting for Autocracy: Hegemonic Party Survival and Its Demise in Mexico*. New York: Cambridge University Press.

Manaev, Oleg, Natalie Manayeva, and Dzmitry Yuran. 2010. "Spiral of Silence in Election Campaigns in Post-Communist Society: The Case of Belarus." *International Journal of Market Research* 52(5): 309–328.

Matovski, Aleksandar. 2020. "The Logic of Vladimir Putin's Popular Appeal." In *Citizens and the State in Authoritarian Regimes: Comparing Russia and China*, ed. Valerie Bunce, Karrie Koesel, and Jessica Chen Weiss. New York, NY: Oxford University Press.

Mazepus, Honorata, Wouter Veenendaal, Anthea McCarthy-Jones, and Juan Manuel Trak Vásquez. 2016. "A Comparative Study of Legitimation Strategies in Hybrid Regimes." *Policy Studies* 37(4): 350–369.

McDonald, Michael D., and Ian Budge. 2014. "Getting It (Approximately) Right (and Center and Left!): Reliability and Uncertainty Estimates for the Comparative Manifesto Data." *Electoral Studies* 35: 67–77.

McFaul, Michael. 1997. *Russia's 1996 Presidential Election*. Stanford, CA: Hoover Institution Press.

Mead, Walter Russel. 2014. "Playing Putin's Game." *The American Interest*. www.the-american-interest.com/2014/04/15/playing-putins-game/ (accessed 05/20/2021).

Meirowitz, Adam, and Joshua A. Tucker. 2013. "People Power or a One-Shot Deal? A Dynamic Model of Protest." *American Journal of Political Science* 57(2): 478–490.

Merolla, Jennifer L., and Elizabeth J. Zechmeister. 2009. *Democracy at Risk: How Terrorist Threats Affect the Public*. Chicago, IL: University of Chicago Press.

Michelutti, Lucia. 2017a. "The Cult of the Boss." *Democratic Authoritarianism: A Symposium on the Fusion of Authoritarianism and Democracy in India and the World* 693: 58–64.

Michelutti, Lucia. 2017b. "'We Are All Chávez' Charisma as an Embodied Experience." *Latin American Perspectives* 44(1): 232–250.

Mickiewicz, Ellen. 1999. *Changing Channels: Television and the Struggle for Power in Russia*. Durham, NC: Duke University Press.

Mickiewicz, Ellen. 2008. *Television, Power, and the Public in Russia*. Cambridge; New York, NY: Cambridge University Press.

Miller, Michael K. 2015a. "Electoral Authoritarianism and Human Development." *Comparative Political Studies* 48(12): 1526–1562.

Miller, Michael K. 2015b. "Elections, Information, and Policy Responsiveness in Autocratic Regimes." *Comparative Political Studies* 48(6): 691–727.

Miller, Michael K. 2016. "Democracy by Example? Why Democracy Spreads When the World's Democracies Prosper." *Comparative Politics* 49(1): 83–116.

Miller, Michael K. 2017. "The Strategic Origins of Electoral Authoritarianism." *British Journal of Political Science* 50(1): 1–28.

Miller, Steven V. 2015. "Individual-Level Expectations of Executive Authority under Territorial Threat." *Conflict Management and Peace Science* 34(5): 526–545. 0738894215600384.

Miller, Steven V. 2016. "Economic Threats or Societal Turmoil? Understanding Preferences for Authoritarian Political Systems." *Political Behavior* 39(2): 457–478.

Missirian, Anouch, and Wolfram Schlenker. 2017. "Asylum Applications Respond to Temperature Fluctuations." *Science* 358(6370): 1610–1614.

Mitra, Pradeep, and Marcelo Selowsky. 2002. *Transition – The First Ten Years: Analysis and Lessons for Eastern Europe and the Former Soviet Union*. Washington, DC: World Bank Publications.

Moffitt, Benjamin. 2014. "How to Perform Crisis: A Model for Understanding the Key Role of Crisis in Contemporary Populism." *Government and Opposition* 50(2): 189–217.

Monroe, Burt L., and Philip A. Schrodt. 2008. "Introduction to the Special Issue: The Statistical Analysis of Political Text." *Political Analysis* 16(4): 351–355.

Moreno, Alejandro Menéndez. 1999. *Political Cleavages: Issues, Parties, and the Consolidation of Democracy*. Boulder, CO: Westview Press.

Morgan, Stephen. L., and Christopher Winship. 2007. *Counterfactuals and Causal Inference: Methods and Principles for Social Research*. New York, NY: Cambridge University Press.

Morgenbesser, Lee. 2016. *Behind the Façade: Elections under Authoritarianism in Southeast Asia*. Albany, NY: SUNY Press.

Morgenstern, Scott, and Elizabeth Zechmeister. 2001. "Better the Devil You Know than the Saint You Don't? Risk Propensity and Vote Choice in Mexico." *Journal of Politics* 63(1): 93–119.

Morrison, Kevin M. 2009. "Oil, Nontax Revenue, and the Redistributional Foundations of Regime Stability." *International Organization* 63(1): 107–138.

Mudde, Cas. 2007. *22 Populist Radical Right Parties in Europe*. New York, NY: Cambridge University Press.

Müller, Jan-Werner. 2017. *What Is Populism?* London: Penguin UK.

Müller, Jan-Werner. 2019. "Populists Don't Lose Elections." *The New York Times*, May 8. www.nytimes.com/2019/05/08/opinion/populists-dont-lose-elections.html (accessed 5/20/2021).

Murray, Damian R., Mark Schaller, and Peter Suedfeld. 2013. "Pathogens and Politics: Further Evidence That Parasite Prevalence Predicts Authoritarianism." *PloS One* 8(5).

Naranjo, Mario. 2012. "Venezuela's Chavez Calls Presidential Foe a 'Pig.'" *Reuters*, Feb. 16. www.reuters.com/article/us-venezuela-election-idUSTRE81F21V20120216 (accessed 7/25/2019).

Negretto, Gabriel L. 2013. *Making Constitutions: Presidents, Parties, and Institutional Choice in Latin America*. New York, NY: Cambridge University Press.

Newell, Waller R. 2016. *Tyrants: A History of Power, Injustice, and Terror*. New York, NY: Cambridge University Press.

Nichter, Simeon. 2008. "Vote Buying or Turnout Buying? Machine Politics and the Secret Ballot." *American Political Science Review* 102(1): 19–31.

Nicolet, Claude. 2004. "Dictatorship in Rome." In *Dictatorship in History and Theory: Bonapartism, Caesarism, and Totalitarianism*, ed. Peter Baehr and Melvin Richter. Cambridge; New York, NY: Cambridge University Press.

Noelle-Neumann, Elisabeth. 1984. *The Spiral of Silence: Public Opinion, Our Social Skin*. Chicago, IL: University of Chicago Press.

Norris, Pippa, and Ronald Inglehart. 2019. *Cultural Backlash: Trump, Brexit, and Authoritarian Populism*. New York, NY: Cambridge University Press.

O'Donnell, Guillermo A. 1994. "Delegative Democracy." *Journal of Democracy* 5(1): 55–69.

O'Donnell, Guillermo A., Philippe C. Schmitter, and Laurence Whitehead. 1986a. "Tentative Conclusions about Uncertain Democracies." In *Transitions from Authoritarian Rule: Comparative Perspectives*, ed. Guillermo A. O'Donnell, Philippe C. Schmitter, and Laurence Whitehead. Baltimore, MD: Johns Hopkins University Press.

O'Donnell, Guillermo A., Philippe C. Schmitter, and Laurence Whitehead. 1986b. *Transitions from Authoritarian Rule: Comparative Perspectives*, ed. Guillermo A. O'Donnell, Philippe C. Schmitter, and Laurence Whitehead. Baltimore, MD: The Johns Hopkins University Press.

Oakes, Amy. 2012. *Diversionary War: Domestic Unrest and International Conflict*. Stanford, CA: Stanford University Press.

Olson, Mancur. 1993. "Dictatorship, Democracy, and Development." *American Political Science Review* 87(3): 567–576.

Oppenheimer, Andres. 1998. *Bordering on Chaos: Mexico's Roller-Coaster Journey Toward Prosperity*. Boston, MA: Little, Brown and Company.

Palairet, Michael. 2001. "The Economic Consequences of Slobodan Milošević." *Europe-Asia Studies* 53(6): 903–19.

Park, Johann, and Valentina Bali. 2017. "International Terrorism and the Political Survival of Leaders." *Journal of Conflict Resolution* 61(7): 1343–1370.

Pavlovsky, Gleb. 2017. "Frontline Interviews: The Putin Files." *Public Broadcasting System*. www.pbs.org/wgbh/frontline/interview-collection/the-putin-files (accessed 11/10/ 2020).

Pearl, Judea. 2009. *Causality: Models, Reasoning, and Inference*. Cambridge; New York, NY: Cambridge University Press.

Pei, Minxin, and Ariel David Adesnik. 2000. "Why Recessions Don't Start Revolutions." *Foreign Policy* (118): 138–151.

Peisakhin, Leonid, and Arturas Rozenas. 2018. "Electoral Effects of Biased Media: Russian Television in Ukraine." *American Journal of Political Science* 62(3): 535–550.

Pejić, Nenad. 2014. "Koja Je Razlika Između Putina I Miloševića? Dvadeset I Dvije Godine (What Is the Difference Between Putin and Milošević? Twenty-Two Years)." *Radio Free Europe*, March 13. www.slobodnaevropa.org/articleprintview/25295670.html (accessed 5/20/ 2021).

Pepinsky, Thomas. 2014. "The Institutional Turn in Comparative Authoritarianism." *British Journal of Political Science* 44(3): 631–653.

Pérez, Orlando J. 2003. "Democratic Legitimacy and Public Insecurity: Crime and Democracy in El Salvador and Guatemala." *Political Science Quarterly* 118(4): 627–644.

Petrocik, John R. 1996. "Issue Ownership in Presidential Elections, With A 1980 Case Study." *American Journal of Political Science* 40(3): 825–850.

Pettersson, Thérése, and Kristine Eck. 2018. "Organized Violence, 1989–2017." *Journal of Peace Research* 55(4): 535–547.

Pew. 2014. "Political Polarization in the American Public." *Pew Research Center*, June 12. www.people-press.org/2014/06/12/political-polarization-in-the-american-public/ (accessed 1/26/2018).

Pipes, Richard. 2004. "Flight from Freedom-What Russians Think and Want." *Foreign Affairs* 83: 9–15.

Plato. 1985. *The Republic*. New York, NY: W. W. Norton and Company.

Politkovskaya, Anna. 2007. *A Small Corner of Hell: Dispatches from Chechnya*. Chicago, IL: University of Chicago Press.

Prosser, Christopher. 2014. "Building Policy Scales from Manifesto Data: A Referential Content Validity Approach." *Electoral Studies* 35: 88–101.

Przeworski, Adam. 1991. *Democracy and the Market: Political and Economic Reforms in Eastern Europe and Latin America*. Cambridge; New York, NY: Cambridge University Press.

Przeworski, Adam, Michael E. Alvarez, Jose A. Cheibub, and Fernando Limongi. 2000. *Democracy and Development: Political Institutions and Well-Being in the World, 1950–1990*. Cambridge; New York, NY: Cambridge University Press.

Przeworski, Adam, and F. Limongi. 1997. "Modernization: Theories and Facts." *World politics* 49(2): 155–183.

Rappard, William Emmanuel. 1938. *The Crisis of Democracy*. Chicago, IL: University of Chicago Press.

Regan, Patrick M., and Sam R. Bell. 2010. "Changing Lanes or Stuck in the Middle: Why Are Anocracies More Prone to Civil Wars?" *Political Research Quarterly* 64(4): 747–759.

Reuters. 2007. "I'm the World's Only True Democrat, Says Putin." *Reuters,* June 4. www.reuters.com/article/us-russia-putin-democracy/im-the-worlds-only-true-democrat-says-putin-idUSL0454405820070604 (accessed 8/3/2019).

Riker, William H. 1986. *The Art of Political Manipulation*. New Haven, CT: Yale University Press.

Riker, William H. 1990. "Heresthetic and Rhetoric in the Spatial Model." In *Advances in the Spatial Theory of Voting*, ed. James M. Enelow and Melvin J. Hinich. New York, NY: Cambridge University Press.

Riker, William H. 1996. *The Strategy of Rhetoric: Campaigning for the American Constitution*. New Haven, CT: Yale University Press.

Robertson, Graeme. 2011. *The Politics of Protest in Hybrid Regimes: Managing Dissent in Post-Communist Russia*. New York, NY: Cambridge University Press.

Rodriguez, Francisco. 2008. "An Empty Revolution: The Unfulfilled Promises of Hugo Chavez." *Foreign Affairs* 87: 49.

Roessler, Philip G., and Marc M. Howard. 2009. "Post-Cold War Political Regimes: When Do Elections Matter?" In *Democratization by Elections: A New Mode of Transition*, ed. Staffan Lindberg. Baltimore, MD: Johns Hopkins University Press.

Rogov, Kirill. 2019. "20 Years of Vladimir Putin: The Rise and Decline of a Regime." *The Moscow Times*, Aug. 9. www.themoscowtimes.com/2019/08/09/20-years-of-vladimir-putin-the-rise-and-decline-of-a-regime-a66782 (accessed 5/20/2021).

Rose, Richard. 2007. "Going Public with Private Opinions: Are Post-Communist Citizens Afraid to Say What They Think?" *Journal of Elections, Public Opinion and Parties* 17(2): 123–142.

Rose, Richard. 2010. *New Russia Barometer I-XVIII Trend Dataset, 1992–2009. [data Collection].* UK Data Service. SN: 6445. http://dx.doi.org/10.5255/UKDA-SN-6445-1.

Rose, Richard, and William Mishler. 2007. "Generation, Age, and Time: The Dynamics of Political Learning during Russia's Transformation." *American Journal of Political Science* 51(4): 822–834.

Rose, Richard, William Mishler, and Neil Munro. 2004. "Resigned Acceptance of an Incomplete Democracy: Russia's Political Equilibrium." *Post-Soviet Affairs* 20(3): 195–218.

Rose, Richard, William Mishler, and Neil Munro. 2006. *Russia Transformed: Developing Popular Support for a New Regime.* Cambridge; New York, NY: Cambridge University Press.

Rosenfeld, Bryn, Kosuke Imai, and Jacob N Shapiro. 2016. "An Empirical Validation Study of Popular Survey Methodologies for Sensitive Questions." *American Journal of Political Science* 60(3): 783–802.

Ross, Michael L. 2001. "Does Oil Hinder Democracy?" *World Politics* 53(3): 325–361.

Ross, Michael L. 2015. "What Have We Learned about the Resource Curse?" *Annual Review of Political Science* 18: 239–259.

Ross, Michael L., and Paasha Mahdavi. 2015. "Oil and Gas Data, 1932–2014." *Harvard Dataverse.* https://doi.org/10.7910/DVN/ZTPW0Y.

Rozin, Paul, and Edward B. Royzman. 2001. "Negativity Bias, Negativity Dominance, and Contagion." *Personality and Social Psychology Review* 5(4): 296–320.

Rundlett, Ashlea, and Milan Svolik. 2016. "Deliver the Vote! Micromotives and Macrobehavior in Electoral Fraud." *American Political Science Review* 110(1): 180–197.

Sambanis, Nicholas. 2004. "What Is Civil War? Conceptual and Empirical Complexities of an Operational Definition." *Journal of Conflict Resolution* 48(6): 814–858.

Sartori, Giovanni. 1976. *Parties and Party Systems: A Framework for Analysis.* New York, NY: Cambridge University Press.

Saxonberg, Steven. 2013. *Transitions and Non-Transitions from Communism: Regime Survival in China, Cuba, North Korea, and Vietnam.* New York, NY: Cambridge University Press.

Schedler, Andreas. 2002. "The Menu of Manipulation." *Journal of Democracy* 13(2): 36–50.

Schedler, Andreas. 2006. *Electoral Authoritarianism: The Dynamics of Unfree Competition.* Boulder, CO: Lynne Rienner.

Schedler, Andreas. 2010. "Authoritarianism's Last Line of Defense." *Journal of Democracy* 21(1): 69–80.

Schedler, Andreas. 2013. *The Politics of Uncertainty: Sustaining and Subverting Electoral Authoritarianism.* Oxford, UK: Oxford University Press.

Schedler, Andreas. 2018. "Disturbing the Dictator: Peaceful Protest Under Authoritarianism." In *Crisis in Autocratic Regimes*, ed. Johannes Gerschewski and Cristoph S. Stefes. Boulder, CO: Lynne Rienner Publishers, 43–74.

Schmitt, Carl. 1988. *The Crisis of Parliamentary Democracy.* Cambridge, MA: MIT Press.

Schmitt, Carl. 2014. *Dictatorship.* Malden, MA: Polity Press.

Seawright, Jason. 2012. *Party-System Collapse: The Roots of Crisis in Peru and Venezuela.* Stanford, CA: Stanford University Press.

Seligson, Mitchell A. 2002. "The Impact of Corruption on Regime Legitimacy: A Comparative Study of Four Latin American Countries." *The Journal of Politics* 64(2): 408–433.

Shevchenko, Olga. 2008. *Crisis and the Everyday in Postsocialist Moscow.* Bloomington and Indianapolis, IN: Indiana University Press.

Shevtsova, Lilia. 2003. *Putin's Russia.* Washington, DC: Carnegie Endowment for International Peace.

Sides, John. 2006. "The Origins of Campaign Agendas." *British Journal of Political Science* 36(3): 407–436.

Sides, John. 2007. "The Consequences of Campaign Agendas." *American Politics Research* 35(4): 465–488.

Simpser, Alberto. 2013. *Why Governments and Parties Manipulate Elections: Theory, Practice, and Implications.* New York, NY: Cambridge University Press.

Singer, J. David. 1988. "Reconstructing the Correlates of War Dataset on Material Capabilities of States, 1816–1985." *International Interactions* 14(2): 115–132.

Singer, J. David, and Melvin Small. 1994. "Correlates of War Project: International and Civil War Data, 1816–1992 (ICPSR 9905)." Ann Arbor, MI: Inter-University Consortium for Political and Social Research.

Singerman, Diane. 2002. "The Politics of Emergency Rule in Egypt." *Current History* 101(651): 29–35.

Slater, Dan. 2010. *Ordering Power: Contentious Politics and Authoritarian Leviathans in Southeast Asia.* Cambridge; New York, NY: Cambridge University Press.

Smith, Benjamin. 2005. "Life of the Party: The Origins of Regime Breakdown and Persistence under Single-Party Rule." *World Politics* 57 (3): 421–451.

Smith, Sebastian. 2006. "The Chechen Wolf." In *Allah's Mountains: The Battle for Chechnya*. New York, NY: Tauris Parke Paperbacks.

Solt, Frederick. 2011. "The Social Origins of Authoritarianism." *Political Research Quarterly* 65(4): 703–713.

Sperling, Valerie. 2014. *Sex, Politics, and Putin: Political Legitimacy in Russia*. Oxford, UK; New York, NY: Oxford University Press.

Sperling, Valerie. 2016. "Putin's Macho Personality Cult." *Communist and Post-Communist Studies* 49(1): 13–23.

Sterling, Joe, and Samatha Beech. 2017. "A Year After Failed Coup in Turkey, Erdogan Says 'Behead Traitors.'" *CNN*, July 16. www.cnn.com/2017/07/15/europe/turkey-coup-attempt-anniversary/index.html (accessed 7/16/2019).

Stevens, Stanley S. 1957. "On the Psychophysical Law." *Psychological Review* 64(3): 153.

Stimson, James. 1999. *Public Opinion in America: Moods, Cycles, and Swings*. Boulder, CO: Westview Press.

Stimson, James, Cyrille Thiébaut, and Vincent Tiberj. 2012. "The Evolution of Policy Attitudes in France." *European Union Politics* 13(2): 293–316.

Stinnett, Douglas M., Jaroslav Tir, Paul F. Diehl, Philip Schafer, and Charles Gochman. 2002. "The Correlates of War Project Direct Contiguity Data, Version 3." *Conflict Management and Peace Science* 19 (2): 59–67.

Stokes, Susan. 2005. "Perverse Accountability: A Formal Model of Machine Politics with Evidence from Argentina." *American Political Science Review* 99(03): 315–325.

Stoner, Kathryn, and Michael McFaul. 2015. "Who Lost Russia (This Time)? Vladimir Putin." *The Washington Quarterly* 38(2): 167–187.

Svolik, Milan. 2008. "Authoritarian Reversals and Democratic Consolidation." *American Political Science Review* 102(2): 153–168.

Svolik, Milan. 2012. *The Politics of Authoritarian Rule*. Cambridge; New York, NY: Cambridge University Press.

Svolik, Milan. 2013. "Learning to Love Democracy: Electoral Accountability and the Success of Democracy." *American Journal of Political Science* 57(3): 685–702.

Svolik, Milan. 2020. "When Polarization Trumps Civic Virtue: Partisan Conflict and the Subversion of Democracy by Incumbents." *Quarterly Journal of Political Science* 15: 3–31.

Tarar, Ahmer. 2006. "Diversionary Incentives and the Bargaining Approach to War." *International Studies Quarterly* 50(1): 169–188.

TASS. 2017. "Volodin Podtverdil Svoj Tezis O Tom, Chto 'Net Putina – Net Rossii' (Volodin Confirmed His Thesis That 'There Is No Russia without Putin.')." *TASS*, October 18. https://tass.ru/politika/4658232 (accessed 1/19/2019).

Taylor, Brian D. 2018. *The Code of Putinism*. New York, NY: Oxford University Press.

Thornhill, Randy, Corey L. Fincher, and Devaraj Aran. 2009. "Parasites, Democratization, and the Liberalization of Values Across Contemporary Countries." *Biological Reviews* 84(1): 113–131.

Thornhill, Randy, Corey L. Fincher, Damian R. Murray, and Mark Schaller. 2010. "Zoonotic and Non-Zoonotic Diseases in Relation to Human Personality and Societal Values: Support for the Parasite-Stress Model." *Evolutionary Psychology* 8(2): 151–169.

Thyne, Clayton L. 2010. "Supporter of Stability or Agent of Agitation? The Effect of US Foreign Policy on Coups in Latin America, 1960–99." *Journal of Peace Research* 47(4): 449–461.

Tir, Jaroslav, and Michael Jasinski. 2008. "Domestic-Level Diversionary Theory of War: Targeting Ethnic Minorities." *Journal of Conflict Resolution* 52(5): 641–664.

Tocqueville, Alexis de. 1840. *Democracy in America*. New York, NY: Harper Perennial.

Tol, Gonul. 2019. "Turkey's Endgame in Syria: What Erdogan Wants." *Foreign Affairs*, Oct. 9. www.foreignaffairs.com/articles/turkey/2019-10-09/turkeys-endgame-syria (accessed 5/20/2021).

Treier, Shawn, and Simon Jackman. 2008. "Democracy as a Latent Variable." *American Journal of Political Science* 52(1): 201–217.

Treisman, Daniel. 2011a. "Presidential Popularity in a Hybrid Regime: Russia under Yeltsin and Putin." *American Journal of Political Science* 55(3): 590–609.

Treisman, Daniel. 2011b. *The Return: Russia's Journey from Gorbachev to Medvedev*. New York, NY: Free Press.

Treisman, Daniel. 2013. "Why the Kremlin Hates Levada Center." *The Moscow Times*, May 23. www.themoscowtimes.com/2013/05/23/why-the-kremlin-hates-levada-center-a24304 (accessed 5/16/2021).

Treisman, Daniel. 2014. "Putin's Popularity Since 2010: Why Did Support for the Kremlin Plunge, Then Stabilize?" *Post-Soviet Affairs* 30(5): 370–388.

Tucker, Joshua. 2007. "Enough! Electoral Fraud, Collective Action Problems, and Post-Communist Colored Revolutions." *Perspectives on Politics* 5(3): 535–551.

Ullrich, Volker. 2017. *Hitler: Ascent, 1889–1939*. New York, NY: Vintage Books.

Ulfelder, Jay. 2007. "Natural-Resource Wealth and the Survival of Autocracy." *Comparative Political Studies* 40(8): 995–1018.

Volkens, Andrea, Pola Lehmann, Theres Matthieß, and Nicolas Merz. 2016. *The Manifesto Data Collection*. Berlin: Wissenschaftszentrum Berlin für

Sozialforschung (WZB): Manifesto Project (MRG/CMP/MARPOR). Version 2016a.

Volkov, Vadim. 2016. *Violent Entrepreneurs: The Use of Force in the Making of Russian Capitalism*. Ithaca, NY: Cornell University Press.

Von Haldenwang, Christian. 2017. "The Relevance of Legitimation – A New Framework for Analysis." *Contemporary Politics* 23(3): 269–286.

Von Soest, Christian. 2015. "Democracy Prevention: The International Collaboration of Authoritarian Regimes." *European Journal of Political Research* 54(4): 623–638.

Von Soest, Christian, and Julia Grauvogel. 2017. "Identity, Procedures and Performance: How Authoritarian Regimes Legitimize Their Rule." *Contemporary Politics* 23(3): 287–305.

Wahman, Michael, Jan Teorell, and Axel Hadenius. 2013. "Authoritarian Regime Types Revisited: Updated Data in Comparative Perspective." *Contemporary Politics* 19(1): 19–34.

Waldner, David, and Ellen Lust. 2018. "Unwelcome Change: Coming to Terms with Democratic Backsliding." *Annual Review of Political Science* 21: 93–113.

Walker, Christopher, and Robert W. Orttung. 2014. "Breaking the News: The Role of State-Run Media." *Journal of Democracy* 25(1): 71–85.

Way, Lucan. 2006. "Authoritarian Failure: How Does State Weakness Strengthen Electoral Competition." In *Electoral Authoritarianism: The Dynamics of Unfree Competition. Lynne Reiner*, ed. Andreas Schedler. Boulder, CO: Lynne Rienner Publishers, 167–180.

Weber, Max. 1918. *Economy and Society: An Outline of Interpretive Sociology*. ed. Guenther Roth and Claus Wittich. Berkeley, CA; Los Angeles, CA; London: University of California Press.

Weber, Max. 1946. *From Max Weber: Essays in Sociology*. ed. Hans H. Gerth and C. Wright Mills. New York, NY: Oxford University Press.

Weyland, Kurt. 2001. "Clarifying a Contested Concept: Populism in the Study of Latin American Politics." *Comparative Politics* 34(1): 1–22.

Whitaker, Beth Elise. 2007. "Exporting the Patriot Act? Democracy and the 'War on Terror' in the Third World." *Third World Quarterly* 28(5): 1017–1032.

Whitaker, Beth Elise. 2010. "Compliance Among Weak States: Africa and the Counter-Terrorism Regime." *Review of International Studies* 36(3): 639–662.

White, Stephen, and Ian McAllister. 2008. "The Putin Phenomenon." *Journal of Communist Studies and Transition Politics* 24(4): 604–628.

Wilkerson, John, and Andreu Casas. 2017. "Large-Scale Computerized Text Analysis in Political Science: Opportunities and Challenges." *Annual Review of Political Science* 20: 529–544.

Williams, T. Harry. 1981. *Huey Long*. New York, NY: Vintage Books.

Windsor, Leah C., Nia Dowell, and Art Graesser. 2014. "The Language of Autocrats: Leaders' Language in Natural Disaster Crises." *Risk, Hazards & Crisis in Public Policy* 5(4): 446–467.

Windsor, Leah C., Nia Dowell, Alistair Windsor, and John Kaltner. 2018. "Leader Language and Political Survival Strategies." *International Interactions* 44(2): 321–336.

Wintrobe, Ronald. 1998. *The Political Economy of Dictatorship*. Cambridge; London: Cambridge University Press.

Wintrobe, Ronald. 2018. "An Economic Theory of a Hybrid (Competitive Authoritarian or Illiberal) Regime." *Public Choice* 177(3): 217–233.

Woloch, Isser. 2004. "From Consulate to Empire: Impetus and Resistance." In *Dictatorship in History and Theory: Bonapartism, Caesarism, and Totalitarianism*, ed. Peter Baehr and Melvin Richter. Cambridge; New York, NY: Cambridge University Press, 29–52.

Wood, Andrew. 2014. "Slobodan Putin." *The American Interest*, May 5. www.the-american-interest.com/2014/05/05/slobodan-putin/ (accessed 5/20/2021).

Wood, Elizabeth A. 2016. "Hypermasculinity as a Scenario of Power: Vladimir Putin's Iconic Rule, 1999–2008." *International Feminist Journal of Politics* 18(3): 329–350.

Wright, Joseph. 2009. "How Foreign Aid Can Foster Democratization in Authoritarian Regimes." *American Journal of Political Science* 53(3): 552–571.

Zakaria, Fareed. 1997. "The Rise of Illiberal Democracy." *Foreign Affairs* 76(5): 22–43.

Zakaria, Fareed. 2007. *The Future of Freedom: Illiberal Democracy at Home and Abroad*. New York, NY; London: W. W. Norton & Company.

Zaller, John. 1992. *The Nature and Origins of Mass Opinion*. Cambridge; New York, NY: Cambridge University Press.

Index

N.B. - locators in **bold** indicate information in tables and locators in *italics* indicate information in figures.

establishing electoral autocracies,
50n13, 58
see also legitimation strategies
EU countries, 3, 20, 83, 91, **94**, 103,
121, 248
European and World Values Surveys
(WVS/EVS), 32
existential anxieties, 226–227
popular opinion trends, 240, 245
survival values, 222–223, 224
voting behavior, 235
event history models. *see* Cox survival
models, survival models
existential anxieties, 190, 201
exploitation of, 71, 133, 169, 184
rise of electoral autocracies, 37,
224–226
support for existing political system
electoral autocracies and
democracies compared,
226–232, **229**, *233*
support for strongman rule, 49
Levada Center survey, 181, *182*
external influence paradigm, 19, 20–22,
23–24, 253
importance of, 24

foreign influence. *see* external influence
paradigm
Freedom House, 3
composite democracy indices, 8–9,
79
Fujimori, Alberto, 4
legitimation strategies, 12, 23

global financial crisis (2008)
democratic norms, impact on, 1–3,
247
Gorbachev, Mikhail, 178, 253
see also Russia

Habermas, Jürgen, 46
social crises definition, 44
hegemonic electoral authoritarianism,
22, 29, 221
economic performance, 22–23
establishment, 58
Russia, 29–30
heresthetics. *see* strongman heresthetics
Hobbes, Thomas, 36

horizontal accountability, 52–53
Hungary. *see* Orbán, Viktor
hybrid nature of electoral autocracies,
1, 4, 76, 232
see also popular appeal of electoral
autocracies; due to hybrid nature

identifying electoral autocracies, 53, 73,
134, 165, 253
ideological homelessness of electoral
autocracies, 13–14, 250
individual freedoms and human rights
(CMP category), 141, 148, 164
Institute for Health Metrics and
Evaluation (IHME)
GDP per capita, 79–80
measuring coercive tactics, 82
measuring economic decline, 79–80
institutional restructuring, 58
see also neo-institutionalism
paradigm
Institutional Revolutionary Party (PRI)
(Mexico), 1, 11, 21, 24
"patriotic" fraud, 51
authoritarian social contract, 43
campaign appeals, 150
rhetoric, 151–156, **153**
legitimation strategies, 11
party manifesto analysis, 138
institutionalized coercion. *see* neo-
institutionalism paradigm
issue ownership, 65–67, 66n31,
204–206
candidate positioning, 204, *207*, 212,
266
political competition, 67

judiciary, repression of, 3, 5, 8, 9

Lee Kwan Yew, 11, 122
see also Singapore
legislatures/parliaments, repression of,
5, 8, 16
legitimation strategies, 11–13, 16–17,
241, 244, 252
campaign appeals, 54
Democratic Legitimacy frame,
51–53, 54, 73, 134–135, 136
see also procedural legitimacy
electoral autocracies